# A PRACTICAL GUIDE TO IT LAW

**BCS, THE CHARTERED INSTITUTE FOR IT**

BCS, The Chartered Institute for IT, is committed to making IT good for society. We use the power of our network to bring about positive, tangible change. We champion the global IT profession and the interests of individuals, engaged in that profession, for the benefit of all.

**Exchanging IT expertise and knowledge**
The Institute fosters links between experts from industry, academia and business to promote new thinking, education and knowledge sharing.

**Supporting practitioners**
Through continuing professional development and a series of respected IT qualifications, the Institute seeks to promote professional practice tuned to the demands of business. It provides practical support and information services to its members and volunteer communities around the world.

**Setting standards and frameworks**
The Institute collaborates with government, industry and relevant bodies to establish good working practices, codes of conduct, skills frameworks and common standards. It also offers a range of consultancy services to employers to help them adopt best practice.

**Become a member**
Over 70,000 people including students, teachers, professionals and practitioners enjoy the benefits of BCS membership. These include access to an international community, invitations to a roster of local and national events, career development tools and a quarterly thought-leadership magazine. Visit www.bcs.org/membership to find out more.

**Further information**
BCS, The Chartered Institute for IT,
3 Newbridge Square,
Swindon, SN1 1BY, United Kingdom.
T +44 (0) 1793 417 417
(Monday to Friday, 09:00 to 17:00 UK time)
**www.bcs.org/contact**
**http://shop.bcs.org/**

# A PRACTICAL GUIDE TO IT LAW
## 3rd edition

Jeremy Holt and Jeremy Newton (editors)

© BCS Learning and Development Ltd 2020

The right of Jeremy Holt, Jeremy Newton, Stuart Smith, Mark Poston, Rachel Anderson, Sam De Silva, Jennifer Pierce, Andy Lucas, Victoria Hordern, Andrew Katz, Michaela MacDonald, Tim Astley, Usha Guness, Jiri Svorc, Chris McCormick, Nicola Cordell, Stewart James and Sara Ellacott to be identified as authors and editors of this work has been asserted by them in accordance with sections 77 and 78 of the Copyright, Designs and Patents Act 1988.

All rights reserved. Apart from any fair dealing for the purposes of research or private study, or criticism or review, as permitted by the Copyright Designs and Patents Act 1988, no part of this publication may be reproduced, stored or transmitted in any form or by any means, except with the prior permission in writing of the publisher, or in the case of reprographic reproduction, in accordance with the terms of the licences issued by the Copyright Licensing Agency. Enquiries for permission to reproduce material outside those terms should be directed to the publisher.

All trade marks, registered names etc. acknowledged in this publication are the property of their respective owners. BCS and the BCS logo are the registered trade marks of the British Computer Society charity number 292786 (BCS).

Published by BCS Learning and Development Ltd, a wholly owned subsidiary of BCS, The Chartered Institute for IT, 3 Newbridge Square, Swindon, SN1 1BY, UK.
www.bcs.org

Paperback ISBN: 978-1-78017-4884
PDF ISBN: 978-1-78017-4891
ePUB ISBN: 978-1-78017-4907
Kindle ISBN: 978-1-78017-4914

British Cataloguing in Publication Data.
A CIP catalogue record for this book is available at the British Library.

Disclaimer:
The views expressed in this book are of the authors and do not necessarily reflect the views of the Institute or BCS Learning and Development Ltd except where explicitly stated as such. Although every care has been taken by the authors and BCS Learning and Development Ltd in the preparation of the publication, no warranty is given by the authors or BCS Learning and Development Ltd as publisher as to the accuracy or completeness of the information contained within it and neither the authors nor BCS Learning and Development Ltd shall be responsible or liable for any loss or damage whatsoever arising by virtue of such information or any instructions or advice contained within this publication or by any of the aforementioned.

All URLs were correct at the time of publication.

**Publisher's acknowledgements**
Publisher: Ian Borthwick
Commissioning editor: Rebecca Youé
Production manager: Florence Leroy
Project manager: Sunrise Setting Ltd
Copy-editor: The Business Blend Ltd
Proofreader: Barbara Eastman
Indexer: Matthew Gale
Cover design: Alex Wright
Cover image: iStock/Lebazele
Typeset by Lapiz Digital Services, Chennai, India
Printed by Hobbs the Printers

# CONTENTS

|   |   |
|---|---|
| List of figures and tables | ix |
| Contributors | x |
| Acknowledgements | xiii |
| Abbreviations | xiv |
| Foreword to the 3rd edition | xvii |

**1. IT CONTRACTS – Jeremy Holt** — 1
- Introduction — 1
- Parts of a contract — 1
- Who are you going to call? — 2
- Checking out the supplier — 3
- Letter of intent — 3
- The supplier's terms — 3
- What contracts are there likely to be? — 4
- Appendix: main points of an IT contract — 11

**2. CLOUD COMPUTING – Stuart Smith, Mark Poston and Rachel Anderson** — 13
- Introduction — 13
- What is cloud computing? — 13
- The evolution of cloud computing — 14
- Factors that contributed to the rise of cloud services — 14
- Cloud formations — 16
- Silver linings — 16
- Thunder clouds — 18
- Summary — 20
- References — 20

**3. CLOUD COMPUTING CONTRACTS – Sam De Silva** — 21
- Introduction — 21
- Pre-contractual steps — 22
- Key commercial and legal issues — 24
- Summary — 35

**4. INTELLECTUAL PROPERTY LAW FOR COMPUTER USERS – Jennifer Pierce** — 36
- Introduction — 36
- Hardware and intellectual property rights — 37
- Software and intellectual property rights — 38

v

| | | |
|---|---|---|
| | Databases and intellectual property rights | 40 |
| | Websites and intellectual property rights | 41 |
| | Domain names and intellectual property rights | 42 |
| | The internet and trade marks | 43 |
| | The internet and copyright and database right | 45 |
| | Appendix: a basic guide to intellectual property and related rights | 45 |
| | Taking advice | 50 |
| | Summary | 50 |
| **5.** | **CYBER SECURITY – Andy Lucas** | **51** |
| | Introduction | 51 |
| | What is cyber security? | 51 |
| | What are the main forms of cyber attack? | 57 |
| | What are the risk areas? | 60 |
| | What laws govern cyber security? | 69 |
| | What practical steps should you consider? | 75 |
| | What guides, frameworks and standards are available? | 85 |
| | Summary | 92 |
| | References | 94 |
| **6.** | **GDPR AND DATA PROTECTION: THE LAW – Victoria Hordern** | **96** |
| | Introduction | 96 |
| | What data are covered? | 96 |
| | Special categories of personal data | 97 |
| | Data protection principles | 98 |
| | Rights of individuals | 104 |
| | Exemptions | 110 |
| | Remedies, enforcement powers and penalties | 111 |
| | Summary | 115 |
| **7.** | **DATA PROTECTION IN PRACTICE – Andrew Katz, Michaela MacDonald, Tim Astley, Usha Guness, Jiri Svorc and Chris McCormick** | **116** |
| | Introduction | 116 |
| | Data protection by design and default | 116 |
| | What amounts to 'processing personal data' under the GDPR? | 117 |
| | Creating a 'record of processing' | 119 |
| | Deciding upon the lawful basis of processing | 120 |
| | Drafting data protection policies | 124 |
| | Data Protection Impact Assessments | 125 |
| | Requests from data subjects | 125 |
| | Children's personal data | 127 |
| | Controllers and processors | 130 |
| | Sub-processors | 133 |
| | Data protection officers | 134 |
| | International transfers | 135 |
| | Processing data of EU data subjects | 138 |
| | Breach notifications | 139 |
| | Summary | 142 |

## CONTENTS

| | | |
|---|---|---|
| 8. | **IT IN THE WORKPLACE: PROTECTING THE EMPLOYER –** <br> **Jeremy Holt** | **143** |
| | Introduction | 143 |
| | Computer and email usage policies | 143 |
| | Social media | 152 |
| | Summary | 155 |
| 9. | **IT IN THE WORKPLACE: AVOIDING EMPLOYMENT PROBLEMS –** <br> **Nicola Cordell** | **156** |
| | Introduction | 156 |
| | Health and safety responsibilities | 156 |
| | Employment law | 161 |
| | Further advice | 163 |
| | Summary | 163 |
| 10. | **OPEN SOURCE SOFTWARE – Andrew Katz and** <br> **Michaela MacDonald** | **165** |
| | Introduction | 165 |
| | What is open source? | 165 |
| | Open source and communities | 171 |
| | Open source software business models | 172 |
| | Businesses as customers of open source | 174 |
| | Open source licensing in greater depth | 182 |
| | Procuring on-premise open source | 185 |
| | Licensing requirements | 186 |
| | Open source in the supply chain | 189 |
| | Open source compliance policies and procedures | 190 |
| | Open source software: employees and contractors | 191 |
| | Open source software and patents | 193 |
| | Summary | 194 |
| | Further information | 195 |
| | References | 195 |
| 11. | **AGILE SOFTWARE DEVELOPMENT– Stewart James** | **197** |
| | Introduction | 197 |
| | The Agile Manifesto | 198 |
| | Commercial challenges | 201 |
| | Commercial models | 207 |
| | Contract drafting | 209 |
| | Template examples | 210 |
| | Summary | 211 |
| 12. | **SETTING UP JOINT VENTURES – Andrew Katz** | **212** |
| | Introduction | 212 |
| | Joint ventures and IT projects | 212 |
| | Establishing a joint venture | 214 |
| | Structure of a joint venture | 216 |
| | The operating agreement | 222 |

## CONTENTS

  Competition law   223
  Summary   224
  Appendix: checklist for a joint venture operating agreement   225

**13. RESOLVING DISPUTES – Sara Ellacott**   **227**
  Introduction   227
  Overview of dispute resolution methods   227
  Key factors in dispute resolution   228
  Specific dispute resolution methods   228
  Summary   238

  Index   239

# LIST OF FIGURES AND TABLES

| | | |
|---|---|---|
| **Figure 11.1** | Comparison of software development methodologies | 199 |
| **Figure 11.2** | Cone of uncertainty | 202 |
| | | |
| **Table 3.1** | Key contractual issues with SaaS contracts | 30 |
| **Table 10.1** | Comparison of typical open source licences with typical proprietary software licences | 167 |
| **Table 10.2** | Summary of the key provisions of popular open source software licences | 176 |
| **Table 12.1** | Factors to consider when forming an entity | 217 |
| **Table 13.1** | Negotiation | 229 |
| **Table 13.2** | Expert determination | 230 |
| **Table 13.3** | Litigation | 232 |
| **Table 13.4** | Arbitration | 234 |
| **Table 13.5** | Mediation | 237 |

# CONTRIBUTORS

**Rachel Anderson** is an in-house paralegal at Natixis Investment Managers. She was previously a paralegal at software company Beamery, and at Algomi, a fin-tech company that provides cloud-based technology to bond market participants and where she worked alongside contributor Stuart Smith. Prior to working as a paralegal, Rachel read law (LLB) at the University of Manchester, where she developed a particular interest in commercial and intellectual property law.

**Tim Astley** is a partner in the Moorcrofts technology department. He is a solicitor with postgraduate qualifications from both Strathclyde University and Queen Mary, University of London in technology and communications law. He has worked on private, public and regulated sector transactions. He has extensive cloud computing contract experience, and has negotiated high-value complex agreements in many jurisdictions around the world. His practice involves providing specialist advice on data protection and open source compliance.

**Nicola Cordell** is a specialist occupational physician, researcher and educator, passionate about developing further understanding of employee health. She is the managing director of a social enterprise, Cordell Health Ltd. The organisation provides workplace health and wellbeing services, such as specialist advice on health and safety and employment issues relating to health across sectors, including the science and technology sector. In her education role, she develops training, in partnership with other professional groups including legal, IT and accountancy specialists, that is delivered to organisations and occupational health professionals, ensuring that advances in the knowledge base in this area are widely known.

**Sam De Silva** FBCS, CITP is a partner at CMS Cameron McKenna Nabarro Olswang LLP and specialises in complex and strategic IT and telecommunication projects. Sam is the Law Society's representative on the European Commission's Expert Group on Cloud Computing Contracts. Sam was elected to the Trustee Board of BCS in 2019 and has been on the Council of BCS since 2016 (vice-chair 2016–2017). In October 2020 Sam was elected as chair of BCS Law Specialist Group. Sam has also recently been appointed as the inaugural chair of the Diversity and Inclusion Advisory Board of the Society of Computers and Law.

**Sara Ellacott** is EMEA Assistant General Counsel for Litigation at Oracle Corporation. Sara advises on issues arising in the IT sector and has experience of a wide range of dispute resolution procedures, including negotiated settlements, High Court litigation, arbitration and mediation. Sara speaks regularly on issues relating to legal risk and dispute management.

CONTRIBUTORS

**Usha Guness** is a dual qualified barrister and solicitor. She has over fifteen years' experience in the commercial and technology field, which includes private practice as well as international experience working for several companies including a major global telecommunications company. She has a wide breadth of experience in advising, drafting and negotiating commercial and technology contracts as well as regulatory and compliance matters. She holds a Masters and recently obtained a certificate in US Copyright Law from the Berkman Center at Harvard University.

**Jeremy Holt** is the former senior partner of Clark Holt Commercial Solicitors (www.clarkholt.com). He has specialised in IT and e-commerce law for over 30 years. In 2003 Jeremy helped set up in Swindon the first museum in the country dedicated to the history of computing. He has co-authored two other books on IT law.

**Victoria Hordern** is a partner at London law firm Bates Wells, where she is Head of Data Privacy. She advises on a wide range of data privacy issues, including all types of GDPR-related obligations (from DPIAs to responses to data security breaches), as well as online privacy issues connected with the e-privacy legal framework. Her experience includes UK, pan-European and global privacy matters for commercial businesses and non-profits/charities. Victoria advises on international data transfers, whistleblowing, outsourcing, cookie compliance and employee monitoring. She holds the International Association of Privacy Professionals' CIPP/E and CIPT certifications and is a member of the IAPP's Privacy Faculty providing training on data privacy.

**Stewart James** is a director and the founder of Agillex, an alternative professional services consultancy that was established to work collaboratively with clients and enable the realisation of outcomes instead of imposing solutions. Previously, Stewart, a lawyer with over 20 years' experience, was a partner at DLA Piper LLP.

**Andrew Katz** is CEO and partner at Moorcrofts LLP, a niche corporate and technology legal practice based in Marlow, Buckinghamshire, where he heads the technology team. Andrew qualified as a barrister and subsequently re-qualified (and now practises) as a solicitor in England and Wales. He is also a solicitor (non-practising) in Ireland. He is a founder editor of the *International Free and Open Source Software Law Review* (now the *Journal of Open Law, Technology and Society*), a fellow of the Free Software Foundation Europe and a fellow of the Open Forum Academy. He is also founder and CEO of Orcro Ltd, a consultancy specialising in compliance issues, with special emphasis on open source supply chain licence compliance.

**Andy Lucas** is Head of the Technology, Media and Telecommunications department at Dentons. Prior to becoming a lawyer, he was a software programmer and project manager. During his 20-plus years in the legal profession, Andy has specialised in advising government and private sector companies on their technology implementations and cybersecurity. As well as advising clients, Andy lectures on a wide variety of technology law issues including blockchain, artificial intelligence and augmented reality.

**Michaela MacDonald** is a lecturer at Queen Mary University and Beijing University of Posts and Telecommunications. She teaches Interactive Entertainment Law, AI, Robotics and the Law, Cybersecurity Law and Product Development. Michaela's main research interests are in the legal, regulatory and societal effects of disruptive technologies. She has been involved in projects exploring the legal and regulatory implications of cloud computing, and, most recently, investigating the legality of smart contracts. Michaela is also working at Moorcrofts LLP as a consultant, collaborating on projects that have focused on the legality of data and text mining activities, open source licences classification and contract automation.

**Chris McCormick** is an experienced contracts manager, having previously worked at a large technology company in the Thames Valley handling their contract administration. In addition to his legal and process experience, he has particular interest in SalesForce implementation and is currently working with a number of Moorcrofts' clients to provide contracts management services and also help to develop the clients' processes around SalesForce. Chris has completed the LPC and is in the process of qualifying as a solicitor. Prior to his career in law, Chris worked as a freelance IT consultant specialising in enterprise storage and storage area networks.

**Jeremy Newton** is a director of Technology Law Alliance, a specialist IT/outsourcing law firm based in London. He has over 25 years' experience of IT and outsourcing contracts, both in private practice and as an in-house lawyer within the IT sector, and is ranked as one of the leading IT lawyers in London by the current Chambers directory. Jeremy advises a wide variety of IT businesses on their contracts, ranging from start-ups through to Tier 1 global outsourcing service providers. He also advises customer organisations including financial institutions, housebuilders, charities and public sector bodies. Jeremy has written and lectured widely on IT law and contracts, outsourcing, data protection and e-commerce matters, and is a past secretary of the Financial Services Specialist Group of BCS.

**Jennifer Pierce** is a partner in the City law firm, McCarthy Denning, where she specialises in intellectual property and information technology. This includes strategies for protection of software and hardware, including patenting (where possible), the use of open source, Internet of Things and work on the overlap with mechanical engineering as well as issues arising from the internet. Her clients range from multinational companies to research institutes to start-ups. She is ranked as a Global Leader by Intellectual Asset Management and is a past president of the Licensing Executives Society Britain & Ireland, the influential IP commercialisation society.

**Mark Poston** is Commercial Manager at Tempora, a software company that provides time tracking, cost and profitability analysis solutions via the cloud to a wide range of market sectors in the UK, US and Asia. Mark graduated from the University of Brighton in 2014 (BSc Computer Science) and 2015 (MSc Marketing & Behaviour Science).

**Stuart Smith** has run the legal operations at both Beamery and Algomi, each providers of B2B cloud services (respectively in the recruit-tech and fin-tech sectors). Previously, Stuart worked in private practice law firms including Clark Holt, Osborne Clarke and Technology Law Alliance. He has had long-standing involvement in his family business, Tempora, a provider of cloud-based time-tracking services.

**Jiri Svorc** has participated in advising businesses as well as public sector organisations on technology, intellectual property and complex commercial law matters, as well as on personal data protection, cyber security and open source licensing and compliance. Most notably, Jiri has participated in cross-border technology transfers, and advised leading global technology companies as well as technology disruptors. Jiri has obtained LLM from Queen Mary, University of London and has worked with a number of law firms in the UK and EU, as well as with DG Connect of the European Commission.

# ACKNOWLEDGEMENTS

The authors wish to acknowledge the contributions made by the following:

Jane Bright
Julieta De Silva
Leonardo De Silva
Stella De Silva
Lizzy Gagan
Dawn Holt
David Hudson
Nathan Hudson
Nia Hudson
George Johnson
Lucy Katz
Andrew Kite
Paul Langford
Antonia Newell
Lucy Newton
Arthur Smith
Christopher Smith
Theodore Smith
Wilbur Smith
Heather Stewart

# ABBREVIATIONS

| | |
|---|---|
| **AGPL** | Affero GPL |
| **ASP** | Application Service Provider/Provision |
| **AUP** | Agile Unified Process |
| **AWS** | Amazon Web Services |
| **BCR** | Binding Corporate Rule (GDPR) |
| **BSD** | Berkeley Software Distribution |
| **BYOD** | Bring Your Own Device |
| **CAA** | Copyright Assignment Agreement |
| **CC** | Creative Commons |
| **CCS** | Crown Commercial Services |
| **CCTV** | Closed-Circuit Television |
| **CEO** | Chief Executive Officer |
| **CIF** | Cloud Industry Forum |
| **CIO** | Chief Information Officer |
| **CISQ** | Consortium for IT Software Quality |
| **CLA** | Contributor Licence Agreement |
| **CPR** | Civil Procedure Rules |
| **CPU** | Central Processing Unit |
| **CRM** | Customer Relationship Management |
| **CSCC** | Cloud Standards Customer Council |
| **CSO** | Chief Security Officer |
| **CTO** | Chief Technology/Technical Officer |
| **DDoS** | Distributed Denial of Service |
| **DoS** | Denial of Service |
| **DPA** | Data Processing Agreement |
| **DPIA** | Data Protection Impact Assessment |
| **DPL** | Data Protection Lead |
| **DPO** | Data Protection Officer |
| **DSDM** | Dynamic Systems Development Method |
| **DSE** | Display Screen Equipment |

## ABBREVIATIONS

| | |
|---|---|
| DSP | Digital Service Provider (NIS Directive) |
| EEA | European Economic Area |
| EEIG | European Economic Interest Grouping |
| ENISA | European Union Agency for Network and Information Security |
| ERP | Enterprise Resource Planning |
| EU | European Union |
| FDD | Feature-Driven Development |
| FLOSS | Free, Libre and Open Source Software |
| FOSS | Free and Open Source Software |
| FSF | Free Software Foundation |
| GDPR | General Data Protection Regulation 2016/679 |
| GPL | General Public License |
| HSE | Health and Safety Executive |
| IaaS | Infrastructure as a Service |
| IASME | Information Assurance for Small and Medium Enterprises |
| ICO | Information Commissioner's Office |
| ICS | Industrial Control System |
| IEC | International Electrotechnical Commission |
| IEEE | Institute of Electrical and Electronics Engineers |
| IoT | Internet of Things |
| IP | Intellectual Property or Internet Protocol (address) |
| ISMS | Information Security Management System |
| ISO | International Organization for Standardization |
| ISP | Internet Service Provider |
| ISS | Information Society Service |
| IT | Information Technology |
| ITU | International Telecommunication Union |
| LGPL | Library/Lesser General Public License |
| LIA | Legitimate Interest Assessment |
| LLC | Limited Liability Corporation |
| LLP | Limited Liability Partnership |
| MAC | Media Access Control |
| MFA | Multi-Factor Authentication |
| MIT | Massachusetts Institute of Technology |
| MitM | Man in the Middle (attack) |
| MPL | Mozilla Public License |
| MVP | Minimum Viable Product |
| NA | Network Administrator |
| NCSC | National Cyber Security Centre |

**ABBREVIATIONS**

| | |
|---|---|
| **NDA** | Non-Disclosure Agreement |
| **NHS** | National Health Service |
| **NIS** | Network and Information Systems (Directive/Regulation) |
| **NIST** | National Institute of Standards and Technology (USA) |
| **OEM** | Original Equipment Manufacturer |
| **OES** | Operator of Essential Services (NIS Directive) |
| **OFT** | Office of Fair Trading |
| **OIN** | Open Invention Network |
| **OSI** | Open Source Initiative |
| **PaaS** | Platform as a Service |
| **PCI DSS** | Payment Card Industry Data Security Standard |
| **PECRs** | Privacy and Electronic Communications Regulations 2003 |
| **PIN** | Personal Identification Number |
| **RDSP** | Relevant Digital Service Provider |
| **RFID** | Radio-frequency Identification |
| **SA** | Sharealike |
| **SaaS** | Software as a Service |
| **SAFe** | Scaled Agile Framework |
| **SAR** | Subject Access Request |
| **SCC** | Standard Contractual Clause |
| **SEQOHS** | Safe and Effective Quality Occupational Health Service |
| **SIS** | Safety Instrumented Systems |
| **SLA** | Service Level Agreement |
| **SQL** | Structured Query Language |
| **SSD** | Solid-state Drive |
| **SSL** | Secure Sockets Layer |
| **T&M** | Time and Materials |
| **TCC** | Technology and Construction Court |
| **ToS** | Terms of Service |
| **UPS** | Uninterruptible Power Supply |
| **VAT** | Value Added Tax |
| **VoIP** | Voice over Internet Protocol |
| **VPN** | Virtual Private Network |
| **XP** | Extreme Programming |

# FOREWORD TO THE 3RD EDITION

This book is a practical guide to IT law. The authors felt the law in England in this area should be summarised in a way that is easy to understand. Things have changed so much and so quickly since the last edition that it was felt that the book should be updated to reflect these changes.

The book is not designed to be read from cover to cover. Readers can dip into the various self-contained chapters to find the answers that they seek. It provides practical advice on the appropriate steps that should be taken.

We hope that it will be a valuable guide to IT professionals as well as being of interest to managers, legal practitioners and students.

Jeremy Holt and Jeremy Newton

# 1   IT CONTRACTS

## Jeremy Holt

This chapter outlines the contents of a contract and lists the matters that should be covered by different types of contract. If you do not have time to read the rest of the chapter, the appendix lists the main points that you should consider.

### INTRODUCTION

Pity the unfortunate manager. It has been bad enough trying to get the computer project organised. Now, possibly at the last moment, the contracts have arrived, some with print small enough to make the reader go blind. The manager suspects (rightly) that these contracts are one-sided in favour of the supplier, but knows that the project will only proceed if those contracts (or something similar) are signed. How does the manager work out what needs to be done and from whom advice can be obtained? This chapter provides a practical framework of help in this situation. If you are looking for an academic guide to computer contracts, you will need to look elsewhere.

### PARTS OF A CONTRACT

The first point to consider is the form that contracts normally take. At its simplest, a contract consists of:

1. the date on which the contract was entered into;
2. the names and addresses of those entering into the contract;
3. a short description of what the contract is about (generally entitled 'Background', 'Recitals' or even, regrettably, 'Whereas');
4. definitions of terms used in the contract;
5. what the supplier is going to do for you;
6. what you must do for the supplier;
7. what you must pay the supplier.

Do not forget we are engaged in contract first aid here. If all else fails, concentrate on points (5) and (7), that is, what the supplier is going to do for you and what you are expected to pay. Standard terms that are not specific to this individual contract (what lawyers call 'boilerplate') are generally grouped together at the end of the contract.

## IMPORTANT BOILERPLATE TERMS

These are some of the more important boilerplate clauses you may come across.

**Force majeure** – this says that neither party shall be liable for any failure to perform the contract because of circumstances beyond its control such as an Act of God, fire, flood and so on. This is more likely to be invoked by the supplier than the client because this clause effectively absolves the supplier from responsibility.

**Entire agreement** – this says that the entire agreement between the parties is set out in the written contract and so no other previous representations by the supplier may be relied upon by the client. This is a reasonable principle, but the client must make sure that the contract deals with all the important points.

**Notices** – this specifies the agreed means of sending formal notices. Normally, this requires a notice to be in writing, to avoid issues surrounding an oral notice (i.e. proving delivery and contents). However, what qualifies as 'writing' may differ from contract to contract. For example, some clauses may expressly state that a notice is not valid if sent by email. A notices clause may also specify the personal details of a party on whom a notice must be served to ensure it comes to the attention of the appropriate party.

**Dispute resolution** – it is sensible to agree an alternative dispute resolution procedure (such as mediation) that must be carried out before any dispute is referred to the courts or to arbitration.

**Governing law and jurisdiction** – ideally this should be English law enforced in the English courts. An alternative is to agree arbitration, but as this happens behind closed doors then the supplier may worry less about bad publicity.

## WHO ARE YOU GOING TO CALL?

You are not going to be able to do all this on your own. You are going to need professional advice. Computer law is a specialist area, and a rapidly changing one (it did not even exist as a field of legal practice 30 years ago) and the correct advice from a lawyer experienced in this field can save a great deal of trouble later. The function of a good lawyer is to assess risk, help the client to understand the level of risk and then reduce it.

There are two directories of lawyers that you might like to consult: *Chambers' Guide to the Legal Profession* and *The Legal 500*. New versions are published each year, and each has sections on lawyers who specialise in computer law (sometimes called 'information technology law'). These two books can generally be found in the reference section of a public library, and can also be searched without charge on the web. Alternatively, you can ring the Law Society or the Society for Computers and Law for suggestions of lawyers who work in this field and who could help you.

## CHECKING OUT THE SUPPLIER

It may seem like an obvious point but make sure that you know who you are dealing with. This will mean, at least, doing a company search. A credit check would do no harm. As the Army maxim has it, 'time spent on reconnaissance is seldom wasted'. If you discover that the supplier company was set up last year and has an issued capital of £1, you may like to consider asking for a guarantee of the contract from a more substantial body.

Business is not all about making rational decisions on paper. Do you get good vibes from the supplier? On small things, do they do what they say that they will do? If, for whatever reason, you do not trust them, do not go ahead with the contract under any circumstances, as this will only lead to worry and tears later.

## LETTER OF INTENT

As the supplier may need to start work on your project before contracts are signed, and because the negotiation and agreement of the contract terms may take a little while, the supplier may ask for a letter of intent from you. Alternatively, you may like to suggest one so that you are not pressurised into signing the contracts before you have reviewed them properly.

A letter of intent is no more than written confirmation from you of your intention to enter into a contract with the supplier. What is critical, however, is that your letter of intent states that the letter is not intended to be contractually binding. Otherwise, you may unwittingly enter into a contract earlier than you intended.

Where there is a non-binding letter of intent and the supplier, at your request and to save time, starts work on the project, it is reasonable for the supplier to ask to be paid for this initial work carried out regardless of whether the project proceeds or not. There are two important matters to agree here. The first is the rate for the work carried out (e.g. a daily rate). Work normally starts under a letter of intent on a time and materials basis; the definitive contract may include a fixed price for a specified deliverable. The second is an overall cap on the total amount of payment to the supplier for this work. This obligation to pay the supplier should be contractually binding (unlike the rest of the letter of intent).

## THE SUPPLIER'S TERMS

It is a good idea to ask for the supplier's proposed terms at as early a stage as possible. Do not wait until you have told them that they have been awarded the contract. There is of course no obligation on you to accept that you will purchase a new computer system on the basis of the supplier's terms. You could propose your own terms entirely – this is certainly an approach taken by large organisations with extensive experience of computer contracts. However, it is generally better to use the supplier's contract terms (unless they are completely unreasonable) as a starting point and amend them to your satisfaction.

If a particular point is important to you, make sure that you get it in writing from the supplier. It may well be that a critical aspect is not dealt with in the supplier's draft contract at all. If so, you must, for evidence's sake, get it in writing from the supplier. An ordinary letter from the supplier is sufficient provided that it is either referred to in the main contract or included as a schedule or as an attachment. If the supplier drags their heels and, despite repeated requests from you, refuses to confirm a point in writing, you should write to the supplier saying that you are only entering into the main contract on the basis that this point is agreed. If the matter ever goes to court, the production of your letter will be of great assistance to your case.

## WHAT CONTRACTS ARE THERE LIKELY TO BE?

Any computer system will require the purchase, licence and maintenance of hardware (the server, PCs, printers, etc.), software (the application software and the operating system software) and services (such as support and maintenance). Previously, the emphasis was very much on the hardware, but nowadays the focus is much more on the software and services. Nevertheless, this chapter discusses all the contracts you are likely to need.

Generally, it is better to decide upon the software first and then to choose the appropriate hardware. Alternatively, you may enter into a contract for consultancy services first, to assist with this process. Consequently, this chapter will deal with such contracts in this order.

### Contracts for consultancy services

Long before the order for a new system is placed, the client may enter into a consultancy contract, perhaps relating to a feasibility study, analysing requirements, recommending a system to meet those requirements, helping to select the appropriate suppliers, or assisting with preparation of an invitation to tender. A large part of the work carried out in the computer industry is under consultancy contracts. The client may need help on a one-off basis or require skills that do not exist within the client's workforce, so need an outside consultant to carry out the work. Sometimes the consultancy arrangement is dealt with by means of an exchange of letters; a formal consultancy agreement, however, is a better option for both parties.

- **Defining the deliverables** – one of the most important issues that must be dealt with in such a contract is a detailed description of what the consultant is expected to do. If the description is loose or inexact, this can give rise to differences between what the client is expecting to receive and what the consultant is expecting to deliver – which can, predictably, lead to disputes. So, defining the nature and quality of the deliverable is particularly important.
- **Payment arrangements** – the payment to the consultant by the client may be on a time and materials, fixed price or estimated maximum price basis. It is an aspect of consultancy that the amount of work required will be uncertain. The disadvantage of a fixed price payment mechanism (as with any other contract) is that the consultant will inevitably include a contingency element in the price quoted. If the consultancy can be broken down into a series of stages, payment against milestones will allow each party to gauge how the work is going.

- **Copyright** – copyright will almost always be an issue. Broadly speaking, there is a simple choice as to how the parties deal with ownership of copyright in the consultant's work. Either the consultant can assign to the client all intellectual property rights in whatever is produced (provided that the consultant has been fully paid) or the consultant can grant a perpetual licence to the client to use such intellectual property rights for the purposes of the client's business (see Chapter 4 for more details). It is important to note that if there is no agreement with a consultant about copyright, the client does not automatically get ownership of such copyright. It stays with the consultant (although there may also be an implied licence for use of the copyright by the client).

- **Confidentiality** – it goes almost without saying that the consultant should be obliged to keep confidential any information given by the client about its business. The problem is that once a consultant has carried out an assignment for one client in an industry, the consultant may be ideally placed to carry out assignments for other clients within that same industry. Sometimes, therefore, clients go further and stipulate in the contract that not only must their own information be kept confidential, but the consultant must agree not to carry out projects for the client's competitors for a period (perhaps a year) after the work is completed.

- **Insurance** – in order to provide peace of mind to the client, the client may require the consultant to take out professional indemnity insurance. This is still relatively inexpensive as, in practice, it is rare for claims to be made under such policies.

- **Key personnel** – the client will want to know the identity of the staff who the consultant will be using to carry out the work. It is normal for the client to be able to veto any staff members of whom they disapprove for whatever reason.

- **Termination** – the client will want to retain the right to terminate the consultancy contract if the consultant is guilty of serious misconduct or any other conduct likely to bring the client into disrepute.

## Contracts for software licences

At its simplest, any contract for software should allow you to use the software in the way that you envisaged without the risk that anyone can come along later and say either that you cannot use it any more or that you have to pay more money. It follows, therefore, that one of the first checks you should do is to confirm that the software supplier either owns the copyright in the software or has the right to license it to you. It is a feature of the computer industry that software is often licensed to end users by organisations other than the actual owner (for example it may be sub-licensed by a distributor or channel partner). You should not put up with oblique answers to your demand for evidence that the supplier can license the software to you. They should be able to produce it immediately.

At this point you may wonder why a licence agreement is necessary at all; why can the supplier not simply sell you the software? The supplier is not actually selling you ownership of the software because they would like to continue to license it to other people. The licence is only a permit for you to use the software for your own purposes.

This leads onto the next important point. You must check in the licence agreement to whom the software is licensed and for what purpose. Is the software to be licensed to your particular company or can it be used by the whole of your group (in which case the software supplier will want more money)? Alternatively, is the software to be restricted to a limited number of users and, if more than that number use it, then do you have to pay an additional licence fee? This is one of the oldest tricks in the software supplier's book. They allow the client to sign up for a very limited number of users and then the supplier makes a considerable profit from the additional users that will almost inevitably be required by the client later. The supplier, of course, responds that this simply reflects the extra use (and, as a result, commercial benefit) that the client is making of the software.

It is also possible that, at some time in the future, the client may want to outsource its computer operations. Consequently, provision for the transfer of the licence from the client to an outsourcing company should be made in the original software licence agreement.

Additionally, make sure that the procedure for acceptance testing is known and agreed. If this has not been sorted out in the contract, how are you going to stop a bad system from being installed? In the past, the test data were generally supplied by the client; nowadays it is more acceptable for it to be provided by the supplier.

## Contracts for software maintenance

No software of any complexity is ever free from errors. The older the system, the more likely that it will need maintenance. Furthermore, if a system is installed in a rush (e.g. to meet a particular deadline), then it is likely not to have been tested properly so may require more attention after it has been installed. In some ways, future charges for maintenance are the icing on the cake for software developers. If they can generate sufficiently wide sales of the software, then support fees can be guaranteed for years to come. It is important for managers to be aware of this as three-quarters of a budget for software may be for future software maintenance. The client is well advised to check how wide the maintenance supplier's client base is (the wider the better) and to look at the offices from which the supplier will be providing the support (and how many people will be providing such support). The maintenance contract will almost certainly be prepared by the supplier. Some of the most common provisions are discussed below.

- **Charging arrangements** – sometimes the cost of the software licence is bundled with the first year's maintenance charges. One interesting point is from when the support charges should run. Some clients argue that they should start from the end of the warranty period for the software. However, it is now generally accepted that they should begin from acceptance of the system, as warranty and support are separate matters.

- **Scope of maintenance services** – maintenance or support will normally cover the investigation by the supplier of errors in the system reported by the client as well as updated documentation and telephone or, more frequently nowadays, online advice. It will, in most cases, cover updates to the software (but not necessarily new versions of the software). The client may want to categorise different kinds of problems into those that could be critical for its business and those that are no more than an irritation and could be dealt with next time a new version of the software comes out. The supplier's response time will be different depending on the severity of the problem. The supplier will not normally commit to a fix within a particular period – only that they will start to fix it within a particular time.

- **Length of maintenance** – make sure that you get the supplier to agree to supply support and maintenance for the products purchased for a decent length of time, for example five years. You do not want the supplier cancelling support after a couple of years just when your new system is working well. Note that you do not have to commit to take the support and maintenance for five years – ideally your commitment should be on a year-by-year basis. It is just that the supplier agrees to make the support available to you for at least five years if you want it.
- **Exclusions from scope** – the maintenance supplier will also be keen to list in the contract what maintenance does **not** cover. Most of these exceptions are reasonable. They generally include problems arising from changes to the software made by people other than the supplier, incorrect use of the software by the client, or events beyond the control of the maintenance supplier such as hardware failure, fluctuation of electrical supplies or accidents. Normally, the maintenance supplier will still seek to help the client where the exceptions apply (indeed there should be a contractual obligation to do so). However, the supplier may want to make an additional charge for such work and will not guarantee any particular recovery time. From the supplier's point of view, it becomes difficult to manage support if the client base is using several different versions of the software. Consequently, the supplier normally restricts support to the latest two versions of the software and will refuse to support earlier versions.
- **Charge increases** – the client will want to ensure that the maintenance charges will not rocket up. One means of doing this is to tie the maintenance charges to a percentage of the list price of the software (e.g. 10–15 per cent) but, of course, the supplier has control over the list price. Alternatively, any increase in maintenance charges can be tied to a recognised index. Clients sometimes suggest the Consumer Price Index. However, suppliers (who know that increases in salaries are generally greater than increases in retail prices) prefer to tie them to an earnings index. There is some logic in this, as the bulk of the supplier's expenses are salaries.
- **Payment arrangements** – payment is almost invariably made three to six months in advance. This is so that if the supplier goes into liquidation the client will not have overpaid very much and the client can also swiftly withhold the payment of maintenance charges if there is a problem with the service provided.
- **Termination** – it is important for the client to look at the termination clauses of the contract offered by the supplier. The client will want to know how much notice they have to give to end the maintenance contract. This is often three or six months. It is a good idea for the client to ask the supplier to commit on its part to supply maintenance (if the client wants it) for the potential life of the software (e.g. five years).

## Contracts for software development

Software will often need to be customised for the client by the supplier. However, this is really only a tinkering with the main programs. In certain circumstances, it may be necessary for the client to commission new software because there is no existing software that meets the client's needs.

Contracts for software development are complex and it is wise for the client to seek professional advice both about the specification for the software and the contract under which the software will be written. This is all the more important because software development projects have a reputation for taking longer, and costing more, than originally forecast. Consequently, background research by the client into the proposed supplier is particularly worthwhile. Pricing for the project will be either for a fixed price or for time and materials. Payments will normally be made conditional upon project milestones being reached. The client should seek to ensure the quality of the software product delivered by the supplier by requiring acceptance tests of the software and a warranty from the supplier that the product will be in accordance with the agreed specification.

A thorny question is whether the client should own the copyright in the software program produced. At first glance, it might be thought that this should obviously belong to the client who has paid for it. However, the client only needs to use the software, not to own or develop it. It may benefit the client if the supplier has an incentive to carry out further development of the software program and license it to other clients; the original client does not then pay the total cost of all the subsequent fixes and has the benefit of the faults reported by other users. However, if the supplier becomes insolvent, then the client needs access to the source code of the software in order to maintain it. For this reason, the client should require the supplier to put a copy of such source code in escrow with an independent third party so that it is available if required. The supplier will normally provide a warranty that defects in the software reported within a particular length of time after the start of its use will be rectified. This is frequently 90 days after acceptance of the software by the client.

**Contracts for hardware purchase**

Since computer hardware is so much more reliable than it used to be, contracts for the supply of hardware are not generally contentious. A hardware purchase contract requires the following details:

- a detailed description of the hardware (this is likely to be in a schedule);
- a warranty about the quality of hardware (normally this warranty applies for a year after acceptance of the hardware by the client);
- delivery dates;
- price;
- acceptance testing;
- future maintenance;
- training.

Problems can arise if the hardware is not large enough for anticipated demand, and with the integration of hardware (such as servers and printers) that may have been supplied by different suppliers.

In many cases the cost of the hardware is not a large percentage of the total system cost. As profit margins on hardware are relatively low, the software supplier may be relaxed about whether the client obtains the hardware from the software supplier or from a third-party supplier. It is always worth asking the software supplier to quote for supplying the hardware as they may have better bargaining power than you would have on your own.

At the end of the day, the two most important matters in a contract for hardware are to check that there is an exact description of what you are buying and that there is an obligation on the supplier to repair or replace it if it does not work properly.

## Contracts for hardware maintenance

Hardware maintenance is more of a commodity than software maintenance and there are likely to be more suppliers for the maintenance of hardware (and so prices are keener). There are two different types of hardware maintenance: preventive maintenance and corrective maintenance. Preventive maintenance covers the regular testing of the hardware (e.g. once every six months) before any problem is reported. Corrective maintenance deals with faults as and when they arise, normally in response to a service call from the client.

With corrective maintenance, the key element is the response time – how quickly will the supplier start to respond to the problem once it is reported? This is generally within a fixed number of working hours. For example, an engineer may have to arrive at the site no more than eight working hours after the problem has been reported by the client. This does not mean that the engineer will solve the problem within eight hours – merely that a start will be made to try to solve it. Sometimes online diagnosis is used: the client's hardware is linked by telecommunications to the supplier who can solve the fault at a distance. (The impetus for online diagnosis came from the US, where the distances were so great it was often not practicable to send an engineer in person.)

Payment for hardware maintenance is generally made in advance on a monthly or quarterly basis. Other points that will normally be covered in a hardware maintenance contract include a right for the supplier to:

- make an additional charge for frivolous or unnecessary call outs;
- increase the charges from time to time, perhaps in accordance with a recognised index (such as the Consumer Price Index);
- refuse to cover equipment that is more than five years old or is past its reasonable working life.

The client will be under an obligation to:

- pay for corrections that are not caused by the equipment itself (e.g. faults arising from electrical fluctuations);
- notify the supplier of problems promptly after they arise (so that time does not make them worse);
- allow the supplier reasonable access to the equipment.

## Service level agreements

Service level agreements (SLAs) are critical to the computer industry, but they are rarely fully understood. Under an SLA, a supplier undertakes to supply a service to a client at a particular level.

Perhaps because so few lawyers have a reasonable working knowledge of the computer industry, SLAs are often drawn up by the participants without legal advice.

A service level agreement should cover:

- the service required (i.e. what the client wants and what the supplier is prepared to commit to supply);
- quality standards (i.e. the standards or levels the supplier must achieve), such as host/terminal response times, batch processing times, 'uptime', or processor availability, by specifying what? when? how? and by whom?
- deliverables (e.g. regular reports);
- the consequences of failing to meet service procedures or standards (e.g. compensation in the form of service credits);
- procedures for the client to monitor performance of obligations by the supplier;
- procedures for change control (i.e. changing part of the service that is being provided by the supplier under the agreement);
- terms dealing with access to, and security of, the client's site and data;
- procedures for disaster recovery (either upon a system failure or following a catastrophe);
- the agreed frequency of meetings between the client and the supplier to review the supplier's performance of the agreement, properly minuted with subsequent action plans and awards of priority.

Ideally, an SLA should be a self-enforcing agreement within a continuing relationship. There should be no need for either side to litigate and changes required should be dealt with through a change control procedure. For example, a clause may specify that any additional features requested by the client would require an extra cost to be paid to the supplier, and for this to be confirmed in writing by both parties. In some ways the process of creating the SLA is as valuable as the agreement itself.

### *What form should a service level agreement take?*

SLAs can be between different businesses or between different parts of the same organisation (such as the IT department and its users). Facilities management agreements, software maintenance agreements and managed data network agreements are all examples of SLAs. Alternatively, the SLA may be one aspect of a larger agreement for services, that is, it may be the schedule that stipulates how well the services have to be provided and what happens if the supplier does not provide this.

At its weakest, an SLA may be a simple oral understanding, documented by an exchange of letters. The best form is a formal legal agreement with the technical procedures and specifications annexed as separate schedules.

### *What happens if the terms of a service level agreement are broken?*

If the breach is fundamental, the party not in breach will be entitled to terminate the agreement and sue for the loss suffered as a result of the breach. In other circumstances there will be a system for measuring the breach and apportioning costs. These systems range from an event-based system (i.e. if ... then ...) to a more sophisticated system of 'failure points' (i.e. if there are more than five examples of ... then ...). The functions of such compensation systems vary from simply drawing attention to a problem to compensation for loss. Compensation for loss is difficult to quantify and, if it is excessive, will be unenforceable by a court. In practice, the right to withhold payment is a valuable weapon. The end (or slowing down) of payments by the client into the supplier's accounts department is likely to put pressure on the supplier.

Escalation clauses are undervalued and should be more widely used. These provide for a problem to be escalated up the various tiers of management on both sides if it cannot initially be resolved. Even the best SLA does not last for ever and there must be a procedure for orderly termination and (if necessary) migration from the supplier's system to another system. The failure to include such clauses was a frequent weakness of early SLAs. Migration is critically important in relation to facilities management contracts and, as a rule of thumb, a year is generally allowed for this. The supplier should also be required to provide all reasonable assistance to the client with the migration to another system.

### Contracts relating to cloud computing

Cloud computing is sometimes called software as a service. It appears likely to continue to revolutionise the computer industry over the next few years. For a description of what cloud computing is and the contracts that you are likely to need, see Chapters 2 and 3.

### Contracts relating to Agile computing

Agile is a particular form of software development that uses short iterations of effort to produce incremental results. This differs from the sequential or 'waterfall' approach to development, which requires a detailed description of the subject matter of the contract to be established at or prior to the start of the project. Agile methodologies use a different cultural approach to the development of software, with the expectation of greater participation by the customer. Consequently, Agile requires an alternative form of contract. The use of Agile and the development of contracts using Agile methodologies is described in greater detail in Chapter 11.

### APPENDIX: MAIN POINTS OF AN IT CONTRACT

Read this on its own if you do not have enough time to read the rest of this chapter. But read it carefully.

- Make sure that you know exactly what you want and what is achievable, because if you do not know then you are not going to get the contract right. Among the most common causes of computer project failure are unclear client requirements and unrealistic client expectations.

- Make sure that all the prospective suppliers sign a confidentiality agreement with you. If you are going to give them a detailed functional specification of what you want and information about your business, you do not want there to be any question of that confidential information being obtained by your competitors.

- Beware of falling into the trap of entering into a contract before you intend to. There are no legal formalities in the UK about entering into a computer contract, so make sure that all pre-contract correspondence is headed 'subject to contract'. If you leave discussions about a written contract incomplete (e.g. lots of draft contracts sent between you and the supplier but nothing ever signed), then a court is likely to take the last undisputed draft as being the basis of the contract between you and the supplier.

- If a particular point is important to you, make sure that you get it in writing from the supplier. It may well be that a critical aspect is not dealt with in the supplier's draft contract at all.

- Make sure that you get the supplier to agree to supply support and maintenance for the products purchased for a decent length of time, for example five years. You do not want the supplier cancelling support after a couple of years just when your new system is working well.

- Make sure that the procedure for acceptance testing is known and agreed.

- Make sure that you can get access to the source code of the software programs supplied if the supplier either goes into liquidation or stops supporting the software. Ideally, this source code should be deposited with an independent third party and kept updated by the supplier as each new version comes out.

- Finally, never forget that the contract is a delivery mechanism for ensuring that a project is completed in the right way at the right time by the right person and for the right price. No more, no less.

# 2   CLOUD COMPUTING

## Stuart Smith, Mark Poston and Rachel Anderson

**INTRODUCTION**

Cloud computing is everywhere. Governments, business and not-for-profit organisations all make use of cloud computing for offsite data storage or to access 'on demand' computing power when capacity is required, via services such as Amazon Web Services, Microsoft Azure and Google Cloud. Individuals too use cloud computing services when they access social media such as Facebook or WhatsApp. This chapter deals with the technical and business benefits of cloud computing, and explains what it is, how it developed and why it has become so ubiquitous in both our business and our personal lives.

**WHAT IS CLOUD COMPUTING?**

Cloud computing is described by the National Institute of Standards and Technology (NIST) as 'a model for enabling ubiquitous, convenient, on-demand network access to a shared pool of configurable computing resources ... that can be rapidly provisioned and released with minimal management effort or service provider interaction' (NIST 2019).

Gartner describes clouding computing as being 'a style of computing in which scalable and elastic IT-enabled capabilities are delivered as a service using internet technologies'.[1]

There are many types of cloud computing, often referred to by acronyms ending in 'aaS', meaning 'as a service'. Three examples are the provision of software (SaaS), platform (PaaS) and infrastructure (IaaS). All are IT resources provided as services hosted remotely from a user's computing device and accessed through a network connection – very often a user's web browser – rather than being installed locally on a customer's computer.

To elaborate on the three types of services above:

- **SaaS** refers to the provision of software applications that formerly might have been installed on a desktop or network, in the cloud.
- **PaaS** refers to the provision in the cloud of services that enable customers to deploy applications created using programming languages and tools supported by the supplier.

---

[1] https://www.gartner.com/en/information-technology/glossary/cloud-computing#:~:text=Cloud%20computing%20is%20a%20style,a%20service%20using%20internet%20technologies

- **IaaS** refers to services in the cloud that provide computer processing power, storage space and network capacity – enabling customers to run arbitrary software (including operating systems and applications). The most well-known are Amazon Web Services (AWS), Microsoft Azure and Google Cloud. IaaS is the platform upon which PaaS and SaaS are frequently built.

These three elements are together sometimes referred to as the cloud computing 'stack'. This chapter is written primarily with the issues surrounding the provision of SaaS in the business-to-business sector in mind, but the themes touched upon below are generally applicable to other forms of cloud service provision and in other sectors.

## THE EVOLUTION OF CLOUD COMPUTING

Long before the term 'cloud computing' was coined, software suppliers were providing services to their customers from remote servers via internet-enabled computers. This was called Application Service Provision (ASP) and was the original platform of IT service delivery to emerge from the convergence of computing and communications in the mid-1990s. However, the ASP model had certain limitations. First, it involved more complicated initial installation and configuration (at the customer end) than today's on-demand cloud services. Second, it arose as a means of providing software on a one-to-one basis, rather than on the one-to-many (multi-tenant) basis. This is a key feature of most cloud computing services nowadays, where one supplier has many customers. Consequently, ASP lacked the huge advantage that cloud computing enjoys, both on the buy and the sell sides, of being very scalable.

The emergence of SaaS at the turn of the 21st century signified the beginning of software delivery based on multi-tenant architecture and involving network-based access to software managed from a central location, thus removing the need for customers to install patches or upgrades. Rather than traditional software licensing with local installation, we entered an era where software was made available as a web-based service, usually under a subscription agreement.

## FACTORS THAT CONTRIBUTED TO THE RISE OF CLOUD SERVICES

Sophisticated and large-scaled data centres can (to an extent) take advantage of low-cost locations and the widespread access to improved internet bandwidth. This has allowed data centre providers, like AWS, Microsoft Azure and Google Cloud, to sell hosting services at a price point that enables the cloud model to dramatically rival the locally deployed IT services on cost alone. This effect is likely to have been magnified by a breakthrough in solid-state drive (SSD) storage technology in 2017, which has facilitated faster and cheaper data processing. ASP was also static in its processing, whereas cloud computing can scale data processed as required, leading to flexible server configurations.

'Bandwidth' is the term coined to describe the maximum amount, in bits (not to be confused with bytes) of information, that can be transferred across a predetermined path in a single transaction. This originally began at 56 kilobits per second with Dial-up, which is the size of a small text document. Modern technologists are currently able to offer 100 gigabits per second (the size of an entire music album) and there is legislation planned to make this speed available across the UK by 2025. This improvement has largely been brought about with the switch from copper cabling, which is susceptible to interference and corruption, to fibre glass cabling, which is also cheaper to repair. For cloud computing, this has meant that the services have been transformed from being able to send and receive small instructions or text files to large documents or media files, within seconds.

It has been suggested that the growth of the cloud services sector owes something to the financial crisis of 2007/8. As well as having a dramatic impact on the global economy, it forced large organisations to rethink cost reduction, the outcome being a preference for the lower operating expense model of cloud services to the higher capital expenditure model of on-premise deployed solutions. As a result, cloud technology became an area of focus for investment. It is worth highlighting, however, that some sectors – including areas of financial services – continue to lag behind more innovative parts of the economy. Many banks are still trying to establish 'cloud strategies' that can leverage the benefits of this technology while also satisfying their information security concerns. However, this may change in an effort to tap into the value of the financial services sector; for example, IBM are expected to offer a financial services-specific set of cloud services to help adoption within that market.

Cloud computing adoption has also been driven by the convenience that it provides for the user and the provider. Cloud technology means that users no longer need to ensure that their hardware is powerful enough to operate the software. The user can rely on the supplier to be responsible for everything that sits behind the service consumed via a device, and all the user is faced with is managing their internet/network access and the device itself. Equally, from the providers' point of view, there is less concern over ensuring their service works when deployed locally on a wide variety of hardware configurations, meaning less time and resources are spent on testing and compatibility checks. However, it is worth noting that cloud providers do encounter challenges as a result of the changing nature of the various browser technologies. This has led to a burgeoning industry in cross-browser testing, as it is important that cloud products will perform on multiple browsers and new versions of those browsers.

Customers are now able to access a multitude of IT services from any computer connected to the internet/network (whether a desktop PC or a mobile device – of which approximately four billion are now in global use). Gone are the days of being limited to using locally installed software and being dependent on the capacity of storage and processing power within their local computer network.

Statista (2019) suggests that the yearly value of the global cloud services market has developed from around 13.4 billion US dollars in 2010 to around 157 billion US dollars in 2020. And PR Newswire (2020) has reported that the global Software as a Service (SaaS) market size is projected to reach USD 307.3 billion by 2026. It is also expected that from 2020 many major software providers (such as Microsoft and Adobe) will switch their sales models to cloud-based subscriptions, contributing to this booming market.

## CLOUD FORMATIONS

The cloud environment is subdivided into public, private, hybrid and community clouds.

- **Public clouds** are those in which services are available to the public over the internet in the manner already described in this chapter.
- **Private clouds** are essentially private networks used by one customer for whom data security and privacy is usually the primary concern. The downside of this type of cloud is that the customer will have to bear the significant cost of setting up and then maintaining the network alone.
- **Hybrid cloud** environments are often used when a customer has requirements for a mix of dedicated server and cloud hosting. For example, they may be appropriate if some of the data that are being stored are of a very sensitive nature. In such circumstances the organisation may choose to store some data on its dedicated server and less sensitive data in the cloud. Another common reason for using hybrid clouds is when an organisation needs more processing power than is available in-house and sources the extra requirement from the cloud. This is referred to as 'cloud bursting'. Additionally, hybrid cloud environments are often found in situations where a customer is moving from an entirely private to an entirely public cloud set-up.
- **Community clouds** usually exist where a limited number of customers with similar IT requirements share an infrastructure provided by a single supplier. Since the cost of the services are spread between the customers, this model is more cost-effective than a single tenant arrangement. Although the cost savings are likely to be greater in a public cloud environment, community cloud users generally benefit from greater security and privacy, which may be important for policy reasons.

## SILVER LININGS

The main benefits of cloud computing are as follows.

### Access to resources

One of the greatest advantages of cloud computing is the access it provides to the processing power of multiple remote computers. This enables customers to take advantage of greater computation speed and larger storage capacity than most organisations can provide on their premises and at a fraction of the cost.

### Mobility

Customers can access the services from almost any location in the world because the services are web/network-based (and because of the proliferation of mobile devices). This can enable users to access important business tools while they are on the move. With the processing taking place remotely, the user can have a seamless experience between desktop and mobile device – even with relatively low-cost technology. Immediate synchronisation ensures all relevant files and components are available in a multi-device environment.

### Easily scalable

Both the monthly subscription and 'pay as you use' charging models make it easy for the amount of service being provided to be increased or decreased. Should a customer want to vary the number of 'seats' included in its subscription or the amount of megabytes of storage space rented from AWS, this can usually be done easily, often through a provider portal. The scalability of the cloud computing model makes it especially attractive to growing organisations with varying levels of demand for computer resources (e.g. where an organisation's platform receives higher volumes of visitors at certain times of year).

### Data security and storage capacity

Data security is of particular importance as lapses in procedure can cause severe financial and reputational damage for the customer and provider of cloud solutions. Historically, this has accounted for much of the reluctance of the financial services sector in adopting cloud technology. However, for the majority of organisations with limitations on resources, cloud data centres offer data security and data storage capacity that might not be afforded in-house; data centres can generally afford better measures of real-time monitoring, intrusion detection and complex encryption. Many businesses using cloud services feel that the adoption of cloud services had further optimised their security standards.

### Cost savings

Many business leaders see cloud services adoption as offering an overall cost saving.

With business-orientated cloud computing services, the payment model is usually a rental arrangement based either on monthly subscription charges (per user or 'seat') or a 'pay as you use' system. This means that there is no large up-front payment as there would be with the purchase of a licence in the orthodox software licence model. Although there may be an initial set-up, training or configuration fee, this is usually relatively low by comparison; increasingly, providers are factoring these costs into their subscription prices to remove a barrier to entry.

The monthly subscription charges will also usually include support and maintenance fees, which would be significantly higher (typically 17–20 per cent of the relevant licence fee, each year) in the traditional software licence model.

The 'pay as you use' system is of particular benefit to an organisation with peaks and troughs in its demand for computing resources. It is cheaper than paying for exclusive use of enough resources to meet peak demand when it is not required, as is the case where all computation is carried out by an organisation in-house.

Cloud services also reduce the need for an organisation to maintain in-house expertise in their own technological infrastructure, which can reduce IT costs to a degree.

### Maintenance and support

Remote hosting of IT services makes the process of maintaining and supporting the services less intrusive for the customer. The supplier can handle backups, updates and upgrades automatically and remotely, often without any technical need to visit a customer's site. This will generally mean that application maintenance and support can be carried out more quickly. In addition, customers are able to piggy-back instantly on their suppliers' upgrades in computing resources and are not locked into using infrastructure purchased at great cost several years previously.

**Free trials**

Some suppliers offer the opportunity to trial part of their product for a period without charge with highly desired functionality hidden behind a paywall in the hope of persuading a customer to update to a fuller version on a paid basis once the customer is hooked to the product.

**Environmentally friendly (this actually has advantages and disadvantages)**

It has been suggested that data centres are a 'green' alternative to in-house computing, but this is a hotly debated topic because servers in very large data centres typically run at around 80 per cent capacity, while an in-house server might run at 5 per cent capacity to allow for peaks in resource demand; a server running at 5 per cent capacity uses only slightly less energy per hour than one running at 80 per cent, while doing 16 times less computation. Nevertheless, it is probable that the existence of cheap and more easily accessible cloud computing architectures has increased the overall demand for computation, outstripping the energy-efficiency gains that have been made in data centres. One option is to choose a supplier using a data centre that makes use of solar technology or wind cooling, or a data centre that is based in an area where local electricity comes from a renewable energy resource.

Computerworld reported in a recent article that in 2016 data centres accounted for 3.2 per cent of global power consumption; however, it is expected this will increase to 20 per cent by 2025 and that by 2040 data centres could create 14 per cent of global emissions (Computerworld 2019).

## THUNDER CLOUDS

The main disadvantages of cloud computing are as follows.

**Internet reliability**

Clearly, where IT services are provided over the internet, lack of internet access or slow connections may render those services inaccessible. When those services are business critical, this can be a major problem; however, this should be a diminishing concern as internet access improves. It should be remembered, though, that there is no guarantee of uninterrupted service even with locally hosted software applications or data storage, which can be rendered inoperable by defects or bugs.

**Dependence on the supplier**

With cloud computing, the customer is dependent on the supplier for day-to-day access to the IT services rather than just for support and maintenance when required. However, dependence on a supplier is a common concept for most organisations and the usual risk assessments can be carried out. Due diligence checks on the supplier can establish whether the supplier has a history of reliability. Cloud providers will sometimes agree contractually to an uptime guarantee for the service and even service credits (refunds or discounts on future invoices) where service uptime targets are missed; however, smaller cloud providers may struggle to negotiate this kind of upstream service guarantee from the data centre providers like AWS and will, therefore, provide more of an 'as is' service, particularly for non-business critical services.

One key concern is how the customer's data will be retrieved from the provider-controlled servers (including in what format) and what level of migration assistance is available from the supplier at the end of the relationship with the provider. Providers will often charge extra for data porting services.

## Resistance to adoption

There is still concern among certain sectors about relying on the cloud, particularly where a customer would need to trust a cloud supplier with data that are highly confidential or of a sensitive or personal nature. When those cautious customers do enter the market, they will sometimes do so on the basis of having become comfortable with a specific hosting provider – for example, where Microsoft's Azure hosting service has passed internal security and compliance checks, but AWS and Google have not. Unfortunately, not many cloud service providers are 'cloud agnostic' – that is, able to run their services on any major hosting provider's platform.

## Data protection

There are significant data protection and security concerns associated with cloud computing, for both customers and providers of cloud services.

Of particular note since the first edition of this book was published: the level of responsibility placed on cloud providers is now very different. The General Data Protection Regulation 2018 (GDPR) has changed the landscape that existed under the Data Protection Act of 1998. In respect of the data they processed for their customers, providers were largely protected from the older legislation, except to the extent that their customer flowed down their obligations contractually. GDPR now means that providers can be liable to individual users of cloud services for breaches of the law, as well as subject to the fines and enforcement notices passed by local supervisory authorities in certain cases. In the UK, the relevant authority is the Information Commissioner's Office (ICO).

Obligations that the law now places directly on cloud providers (as data processors) include:

- implementing technical and organisational measures to ensure appropriate security for the data being processed;
- maintaining records of processing activities, which in the UK the ICO may demand to see;
- including certain prescribed concepts in the provider/customer contracts;

- notifying the customer (as data controller) of breaches without undue delay upon becoming aware of them; and
- appointing a Data Protection Officer (for certain types of services and businesses).

A further significant implication is that there are now restrictions on a cloud provider's ability to subcontract the processing services without 'specific or general consent' from the customer. This means that providers can find themselves being restricted from switching the hosting of their services – for example from AWS to Microsoft Azure – even though it might benefit from cost reduction offers between competing hosting providers. Where providers obtain general consent to subcontract, they will be able to reserve some flexibility, provided they inform their customers of any changes in subcontractors used. However, many customers are now using the GDPR as leverage to demand specific consent for any subcontracting.

These and other matters relating to data protection are discussed more fully elsewhere in this book.

## SUMMARY

Cloud computing usage will continue to increase rapidly in the future. With the internet/network connections becoming more reliable and offering users more flexible, agile and cost-effective technologies, the concerns over data security, confidentiality and data protection are likely to be outweighed. As a result, organisations will increasingly be able to take advantage of the benefits offered by this unstoppable trend in IT service provision. The cloud has set in.

## REFERENCES

Computerworld (2019) 'Why data centres are the new frontier in the fight against climate change'. Computerworld UK. https://computerworld.com/article/3431148/why-data-centres-are-the-new-frontier-in-the-fight-against-climate-change.html.

NIST (2019) 'NIST Cloud Computing Program – NCCP'. National Institute of Standards and Technology. www.nist.gov/itl/cloud/index.cfm.

PR Newswire (2020) 'Software as a Service (SAAS) market size is projected to reach USD 307.3 billion by 2026 - Valuates reports'. https://www.prnewswire.co.uk/news-releases/software-as-a-service-saas-market-size-is-projected-to-reach-usd-307-3-billion-by-2026-valuates-reports-875840023.html.

Statista (2019) 'Total size of the public cloud software as a service (SaaS) market from 2008 to 2020 (in billion U.S. dollars)'. https://www.statista.com/statistics/510333/worldwide-public-cloud-software-as-a-service/.

# 3 CLOUD COMPUTING CONTRACTS

## Sam De Silva

The purpose of this chapter is to help companies navigate through the typical contractual issues in cloud computing contracts. Some of these issues should be familiar to those who deal regularly with other types of information technology contracts. However, even in relation to those issues, the nature of cloud computing can create new or different risks, and organisations may need to consider those issues afresh in the cloud computing context.

## INTRODUCTION

Like cloud computing models, cloud computing contracts appear in a wide variety of forms. These can range from simple standardised click-wrap agreements to framework and multi-layered sets of terms and conditions. However, there are a set of core contractual issues that a customer should consider in any cloud computing contract as part of its procurement exercise.

There are some points of terminology that we need to make clear at the start:

- When we refer to 'cloud computing contracts', we mean contracts in relation to Software as a Service (SaaS) solutions.
- The service providers that are providing the cloud services are referred to as 'cloud providers'.
- The organisation that is procuring the cloud services from the cloud provider is referred to as the 'customer'.

Data protection issues are also relevant for cloud computing. However, given the complexity of the subject matter and the coverage that would be required to explain the issues, data protection in relation to cloud computing contracts is beyond the scope of this chapter.

Prior to exploring some of the key commercial and legal issues with procuring cloud computing services, this chapter discusses pre-contractual steps: risk management approaches to click-wrap agreements, the role of the business case and various negotiation approaches for concluding a cloud computing contract.

## PRE-CONTRACTUAL STEPS

Since the customer may not be able to negotiate the cloud computing contract to the same extent as other types of IT agreements, it is important to be aware of certain common features of the cloud computing contract process.

### Risk management – click-wrap agreements

Many cloud provider contracts are presented as 'click-wrap'. Under this type of agreement, users consent to the terms and conditions by clicking the 'I agree' button prior to having access to the cloud services. However, commentators have said the 'click-through' model poses risks for customers, such as encouraging users to avoid institutional procurement processes.

It is possible that some employees attempt to circumvent internal procurement procedures where services are free of charge. From the user organisation's point of view, however, 'free of charge' or 'low cost' does not necessarily mean 'free of risk' or 'low risk'. Legal, regulatory or reputational risks may exist. This is particularly true if the data being processed using the cloud service are 'real' data (i.e. actual live data as opposed to 'fake' test data), and especially when they are confidential or personal data. Furthermore, organisations may still be charged for essential supporting services or 'extras' beyond the 'free' component.

There may accordingly be internal governance and cultural issues that a customer organisation needs to consider and address as part of its overall risk management strategy. Approaches to manage risk include the review of procedures and practices and training. Without implementing such measures, customers may find themselves committed to cloud computing contracts on terms not favourable to them, because of the ease with which individual staff members can sign up to cloud services.

### Business case

It is, of course, a fact of business life that there are many immediate and potential risks in entering into any IT contract (and cloud computing contracts are no different). The terms and conditions of a contract can address some of those risks through placing legal obligations on the cloud provider and having the appropriate remedies available. However, the success of the contract will ultimately depend on the planning and investigation that is done in relation to:

- the needs of the customer's business;
- the services the customer requires to fulfil those needs; and
- the cloud provider and its ability to supply those services on acceptable terms.

Before entering into negotiations for a cloud computing contract, you should consider the following factors:

- Whether the cloud provider owns the intellectual property in the software or technology, or otherwise has power to grant the necessary rights for the customer to receive the benefit of the services.
- The functional specifications that will be used to assess the performance of services.
- The plan for assessing whether the service does what it should – performance testing and acceptance testing.
- Who will do the performance assessment and whether they are independent of the authors of the business case.
- Whether the customer is adopting services that are widely used.
- Risk measures, such as considering whether the service is a commoditised offering readily available from a number of cloud providers, so that the service can be switched quickly if required.
- The cloud provider's security arrangements.
- The financial viability of the cloud provider.

## Negotiating approach

A customer may decide that, for non-strategic applications or where personal data or other sensitive data are not involved, the time and costs of negotiating a cloud provider's standard terms are not worthwhile. This can be a reasonable approach to adopt. However, for applications that are fundamental for the ongoing business of the customer and/or where personal data are involved, a customer should consider negotiating the cloud computing contract with the cloud provider.

The extent to which a customer may need to negotiate the cloud computing contract will obviously depend on how much relative control the particular system's design affords users and cloud providers over users' applications or data, and how 'customer friendly' a cloud provider's standard terms are. With paid-for services, providers are generally more willing to accept liability (or greater liability) and agree other user-requested commitments or measures than with free services. It appears that the more the cloud providers are paid, the more they are willing to concede.

However, it may be the case that the cloud provider simply refuses outright to negotiate on its terms and conditions. As with any commercial agreement, much depends on the relative bargaining power of each party. Large cloud providers generally decline any changes to their standard terms, insisting their services are provided on a 'take it or leave it' basis. In this case, the customer has only two options: either sign and accept the risks inherent with the cloud provider's terms and conditions, or walk away.

One approach to getting more favourable terms and conditions is to procure the solution from what the Cloud Industry Forum refers to as 'Reseller, Cloud provider and Outsourcer', comprising information technology consultancies, managed services providers, systems integrators, specialist resellers, technical value-added resellers, information technology outsourcers, distributors and volume resellers, and information technology retailers (collectively referred to as 'Integrators').

In essence, Integrators are like cloud providers who use other providers to offer services to their own end users (i.e. the customer). Integrators are potentially very large users of Infrastructure as a Service (IaaS) or Platform as a Service (PaaS), based on which they provide services (particularly SaaS) to their end users. Integrators are often better able than customers to negotiate improved terms with providers. This might be because Integrators may have ongoing relationships with the cloud providers, and perhaps a better bargaining position because of their large business volumes, as they may use the same cloud provider to service multiple customers.

## KEY COMMERCIAL AND LEGAL ISSUES

The following issues are considered in this section:

- liability for service failure;
- service levels;
- security and protection of information;
- business continuity and disaster recovery;
- other contractual issues, including:
  - automatic renewal;
  - responsibility for end users;
  - unauthorised or inappropriate use;
  - suspension of end-user accounts;
  - emergency security issues;
  - suspension and termination of service;
  - ownership of data;
  - disclaimer of warranty;
  - indemnification by customer;
  - indemnification by cloud provider;
  - modifications to the contract;
  - incorporation into the contract of other documents via website links;
  - data protection/privacy;
  - location of data;
  - access for data for e-discovery or regulatory purposes;
  - governing law and jurisdiction.

### Liability for service failure

Liability provisions are, without doubt, the most contentious and fiercely negotiated provisions in almost any technology contract. The reason is the potential financial impact that non-performance might have on the user organisation's business, which may be many times the level of fees being paid under the contract itself.

Customers and cloud providers vary enormously in the extent to which they expect the other party to accept liability or seek to exclude liability, respectively. Customers are generally keen for the cloud provider to be 'on the hook' for the potential damage that can be caused by the failure of a business critical service. Cloud providers, on the other hand, argue with some justification that it would only be a matter of time before they were out of business if they accepted unlimited liability on every transaction.

### Approach to direct losses in cloud computing contracts
Most US-based cloud providers seek to limit liability for direct damage as far as possible, be it in very general terms or phrased as relating to the consequences of inability to access data. In this context, 'direct liability' is taken to mean liability for losses to the customer relating to the loss or compromise of data hosted on the cloud service.

Cloud providers based in Europe tend to be less overt about seeking to exclude direct liability. This presumably is on the basis that in most European legal systems it is difficult to do so. Such exclusions as there are tend to be based on, for instance, force majeure.

### Approach to indirect/consequential losses in cloud computing contracts
Exclusions of indirect liability, such as for indirect, consequential or economic losses arising from a breach by the cloud provider, appear to be even more common. This is no doubt due to the potentially very large scope of such damages. It may prove difficult to quantify the indirect loss, if any, resulting from, for example, the deletion of customer data by a cloud provider.

### Practical application
The issue relating to liability is not academic. Effective cloud architecture should be robust. However, it is not possible to guarantee that the service will be completely immune to outages. Every service (whether run in a cloud or in-house) is susceptible to outages or technical difficulties; and limitations on both the power to control the technical solution and the ability to obtain remedies against the cloud provider may cause some customers to reconsider using cloud services or restrict the parts of its business for which it uses them.

It is extremely unlikely that any cloud provider will be prepared to guarantee compensation for all business disruption that it causes customers. To limit their risk, cloud providers generally seek to impose aggressive limitations or exclusions of their liability to their customers, and often provide little in the way of contractual assurances about the availability and resilience of their cloud architecture. In these circumstances, the best assurance for a customer is to deal with a cloud provider that has:

- a good track record;
- a demonstrable commitment to remain in the cloud computing market; and
- a reputation to protect.

Conducting proper due diligence is accordingly a critical aspect of any cloud service procurement, particularly if the cloud provider is unwilling to offer real contractual assurance.

## Service levels

One of the key service levels for cloud computing contracts is service availability.

### *Service availability*
Service availability measures the amount of time the cloud service is 'up and running'. For example, a cloud provider may agree that the cloud service will be up and available 95 per cent of the time in any given month or during certain key windows during the work week, and that the service will not be down for more than one hour at a time at any given time.

Some of the key issues that need to be considered when negotiating service availability service levels for cloud computing contracts, include:

- point of measurement;
- service measurement period; and
- application availability.

### *Point of measurement*
The point of measurement of service availability can be at a variety of points. For example, it can be at:

- the cloud provider's servers that host the application;
- the cloud termination point (where the link is made between the cloud service and the customers' IT infrastructure); and/or
- the user's computers.

Cloud providers normally aim to establish the point of measurement at their servers. However, this approach needs to be questioned by the customer. Where the transmission is over the internet, there are many different types of internet service provision and the cloud provider should not be allowed to adopt a potentially low-quality and low-cost approach, with the adverse impact on service quality, unless the customer understands the approach and has agreed to it.

From a customer's perspective, service availability measurement at the point of use is more useful and beneficial. However, this approach may not be practicable as it requires the technical expertise or tools to assess availability at the user's computer. A customer needs to have a reasonably sophisticated system infrastructure to make such a measurement.

A cloud provider is likely to argue that service availability measurement at the user computer level is inappropriate, as this will introduce downtime (when the service is not available) resulting from the customer's infrastructure failure rather than from the failure of the cloud service. As an alternative, the cloud provider may propose that the point of measurement should be the cloud termination point at the customer's premises. The limitation with this approach is it will be more difficult for the customer to assess service availability at an individual-user level rather than at the aggregate level relating to all of the users to whom the service is provided.

### Service measurement period

The choice of the service measurement period has an impact on the calculation of service level assessment. While a 24/7 service might appear to be attractive (particularly for international organisations), in practice this can lead to a need for considerable downtime before service credits are incurred. For example, a 98 per cent service level means nearly 15 hours of downtime in a 31-day month is permitted. Comparing this to an 8.00am to 6.00pm weekday service, only around four hours of downtime is permitted. Customers should consider the impact that taking either approach would have on their operations.

### Application availability

A cloud provider may provide a bundled cloud service comprising, for example, email, internet browsing and office applications (such as word processing and presentation applications). To provide maximum protection for the customer, the service availability service level should therefore relate not just to the overall cloud computing service availability, but also to the availability of the individual software applications.

## Security

One of the key issues for any cloud computing contract where the cloud provider holds or is able to access a customer's data is the security of those data. The risk increases where the data are sensitive (such as personal, health or financial data) and/or they are held offshore.

A customer should develop a comprehensive risk assessment to make an informed decision on the suitability of adopting a cloud-based solution. As part of that risk assessment, the customer should consider addressing the following in the cloud computing contract:

- The level of encryption and other security mechanisms to be applied to customer data held and transmitted by the cloud provider.
- The level of access security protocols to be adopted by the cloud provider to defend against unauthorised attempts to access the customer data by third parties, cloud provider personnel and other customers of the cloud provider.
- Requirements for the sanitisation or deletion of data in the damaged media if the relevant physical media is damaged and replaced.
- The approach to storing separate packages of data. For example, the customer may want to specify that the cloud provider does not aggregate separate packages on the same hardware (as such aggregation may increase the sensitivity of data or risks to security of the information).
- Notification requirements on the cloud provider so that the customer is made aware immediately if there are security incidents or intrusions, or requests from foreign governments or regulators for access to the data.
- An obligation on the cloud provider to destroy or sanitise (or de-identify in the case of personal data) sensitive information held by the cloud provider at the end of the contract (where such data are not or cannot be returned to the customer).

- Specific security requirements depending on the nature of the service and the sensitivity of the data.

## Confidentiality

A customer is likely to have contractual obligations to keep particular information confidential. It is important that these obligations are flowed through the cloud provider, where the cloud provider is storing or accessing the customer's data.

In most circumstances, a customer would want the cloud provider to meet a minimum level of confidentiality for the customer's information. In cases where the provider is obtaining access to particularly sensitive information, the level of protection will need to be significantly greater. Customers should consider in a cloud computing contract:

- replicating any obligations placed upon the customer by contract or law;
- for non-sensitive data, an obligation on the cloud provider to be aware of the level of confidentiality required and to commit to protecting those data appropriately;
- for sensitive data, more detailed confidentiality obligations, such as restricting access to the customer's data to a limited set of the cloud provider's personnel only.

## Compensation for data loss/misuse

There is a risk that that data could be permanently 'lost' or corrupted by a cloud provider in a number of circumstances. In addition, there is always the risk of misuse by rogue employees of the cloud provider or by external parties.

While the risk can and should be managed by the cloud provider (e.g. by ensuring offsite data backup, proper technical and security training and hardware maintenance), a customer still should consider how to address data loss or misuse in its contract with the cloud provider. Options to consider include:

- Expressly state that liability for data loss and misuse is a deemed direct loss, otherwise such losses could be caught within the ambit of the exclusion for indirect and consequential losses (which will typically be the type of losses that flow from data loss and misuse).
- Seek an indemnity from the cloud provider in respect of data loss or misuse as a result of the negligent, illegal or wilfully wrong act or omission of the cloud provider or its personnel.
- Include a separate liability cap for data loss or misuse that is sufficiently high to cover potential liability arising from such loss or misuse.

## Audit

The risk management strategies described in this section are likely to be of limited use unless the customer is able to verify the cloud provider's compliance with its confidentiality and security obligations. Audit of cloud computing contracts is one way of checking compliance. However, audit of such arrangements is potentially complicated by:

- the location of the data – because unless the location is specifically identified and locked down in the contract, the customer will not know where to look; and
- the nature of cloud computing itself – which may involve customer data being spread across many different cloud provider computing devices (to achieve the economies of scale and on-demand provision of computing that cloud computing services potentially offer).

Consequently, a customer should consider including the following in a cloud computing contract:

- placing a restriction on the locations/countries in which customer data may be held;
- having a right to audit the provider's compliance with the contract (such right to be exercisable by the customer or its appointed representative) and any regulator to which the customer is subject;
- including the right for the customer to remotely monitor access to its data where technically available.

## Business continuity and disaster recovery

Business disruptions, whether the result of natural disasters, technology failures or criminal acts ('incidents') have the potential to adversely affect the business of a customer. Business continuity generally refers to the capabilities needed in the wake of an incident to restore the functionality and availability of networks, systems and data. An outage at a cloud provider's facility can impact delivery of the services, so customers will want to be assured that the cloud provider has a sound business continuity plan.

The key principles underlying business continuity provisions should be:

- To ensure that, in the event of a failure of or disruption to the services, the customer is able to maintain continuity of service provision or restore services fully within a specified period of time.
- To prevent loss of data.
- To prevent or minimise (as far as possible) any impact on the achievement of the service levels.
- To ensure that normal provision of the services is recommenced as soon as possible.

A customer should therefore consider including protections in the cloud computing contract to ensure business continuity. For example, such protections could include:

- the cloud provider committing to have a geographically separate disaster recovery site and having the process in place for seamless transition to this site;
- having the ability for the cloud provider to operate if the mains power is disrupted (e.g. use of an uninterruptible power supply (UPS) and/or back-up generators);

- ensuring that business continuity is an absolute requirement and not subject to qualifiers such as 'reasonable efforts';
- requiring that the cloud provider submits a draft business continuity and disaster recovery plan for comment and approval by the customer;
- limiting the right for the cloud provider to suspend their service for force majeure reasons only in the circumstances where the business continuity and disaster recovery plan has been properly followed and implemented; and
- ensuring that scheduled maintenance in respect of cloud provider systems does not occur during hours that the customer requires access and use of the services (a common problem if the service is provided from outside the UK owing to time differences).

A customer may also need to take other precautions outside the contract with the cloud service provider itself to minimise disruptions (e.g. to ensure the availability of the customer's internet gateway). Any failure in such related systems might be disproportionately amplified once the customer moves a substantial part of its IT capability into the cloud.

## Other contractual issues

The customer should check that all of the following issues are covered in a cloud computing contract or the customer's internal governance policies (or at least considered, even if then determined to be manageable risks that the customer is prepared to live with). As with any contract, risk assessment will be a matter of balancing up questions of probability, severity and ease of mitigation on the one hand, with the cost and convenience of the service on the other.

**Table 3.1 Key contractual issues with SaaS contracts**

| Issue | Comments |
| --- | --- |
| Automatic renewal | Is there a provision where the contract renews automatically for an additional period of time unless the customer gives prior written notice? |
| | The customer should have an internal process to remind itself when to decide about renewal and give notice of any termination. Ideally, the contract would renew automatically (so the customer does not have to renegotiate every time), but also allow termination for convenience on some reasonably short period of notice. |
| Responsibility for end users | Is there a provision where the contract requires the customer to 'ensure' that any end users (i.e. its employees, etc.) comply with the cloud provider's acceptable use policy, terms of service (ToS) or similar provisions? It is preferable from the customer's perspective (though still potentially problematic) to use 'best efforts' or 'commercially reasonable' efforts to do so. |

*(Continued)*

**Table 3.1 (Continued)**

| Issue | Comments |
|---|---|
| | This approach may be appropriate in relation to employees for whom the customer is vicariously liable, but the better approach is to provide that the customer will 'inform' its end users for whom the customer is not vicariously liable,[1] and over whom the customer has minimal control, of their obligation to do so. |
| | An alternative is to provide that the cloud provider may require end users to agree directly with the cloud provider to comply with any such provisions. |
| Unauthorised or inappropriate use | Does the contract attempt to make the customer responsible for actively preventing any 'unauthorised' or 'inappropriate' use of the cloud provider's service by others, or perhaps to use 'best efforts' or 'commercially reasonable efforts' to do so? Given that these services are 'in the cloud' and therefore largely outside the customer's control, it may be better to provide only that the customer will not 'authorise' or 'knowingly allow' such uses. |
| | The contract also may require the customer to notify the cloud provider of 'all' unauthorised or inappropriate uses of which the customer becomes aware. In relation to cloud providers with broadly stated acceptable use policy or ToS, such expansive obligations could be burdensome and unnecessary. An option to consider is to replace 'all' with 'material' or some similar, higher threshold. |
| Suspension of end-user accounts | Does the contract permit the cloud provider to suspend the customer's end users for breaches of the cloud provider's acceptable use policy or ToS? If so, consider trying to limit any such rights to a more restrictive standard, perhaps only 'material' breaches, or breaches that 'significantly' threaten the security or integrity of the cloud provider's system. |
| Emergency security issues | Is there a provision that allows the cloud provider to have the right to 'immediately' suspend an 'offending use', and possibly the service altogether, in the event of an 'emergency' issue? If so, the standard for what constitutes an emergency should:<br>• be clearly defined;<br>• not give the cloud provider much, if any, discretion or flexibility in its application; and<br>• incorporate a 'materiality' or similar threshold. |
| Suspension and termination of service | Does the contract give the cloud provider the right to suspend the service and/or to terminate it altogether upon certain events or conditions? Such provisions are not unreasonable in principle, but they should:<br>• be limited in scope to truly significant matters only; |

*(Continued)*

## Table 3.1 (Continued)

| Issue | Comments |
|---|---|
| | • provide an opportunity for the customer to remedy the alleged breach, or invoke some form of escalation, rather than be exposed to instantaneous and potentially arbitrary action without any legal protection (except in the case of true emergencies); and |
| | • give the customer adequate time to make alternative arrangements for its data or service. |
| | The customer should also have assurance that the data will continue to be available in a usable format, for at least a specified period post-termination (or, if the cloud provider is unwilling to commit to a specific length, a 'commercially reasonable' period of time), as well as that the cloud provider will return or destroy any copies of the customer's data once disengagement is complete. |
| Ownership of data | The contract should expressly make clear that all data belong to the customer (and/or its users) and that the cloud provider acquires no rights or licences to such data. It also may be useful to provide that the cloud provider does not acquire and may not claim any security interest in the customer's data. |
| Disclaimer of warranty | At a minimum, the contract should warrant: |
| | a. that the service complies with and will perform in accordance with its specifications (which should themselves be as detailed as possible, to avoid misunderstandings and disagreements); and |
| | b. that it does not infringe any third-party intellectual property rights. |
| | Many cloud provider contracts disclaim essentially all warranties. However, without these two warranties, there is minimal assurance for a customer that the service will in fact do what the cloud provider's marketing people claim it will do or that the cloud provider even has the right to provide the services to the customer. |
| Indemnification by customer | Is the customer required to indemnify the cloud provider not only for its own actions (which is not necessarily unreasonable), but also those of its end users, including users for whom the customer may not otherwise be vicariously liable? It is preferable **not** to voluntarily accept that liability. If the indemnity is accepted by the customer then the scope of such indemnity needs to be considered carefully – for example, is it an unlimited indemnity? |
| Indemnification by cloud provider | The contract is not likely to include any form of indemnification benefiting customers. However, such protection is important in at least two key areas: |
| | • infringement of third-party intellectual property rights; and |

*(Continued)*

**Table 3.1 (Continued)**

| Issue | Comments |
|---|---|
| | • inappropriate disclosure or data breach, both of which are largely, if not entirely, in the cloud provider's sole control, and both of which can be extremely costly for a customer to defend and remedy. |
| | If a cloud provider refuses to accept liability for either of these issues, the customer needs to view this as a warning about the cloud provider's lack of confidence in its own service. Effectively, what the cloud provider is really saying is that it expects the customer to accept the risk of these liabilities. |
| Modifications to the contract | Does the cloud provider have the right to make modifications to its services unilaterally? While some form of right to make changes probably is necessary and appropriate (such as improvements), such an approach is risky from a customer perspective and does not provide the customer with any assurance that any such modifications will be beneficial, let alone acceptable. Limiting the cloud provider's right to 'commercially reasonable modifications' would be better. Even better would be to add to that a qualification prohibiting 'materially detrimental' modifications, perhaps something to the effect of 'Cloud provider may make commercially reasonable modifications to the Service, provided that they do not materially diminish the nature, scope, or quality of the Service.' |
| Incorporation into the contract of other documents via website links | Does the contract incorporate by reference additional terms and policies posted to the cloud provider's website? If so, such additional terms and policies are likely to be subject to the cloud provider's unilateral amendment, and those terms and policies may in turn incorporate by reference other terms and policies posted elsewhere on the cloud provider's websites, which also are typically subject to the cloud provider's unilateral amendment. The result is that the contract itself is incomplete, it may well contain provisions that are inconsistent or in conflict with each other and it likely will be difficult or impossible to fully comprehend. It will also be potentially meaningless, in terms of providing contractual certainty to the customer, because the cloud provider will have the right to amend it significantly at any time, and likely even without any more notice to the customer than posting the change to its website. |
| | While it may be reasonable to deal with technical standards and guidelines or other 'non-legal' matters elsewhere, it is strongly preferable that all contractual terms be included in the contract itself. At the very least, the customer should attempt to require the cloud provider to provide direct, individual notice sufficiently in advance of the effective date of any amendments to incorporated terms, along with the right to terminate if such amendments are unacceptable or materially detrimental to the customer's interests. |

*(Continued)*

## Table 3.1 (Continued)

| Issue | Comments |
| --- | --- |
| Data protection/ privacy | Some of the data will constitute 'personal data' for the purposes of data protection legislation and the cloud provider will be a 'data processor' for the purposes of such legislation. Given that the customer will be the data controller, it will need to ensure that it complies with the data protection legislation, including imposing the appropriate contractual provisions in the contract with the cloud provider. |
| Location of data | Some contracts expressly reserve for the cloud provider the right to store customer data in any country in which they do business. Others may not address the issue, but the cloud providers may follow similar practices nevertheless, on the (generally legitimate) theory that what is not expressly prohibited is thereby permitted. The data protection implications of any personal data transferred outside the European Economic Area (EEA) need to be considered. |
| Access for data for e-discovery or regulatory purposes | Although the contract probably will not (and probably need not) expressly address the issue, it is important to understand (ahead of time) the architecture of the cloud provider's system, how and in what format it keeps the customer's data and what tools are available to the customer to access its data so that it will be ready for any e-discovery needs that may arise. |
| Governing law and jurisdiction | The contract is most likely to specify that it is governed by the law of the cloud provider's home state and grant the courts of that state exclusive jurisdiction over any disputes arising out of the contract.<br><br>Better options for the customer to consider include:<br><br>• specifying the law and jurisdiction of the customer's own jurisdiction (large cloud providers likely operate in and are subject to all such jurisdictions, so it is no significant inconvenience for them);<br><br>• providing that disputes must be brought in the defendant's jurisdiction (which is even-handed and tends to encourage informal resolution, as the claimant won't have the 'home court' advantage); or<br><br>• deleting the provision and leaving the question open for later argument and resolution if and when needed. |

1  Vicarious liability is a common law principle of strict, no-fault liability for wrongs committed by another person, in effect a form of secondary liability. Vicarious liability most often occurs in employment relationships, but it may also arise in other areas, including partnerships. In an employment relationship, it involves an employer being liable for the wrongs committed by an employee where there is a sufficient connection between those wrongs and the employee's employment such that it would be fair to hold the employer to be vicariously liable. It does not matter that the employer itself has committed no wrong.

## SUMMARY

There are a number of contractual issues to consider when entering into a cloud computing contract and even if a customer is not able to negotiate the contract, best practice suggests that a risk assessment of the contractual terms should be undertaken.

# 4 INTELLECTUAL PROPERTY LAW FOR COMPUTER USERS

Jennifer Pierce

**INTRODUCTION**

Intellectual property law is a relatively complex subject. This chapter concentrates on the more important aspects for users, so that you are aware of the pitfalls and know when to seek professional advice. The appendix at the end of the chapter provides a basic guide to intellectual property and explains the terminology in use.

Intellectual property is an inescapable element of modern business, especially in the field of information technology. It protects both suppliers' rights in the systems that they provide and users' rights in aspects of their usage. Everybody needs to know roughly who owns each part of a computer system and how that impacts on its use. They also need to know what not to do with the equipment on the internet, so as to avoid being sued.

There are five main types of intellectual property in the UK:

- **Patents** – protect new inventions, which could be found in any part of a computer system. Software as such is not technically patentable, but if it has other features that fulfil the criteria for patentability this will not prevent the grant of a patent.
- **Designs** – there are basically three types of UK right, which also overlap with copyright. They cover items that are as diverse as semiconductors and computer graphics.
- **Copyright** – protects literary, artistic and other works. Software is classed as a literary work for the purposes of copyright law. Graphical user interfaces are artistic works, and may also be treated as literary works.
- **Database right** – covers collections of data that are accessible by electronic or other means.
- **Trade marks** – broadly, protect brands, such as 'Microsoft®' and 'Intel®'.

For those who are not familiar with intellectual property, at the end of the chapter there is a further explanation of these rights. Rights in other territories, even European Union (EU) territories, may be different, although some rights are harmonised throughout the EU. In view of the complexities arising from Brexit, this chapter is confined to UK rights after Brexit and the end of the transition period, to the extent known at 30 September 2020, unless otherwise stated.

## HARDWARE AND INTELLECTUAL PROPERTY RIGHTS

'Hardware' is a bit of a misnomer because much hardware contains systems software too. From an intellectual property perspective, the distinction is very important, because the real hardware element is sold but the systems software is usually licensed (see the next section). If hardware is protected this is generally by patents and/or designs, although brands are also extremely important in this sector.

The non-software element is treated like any other machine. If it is protected, you need authority from the person who owns the intellectual property rights to manufacture, sell or import it, and so on. However, after the first authorised sale of the hardware in the UK, those rights will be 'exhausted' in the UK. This means that if the equipment comes from an authorised source you will be able to do what you like with it, unless there is a special arrangement or you export it from the UK or do drastic repairs that amount to remaking it (or bits of it).

We have yet to see how this will be affected by the outcome of the Brexit negotiations. It is likely that the UK will be outside the European Economic Area (EEA) system, in which case this exhaustion principle would cover the UK and the EEA separately. However, at the time of writing there is no trade agreement between the UK and the EU, and no UK legislation to cover the UK position regarding exhaustion within the UK after the end of the transition period.

### Authorised sales

So everything is fine if you buy from an authorised source, but how do you tell who is authorised and who is not? There are plenty of people who call themselves 'authorised dealers'. Some will be fully authorised under all of the necessary rights, some will have limited rights and others may not be authorised at all. You should ideally check the status of a dealer with the equipment manufacturer when you buy equipment. However, even the larger computer manufacturers may sometimes sell infringing hardware without knowing about it.

Technically, the owner of intellectual property can seize infringing equipment, so it is a serious matter. In practice, though, it is rare for an intellectual property owner to seize equipment from end users.

So what should you do? There should be a relatively low risk if you buy hardware from a reputable supplier who gives you a full indemnity to cover the situation where the hardware infringes somebody else's intellectual property. You should also pick a supplier with a 'deep pocket' who will be sure to meet its obligations under the indemnity.

### Special conditions

Some intellectual property owners attach special conditions to the sale of their equipment. This is not the technical terminology, but is an easy way of describing what happens. For example, they may insist that you do not take it outside a particular territory or that you only use it with another piece of equipment. Some of these conditions are unenforceable because they breach trade laws, but others may be enforceable.

### Repairs

When you have bought equipment you generally have a right to repair it, although repairs by somebody who is not authorised by the manufacturer may affect your warranty and the maintenance contract. If the repair entails replacing parts that are covered by intellectual property, the same rules apply to repairs as applied to the original sale, so this sort of repair must be made by an authorised person.

## SOFTWARE AND INTELLECTUAL PROPERTY RIGHTS

### Copying and adapting: the general rules

Copyright is the main form of intellectual property protecting software, so it is treated differently from hardware. Software can also be protected by some of the rights protecting hardware, including registered rights, so all of the rules relating to hardware may apply, but there are additional things to think about.

Copyright protects against copying, adaptation and distribution. It can protect against other things, but these are the main types of protection in this context. You cannot do any of these things unless you own the copyright or have the authorisation ('licence') of the copyright owner.

It is fairly unusual for a user to own copyright outright. Most software houses want to retain ownership of copyright in the software they produce, and accordingly they generally only grant licences: this is certainly the case with standard software packages, which are licensed to multiple users who then benefit from lower costs for development and maintenance. However, if a supplier is making a bespoke program and you are to pay the full economic costs of this, there are strong arguments that you should own the copyright if the program is stand-alone. If you are to own the copyright you need a document that transfers the rights to you.

Simply running software involves copying it, so if you do not own the rights you need a licence to run it. You also need a licence if you are going to alter it, because that amounts to adaptation. In practice, few software houses will simply allow you to copy and adapt their software. They tend to specify precisely what you can do with it.

You also need a licence if you are going to rent, lend or broadcast copyright material or to communicate a work to the public. The average software user does not want to do any of these things, so they are not covered in this book.

### Backup copies

Whatever the licence says, there are some things that the supplier cannot stop you from doing. So, if you have a licence, the supplier cannot stop you from making backup copies if you need them for your permitted use of the software.

## Maintenance

As a general rule, you can copy or adapt software if that is necessary for you to use the software, provided that the licence doesn't stop you. So, for example, you can adapt software to correct errors, unless the licence specifically says that you cannot do it.

## Decompilation and interfaces

You can decompile a program if you want to create an interface with another program, provided that you do not use the information that you glean from this to do anything else and do not give it to anybody who does not need it to build the interface. Similarly, if you can get the information from another source (such as the supplier) or if you use it to build a copycat program, the decompilation is not permitted.

## What does all this mean in practice?

In many cases, it is just not feasible to change the standard terms that you will be offered in the form of a shrink-wrap or click-wrap licence. The terms may not be enforceable if they are unreasonable, but that is a hard call for you to make without advice.

Have a good look at the scope of the licence and look for anything that you would want to do that is left out or is prohibited. If it says 'copy and adapt' without qualification, you will have no problems, unless you want to sell copies, and most suppliers only allow professional distributors to do that. If it is of more limited scope and sets out a list of things that you can do, you need to scrutinise the list.

Many users cannot and do not want to maintain software, but they may want to know that they can go to another supplier if something goes wrong. This is precisely what many suppliers want to avoid because they do not want anybody else meddling with their trade secrets or depriving them of maintenance fees. So some clients ask for maintenance rights, while many suppliers try to avoid granting them; in the end it is a matter for discussion, although the supplier will often win the argument.

You will encounter similar problems with decompilation to create interfaces, but in that case the supplier can only prohibit decompilation if it provides sufficient information to allow you to build an interface. So this is less of a problem.

In any event, the right to adapt for the purpose of maintenance may well be of limited use unless you have a copy of the source code.

## Transferring a licence

Many licences prohibit the transfer of the licensee's rights to somebody else completely. In other cases, the consent of the licensor is required before the rights can be transferred. According to EU law (which still applies in the UK after Brexit if it was in force before Brexit, unless that EU law is changed by the laws of England and Wales, Scotland or Northern Ireland), this type of prohibition on transferring a copy of software, whether provided as a physical copy or a download, is unenforceable if the licence is for an unlimited period and the licensor has been properly remunerated. This does not, of course, cover software provided as a service.

Before you sell or transfer a computer, you need to check that you can pass on rights under any related maintenance contracts. This can be crucial in the context of outsourcing.

**Non-compliance**

Needless to say, if you do something outside the scope of your licence and the act is prohibited by copyright, technically you are infringing copyright and the copyright owner may sue you and seize the software. In practice, if you do something accidentally and no real harm is done, the copyright owner may give you a warning, or ask for further payment without taking the matter any further.

## DATABASES AND INTELLECTUAL PROPERTY RIGHTS

### Taking a licence of somebody else's rights

The intellectual property rights protecting databases are relatively easy to understand provided that you can envisage the constituent parts of a database.

Databases are usually manipulated by software, which is protected by the law of copyright. Separate intellectual property rights may subsist in the form of the actual database, the collection of data to populate it and, finally, individual items of data.

From a legal perspective, the software is no different from any other software. The form of the database is protected by copyright in a similar way to software. The collection of data will be protected by copyright if the selection or arrangement of the contents constitutes the author's own intellectual creation.

There is also database right, which can protect the contents of the database against substantial extraction and re-utilisation. In order to qualify for protection, there must have been a substantial investment in obtaining, verification or presentation of the contents of the database and the resulting database must be arranged in a systematic and methodical way, with data individually accessible by electronic or other means.

Database right does not, however, protect the individual items of data. These individual items of data, such as photographs, may also be protected by copyright.

So what does this add up to in practice? It means that you need a licence to use any of the rights protecting a database that you do not own. You need to ensure that the licence covers the way that you envisage using the database in terms of extraction and re-utilisation of data. In particular, if you are using a database to extract large amounts of data, you need to watch out for any limits on usage.

### Protecting your own rights

If you are setting up and populating a database of your own, you will acquire rights in the database that you assemble provided that you or your employees do this, or you acquire the rights under a written contract with the person who does.

If you ever need to enforce your rights you will need to prove that they are still current. This entails keeping records of the dates when the database is finished or made available to the public (if earlier), together with a copy of the database at that time. You need to do the same thing each time that it is substantially updated, because major updates may qualify for further protection.

You also need records of the nationality of the person, company or partnership that took the financial risks of making the database (the 'maker'). The database will only qualify for protection in the UK if the maker is from the UK **or** was from the EEA and the database to be protected was made before the end of the transition period. If the maker is a company it must be incorporated in the relevant jurisdiction with either its central administration or principal place of business in that jurisdiction or its registered office and a firm base in that jurisdiction.

It is worthwhile marking all copies of the database with 'database rights', the name of the owner and the date when it was completed or, if earlier, first made available to the public. This may deter infringers and will help you to claim damages from them. It could also, potentially, be used as evidence of the origin of any pirate copies. If the content also merits copyright protection, then add a copyright symbol, the name of the copyright owner and the date of first publication.

## WEBSITES AND INTELLECTUAL PROPERTY RIGHTS

### Make sure that you own your website

Many people spend a great deal of money on websites, but allow the designer to retain the intellectual property rights in them. It is a bit like buying something and leaving part of it in the shop on a permanent basis. Nonetheless, appreciable numbers of people do this, probably because they are now used to somebody else owning the software that they use.

The contents of a website are protected by copyright, which arises automatically when it is created, provided that it is first published in the UK (or another country, such as an EU state that is party to the same treaty as the UK) or fulfils certain other criteria. It is also possible to apply for registered designs in respect of specific graphics such as icons; this is a registered right, so it gives monopoly protection, which means that anybody else using a design within the scope of valid registration will infringe unless they are licensed.

Trade mark protection may be available for signs that are used on your website. These can overlap with registered designs in this context. As a very general rule, in the UK, trade mark applications are more expensive to process than ones for designs. However, trade marks can give broader protection and they can last indefinitely if you pay the renewal fees.

Many websites are dependent on software to assist in navigation and to process data that are input. The same rules apply to this software as to any other software. Similarly, there may be a facility for accessing and searching a database and that database should be treated in the same way as any other database.

## Look after your rights

Copyright, registered designs and trade marks can all be valuable assets of a business, and can be used to protect it against imitators, so you should aim to own rights in your website. Consultants who build websites are likely to use certain generic material on each job. They would be foolish to give this to you, but anything that is specific to your project should be yours and you should protect it.

Before your designer starts work, you should have a written agreement, transferring rights in the material they create to you and obliging the designer to keep the designs confidential in case you want to register them. Otherwise, the designer may be able to argue that they own the copyright and design right, and you just have a licence; or somebody else may try to register the design before you do.

If you own the copyright in your website, it is worthwhile marking it to deter infringers, to ensure that you can claim damages from them and to take advantage of protection under international copyright treaties. You should put the © symbol followed by the name of the copyright owner and the date of first publication on the website.

If you put material onto a website, visitors are entitled to assume that they can use it in some way, so you need to be clear about what they can do. For example, if they can make copies solely for domestic use, but not for a business or any other purpose, you must state that specifically and should ideally include a button to click to signify agreement. The same applies to adaptation and giving other people copies. If you simply include this in the general terms and conditions on a website, then this may well not be enough.

## DOMAIN NAMES AND INTELLECTUAL PROPERTY RIGHTS

### Why there are problems

In the 1990s one of the more memorable rackets was buying up domain names that corresponded to famous trade marks and then holding the trade mark owner to ransom by demanding vast sums to transfer the domain name to them. Courts in many jurisdictions have now put a stop to this by holding that the 'cybersquatters' are infringing trade marks.

Unfortunately, that is not the end of the story. There are still problems with domain names and trade marks. Trade marks are registrable in 45 different classes of goods and services, and it is possible to subdivide each class by specifying only some of the goods or services within that class. So a great many businesses with the same trade mark may co-exist without problems.

This is not so with domain names because it is only possible to register a name once. So, for example, if BCS has registered 'BCS.org' nobody else can register 'BCS' with the top-level domain of '.org'. The situation has improved with the creation of further top-level domains, such as '.biz', but the old ones like '.com' and '.org' are still the most popular.

## Opposing a registration

Domain names are generally allocated to the first person to register (although there may be special arrangements for trade mark owners to have priority when new top-level domains are first allocated). This means that if somebody has already registered the name that you are seeking to register, you will only be able to oppose the registration in limited circumstances.

You can oppose registration if a name:

- is identical or confusingly similar to your trade mark;
- the person using the domain name has no right or legitimate interest in that domain name; and
- the person using the domain name registered it and is using it in bad faith.

In some circumstances it is unclear whether there has been bad faith; but in others, such as cybersquatting, this has been relatively easy to decide. In most cases, obtaining cancellation of a domain name involves bringing proceedings in a court or pursuing arbitration. However, in the case of abusive registrations (such as cybersquatting), the trade mark owner can submit a complaint to an approved dispute-resolution service provider (such as the World Intellectual Property Organization).

## Avoiding disputes

If a domain name is not used or is not commercially important, and where there are no grounds for opposing its continued registration, it may be possible to purchase the domain name for a relatively modest sum.

In practice, the best way to avoid disputes is to register a domain name early. If you can afford it, registering a corresponding trade mark in the same jurisdiction as the domain name registry can help too. If you think that there are grounds for opposing a domain name registration, it is best to seek professional advice.

It goes without saying that if you are registering a domain name you need to be careful to avoid infringing somebody else's trade mark (see the next section).

## THE INTERNET AND TRADE MARKS

### Infringement

The international trade mark system has historically been divided by national boundaries or by trading blocs. Internet use is international by its very nature, so if you use a trade mark on the internet there is a technical possibility of infringing separate trade marks in a large number of territories. Registration in one or more jurisdictions will not protect you from infringement in others.

Trade mark infringement usually occurs when a person uses at least the same or a similar mark, for the same or similar goods or services, as the trade mark is registered for. In Europe, if the mark or services are similar but not identical, and you want to claim infringement, you must show that people would be confused about where the goods or services come from.

Well-known marks are a special case because it is possible to infringe them by trading in different goods or services and, in the EU (including the UK), if without due cause the use would take unfair advantage of the mark or be detrimental to it. In the USA, use of marks that blurs their distinctiveness or tarnishes their reputation may also amount to trade mark dilution.

In practice, it is more likely that somebody will take action if you are actively using a mark in a particular jurisdiction, more especially if you trade there or have assets in that jurisdiction, because the trade mark owner then has a more realistic possibility of suing you successfully.

## What should you do?

There is no easy answer to this because laws and trading methods are still being developed. Full international searches are too expensive for many companies. However, it should be possible to search for trade marks in the major jurisdictions that are targeted before using a mark on the internet. If you cannot afford a professional search by a trade mark attorney, some patent offices, such as the UK, provide limited internet searching facilities. Nonetheless, a professional search is always preferable.

## Examples of infringement

In addition to using a trade mark on a website, or as a domain name, the most likely ways in which trade marks will be infringed on the internet are through linking and framing, and metatags.

## Linking and framing

There are two types of links on web pages: hypertext links and inline links.

With a hypertext link, you click on an icon and your browser retrieves material from a second website. With an inline link, material from a second website is automatically retrieved by and shows as an integral part of the first website.

Framing is an extreme form of linking where material from the linked site is framed by advertising and other material from the first site, so that it appears as if it is all on the same site. Linking technologies allow people to pretend that somebody else's content is theirs. Links that bypass the home page of another site can bypass valuable advertising.

In terms of intellectual property, linking can lead to confusion over whose products are being displayed under which marks. So, for example, the marks from the linked site may appear with products from the first site and the products of the linked site may appear under the trade marks of the first site. This may amount to trade mark infringement, unfair competition or passing off, depending on the jurisdiction – so when dealing with brands it is safest not to skip home pages and to inform users that they are entering another site. Furthermore, if the link itself consists of a trade mark or copyright material, there is a possibility of infringement. There is also a possibility of infringement if the link is to copyright material that is not freely available in that context. When considering whether copyright material is freely available, it is best to seek advice.

## Metatags and advertising keywords

Search engines find and classify websites by reference to keywords. Website owners assist the engines by embedding keywords, to increase use of their sites. Some businesses have embedded competitors' trade marks and well-known marks as keywords to try to divert business to their sites. In the UK, this may amount to trade mark infringement or passing off, if there is a likelihood that those using the search engines would think that the site with the metatag is the site of the trade mark owner. There are similar remedies available in other jurisdictions.

Keyword advertising, where banner advertisements are linked to keyword search terms, presents similar problems, although in many cases generic words will be used so there will be no trade mark infringement or passing off.

## THE INTERNET AND COPYRIGHT AND DATABASE RIGHT

Simply creating links from one website to another is unlikely to infringe copyright, because the material on the other website is not copied or otherwise affected when the link is created. However, if the linked material is not freely available, then there may be copyright infringement.

## APPENDIX: A BASIC GUIDE TO INTELLECTUAL PROPERTY AND RELATED RIGHTS

### Copyright

#### *What is copyright?*
Copyright protects the means of expression of a work, including literary works, fine art, crafts, music, films, broadcasts and so on. In order to qualify, works must be original; that is to say that they have not been copied, although the law for both software and databases states that in order to be original the material must be the author's 'own intellectual creation'. There is usually a requirement that a work is recorded in some permanent form.

Three-dimensional works are not protected by copyright, except for artistic works, such as sculpture or architecture, and works of artistic craftsmanship.

#### *Duration*
In the case of literary, dramatic, musical and artistic works, protection generally lasts for 70 years after the end of the year in which the author dies. There are exceptions, notably for computer-generated works, which are only protected for 50 years after the end of the year in which they were created.

### No registration
Copyright arises automatically on creation, and in the UK and many other jurisdictions there is no need for registration. There are exceptions, most notably in the USA where registration is required in order to claim compensation for lawyers' fees in litigation. As an unregistered right, copyright does not protect against independent creation of the same or a similar work, provided that there is no copying involved.

Computer software generally qualifies for copyright protection as a literary work. Copyright protects the way that code is written, as opposed to the underlying concepts, which are often more valuable. There is a certain amount of overlap between concept and expression, but not much (see 'Patents' section below for protection of technical concepts).

Copyright also protects manuals (in whatever form they are produced), the structure and collection of data (provided it is the author's own intellectual creation), items of data in databases that merit protection in their own right, and the contents of websites.

### Moral rights
With certain notable exceptions, authors of copyright works have moral rights. These rights are, broadly, the right to be identified as the author; the right to object to derogatory treatment of a work; the right not to have a work falsely attributed; and the right to privacy of certain films and photographs. Exceptions to these rights include computer programs and computer-generated works. Employees have limited moral rights. Moral rights cannot be transferred; they can be waived in the UK but not in countries such as Germany.

### Database right
Database right protects the collection of data in a database, provided that the items of data are arranged in a systematic and methodical way and are individually accessible by electronic or other means. There is a further requirement that there has been a substantial investment in obtaining, verifying or presenting the contents of the database; this is taken literally, so other types of investment do not qualify.

The right lasts for 15 years from the end of the year in which the database is completed or the end of the year when it is made available to the public, if that happens before completion.

Database right is another unregistered right, which arises automatically and can be circumvented by independent creation of a similar database.

### Patents

### What is patentable?
Patents protect new inventions that make an inventive step beyond the current technology and which are of use to industry. Some types of invention, such as software and business methods, are unpatentable as such, but they can still be patented if there is another aspect of the invention that is patentable.

So, for example, word-processing software is generally viewed as plain software, but software that has a technical effect, such as control software used in a car, may still be patentable. An appreciable amount of software is now patented, and some of the large software providers have a considerable number of patents.

As a registered right, a patent can be exceedingly powerful, so there are strict requirements for validity. In industrialised countries, inventions are unpatentable if they have been disclosed to anybody before the application is made, with limited exceptions such as certain confidential disclosures. Regarding the inventive step, it must be something that would not be obvious to a skilled but unimaginative worker in the field.

Patents and applications contain a description of the invention together with 'claims' that set out the features of the invention that merit protection. They generally last for 20 years from the date when the application was filed, subject to payment of renewal fees. Patents are always subject to potential revocation on the grounds that they do not meet the requirements for patentability, unless there has been an unappealable decision on the same grounds for challenge in the relevant jurisdiction. In the territories where patents are granted, they provide a monopoly within the scope of the claims.

**Formalities**

Applications for patents must be made for each territory where protection is required. There are international filing systems that assist with delivering the applications and it is possible to postpone dealings with national and regional patent offices for around 30 months.

After patents are filed there is usually a search to determine whether the invention is new or obvious. This is followed by examination of the application in each patent office where the application is made to see whether the invention meets the requirements for patentability. At this stage the scope of the claims may be reduced during negotiation with the examiner in order to avoid objections.

As a result of this procedure and the requirement for translations, patenting can be costly, especially large-scale international filings. However, a patent is the best means of protection for a great many inventions and can be very valuable.

**Confidential information**

In the UK, the EU, the US and many other jurisdictions, it is possible to protect confidential information, such as secret formulae and sensitive commercial information. In the UK and EU, protection arises automatically if the information is genuinely confidential and reasonable steps have been taken to keep it confidential. Protection is lost if the information ceases to be confidential, although there may still be a claim for damages if this results from misappropriation by somebody else. It is possible to get an injunction to prevent disclosure, but after information has become widely known it is only possible to claim damages for the unauthorised disclosure.

Proving that information is confidential and that disclosure is unauthorised can be difficult, but it is much easier if there is a contract which says that it is confidential and that it must not be disclosed.

Strictly speaking, confidential information is not intellectual property.

## Trade marks

### What is registrable?
In the UK and the EU, trade marks protect signs that indicate the origin of goods and services. They are not confined to word marks and logos. Provided that they can be represented graphically, they can even be shapes and smells.

In principle, anything may be registered provided that it is capable of distinguishing the goods of the trade mark owner. However, if a mark is descriptive, in particular if it is descriptive of the goods themselves, it may be refused registration.

Registration may also be refused if a mark is too close to a mark that is already registered, or if use of the mark could lead to passing off (see below).

### Infringement
Trade marks provide a limited monopoly. They can be used to prevent others from using the same mark on the same goods or services, or, if there is a possibility of confusion, a similar mark with similar goods or services. Well-known marks can also be infringed if they are used on different goods that would not be confused where, without due cause, the use would take unfair advantage of the mark or be detrimental to it.

### Formalities
As with patents, an application needs to be made in each territory where protection is required, and there are international conventions that assist with this.

In addition to national marks, in the EU there is a separate Community mark that covers the entire EU. Trade marks are renewable every 10 years, and may last indefinitely with continued renewal. Like patents, they are always subject to revocation on the grounds that they no longer meet the requirements for registration, unless there has been an irrevocable decision on the grounds for challenge in the relevant jurisdiction.

### Passing off

Passing off is a right that protects goodwill. Technically, there must be a misrepresentation made in the course of trade to existing or prospective customers that is likely to make those customers believe that goods are those of another enterprise, in circumstances where this is likely to cause damage.

This is not as complicated as it sounds. It usually involves one business trying to persuade customers of another that they are one and the same, so that the clients of the first business will buy from the second. Selling lemon juice in a plastic lemon that was suspiciously similar to another trader's packaging has been sufficient to give rise to a claim for passing off.

Like confidential information, it is not, strictly, an intellectual property right, but it can be very useful for protecting unregistered trade marks and get-up, and there are no formalities. However, lesser-known enterprises may have difficulty in demonstrating sufficient goodwill to take action.

In other European countries there are similar rights that are known as 'unfair competition'.

## Designs

Currently there are so many rights protecting designs that it can be confusing.

There are three types of right under UK law that are valid in the UK only: there are UK registered designs and two types of UK unregistered design rights.

### UK registered designs

- **Scope** – registered designs protect the appearance of the whole or part of a product resulting from features of lines, contours, colours, shapes, textures and/or materials, and/or ornamentation in particular. They cover graphic symbols such as computer icons, typographic typefaces, packaging and get-up. This right does not protect parts of objects that are dictated solely by their technical function, are hidden from view during normal use, or are features of objects that fit mechanically around other objects so that either object may perform its function.

- **Novelty and individual character** – designs must be 'new' and have 'individual character' in order to qualify for protection. For these purposes, 'new' means that the design has not been disclosed prior to the 12 months before the date of the application in such a way that it would become known to specialists in the industry sector within the UK. (It is unwise to rely on this 12-month period, however, in case somebody else makes a similar design during that period.)

- **Formalities** – registered design rights may be granted on application to the UK Intellectual Property Office. Rights last for a maximum of 25 years provided that they are renewed every five years. In common with patents and trade marks, registered designs are subject to revocation on the grounds that they do not fulfil the requirements for registration. As a registered right, the protection provides a monopoly within the registered specification, although the scope of that monopoly may well be interpreted narrowly, more especially in very popular forms of design. Registered design protection is available in many other territories.

### Supplementary unregistered designs

There are also unregistered designs, named supplementary unregistered designs, which are similar to the registered variety, although they only last for three years from the date when they are first made available to the public within the UK (or in the case of rights arising before Brexit in the UK or the EU).

If the design becomes known to specialists in the design sector concerned, then for these purposes it is deemed to be available to the public. The supplementary unregistered right is intended to protect designs that are short-lived. Like the registered right, designs must be new and have individual character.

A supplementary unregistered design does not qualify for protection unless it is made available to the public; so the first person to disclose a design is entitled to any supplementary unregistered design right, although somebody who develops the design independently and not by copying can still use the design.

### UK design right

UK design right is an unregistered design right that is peculiar to the UK. It protects aspects of shape and configuration (whether internal or external) of the whole or part of an article. It does not protect surface decoration, parts of articles that are designed to fit around other objects or which are designed to match other objects, or principles of construction. In the context of computers, a modified form of this right protects semiconductor topographies (i.e. chip designs).

The right lasts for 15 years from the end of the year in which the design was first recorded in a design document or an article was made to the design, whichever happened first. This 15-year period is reduced if articles made to the design are legitimately marketed in the first five years, in which case the right lasts for 10 years from the date of the first sale or hire. Anybody can apply to the Intellectual Property Office for a licence during the last five years of the right.

### Design rights and Brexit

Technically, there are two other types of design right, which are variants of the UK registered design and the supplementary unregistered design. As a result of Brexit, rights that covered the whole EU were cloned to create a UK equivalent as the EU rights ceased to apply in the UK. So, there are some UK registered designs that have been created from EU registered designs and some rights that are like supplementary registered designs and that were created from EU unregistered designs. There are some differences in these rights, which arose from the way in which they were created, but those differences are outside the scope of this chapter.

### TAKING ADVICE

If you need advice on intellectual property law, it is always worth using a specialist intellectual property practitioner. If you do not know of one, the Law Society should be able to help you to find one. Other sources of information in the UK include the Chartered Institute of Trade Mark Attorneys and the Chartered Institute of Patent Attorneys.

### SUMMARY

Intellectual property law underpins the entire IT industry. It is a specialised area of legal practice and in a chapter of this kind it is difficult to do more than scratch the surface. However, without at least a basic understanding of intellectual property law, individuals and companies will fail to take the necessary steps to protect their rights in the IT systems that they develop, acquire or use. Equally important, from the legal point of view, they will also risk infringing the rights of other people, exposing themselves to potential claims for damages and even criminal sanctions.

The aim of this chapter has accordingly been to outline just some of the most important aspects of intellectual property law for computer users, and to highlight some of the main pitfalls: it is hoped that this will be helpful in alerting readers to situations in which formal professional advice might be needed.

# 5 CYBER SECURITY

## Andy Lucas

### INTRODUCTION

When the National Health Service (NHS) came to a standstill in 2017, it was because of the effects of a global cyber security incident known as a ransomware attack. Exploiting security weaknesses in computer systems, criminals purposely installed malicious software that was designed to spread and infect servers and networks, desktops and laptops, tablets and smartphones, rendering them unusable by corrupting or encrypting the data held in them. With governments and business so dependent on IT systems and networks, and so much financial and personal information about all of us as individuals stored in data centres all over the world, cyber security should be a matter of concern to everyone. This chapter describes the main cyber security threats to be aware of, and the measures that individuals and organisations should put in place to mitigate those risks.

### WHAT IS CYBER SECURITY?

We put in place systems, contracts and policies to deal with risk.

To protect against the risk that your house might be burnt down, you will probably implement a range of measures. These include insurance, for both the building and its contents. You might want to ensure you have smoke alarms and fire extinguishers in place. Fire doors and clear paths to exit are also essential. That totals four or five different measures to deal with one basic risk.

How do you deal with the sort of risk that is far less clear, far more sophisticated, far worse understood and that may come in numerous different guises? You can take out insurance – but what does it need to cover? Practical measures you can take need to deal with what? How can you anticipate and extinguish a problem if you are not sure where it comes from or even what it is?

The first step is to identify and fully understand the nature and extent of any potential risks. Only once you have done this – and are comfortable you understand the extent of the problem you face – can you start to adopt the correct systems, comply with the relevant laws, draft the right contracts and adopt the appropriate policies to deal with them.

The problem in dealing with cyber risks is the breadth of the term 'cyber'. What does this mean in practice? Where are the cyber threats likely to come from?

## What is cyber?

'Cyber' is simply a term relating to computers and IT generally. In its 2011 cyber security strategy (Cabinet Office 2011), the UK government went as far as defining 'cyberspace' as being:

> An interactive domain made up of digital networks that is used to store, modify and communicate information. It includes the Internet, but also other information systems that support our businesses, infrastructure and services.

Things have moved on a lot since 2011. If cyberspace refers to communication over computer networks, those networks are far more complex than ever before. They do not simply comprise the computer on your desk, which is connected to a server in a cupboard in the basement of your organisation's IT department, which connects to the world via the internet. Cyberspace links up practically everything and anything, from the car you drive, to the watch you wear, to the fridge in your kitchen that downloads the latest recipes from Mumsnet.

The question 'What is cyber?' is therefore more accurately answered by saying that it might potentially mean **any** item that has the ability to communicate.

In a work environment, not even the most stringent of IT policies will guarantee that your organisation's employees do not find a way to use their work smartphone to check their social media accounts. What practical measures are required to protect against the risk of employees tethering their own devices with their work ones? How do you eradicate all possibility of your staff accessing email applications intended to be locked down to authorised devices on their own smartphones?

The first step is to understand fully both the extent and the nature of the threats.

## Where are cyber threats likely to come from?

The simple answer to this question is that cyber threats are everywhere and can come from anywhere. It is not necessary to look far for evidence to support this:

- The latest annual UK government survey on cyber security breaches (DDCMS 2020) reported that virtually all UK businesses it interviewed are exposed to cyber security risks; 80 per cent cited cyber security as a high priority for their senior management.
- The National Cyber Security Centre's *Cyber Security Small Business Guide* (National Cyber Security Centre 2018) warns that small or medium-sized enterprises have a 50 per cent chance of experiencing a cyber security breach.
- In the Ponemon Institute's *2018 Study on Global Megatrends in Cybersecurity* (Ponemon Institute 2018), 82 per cent of respondents predicted that unsecured Internet of Things (IoT) devices are likely to cause a data breach in their organisation.

Security breaches are taking up an increasing share of the business headlines. The list of companies that have made front-page news due to massive cyber breaches is long and increasing. It includes the businesses most of us use on a daily basis; Uber, Apple, Yahoo!, eBay, Adobe and Sony PlayStation are among the high-profile names.

## What is the impact of cyber breach?

The scope and impact of these breaches is considerable.

- At least 150 million users of sports giant Under Armour's MyFitnessPal app had their personal details leaked in a data breach including usernames, email addresses and passwords (Tech Advisor 2019).
- The massive pay-out made by the Canadian lifestyle extra-marital dating website Ashley Madison to victims of its data breach demonstrates not only the financial and personal costs suffered by all involved but also the unscrupulous cunning of the modern hacker (Lord 2017).
- In the UK, the NHS virtually ground to a halt following a major security breach in 2017 that affected the medical records of around 26 million patients (Donnelly 2017). This was attributed to the now infamous worldwide WannaCry ransomware attack, which spread rapidly through computer networks, targeting particularly vulnerable operating systems.

### THE DARK SUMMER OF 2017: WANNACRY AND PETYA

#### WannaCry

The WannaCry attack took place on Friday 12 May 2017 (Symantec Security Response Team 2017).

More than 300,000 devices across 150 countries were hit by a virulent strain of ransomware that was designed to self-replicate and spread. The attack targeted the vulnerable, in particular those using obsolete operating systems on their networked computers. It worked by searching for and encrypting 176 different types of file, adding '.WCRY' to the end of the file name. It then asked users to pay a US$300 ransom in bitcoins. The ransom note indicated that the payment amount would be doubled after three days and it claimed that, if payment was not made after seven days, the encrypted files would be deleted.

#### Petya

The main Petya attack took place on Tuesday 27 June 2017 – although its existence was discovered many months earlier.

Petya was a similar ransomware attack to WannaCry. Again, the incident affected organisations worldwide. This time, the organisations that were hit included major international law firms and national banks.

Other targets included energy companies, a power grid, petrol stations and even an airport.

As the numerous high-profile instances of cyber breach demonstrate, the impact can be far-reaching and the disastrous effects can endure long after the actual attack. The immediate disruption to business operations might be merely the tip of the disaster-recovery iceberg. An assessment of the full impact of an attack needs to take into account all of the following:

- The time lost during/cost of the disruption.
- The time/cost in repairing systems and infrastructure.
- The time/cost of dealing with customer complaints and queries.
- The loss or destruction of data (which may include secrets, confidential information, commercially sensitive materials and legally protected information).
- Any possible action by a regulator or governmental body, including any fines or other sanctions.
- The impact on reputation and goodwill.

## What do we mean by cyber security?

How can we protect against the potentially massive impact of a cyber breach? Given the sophistication of the perpetrators and the proliferation of threats, what is the key to effective prevention? Is prevention even a realistic possibility? If no system is completely resistant to unauthorised access or manipulation, is effective cyber security more a case of putting resources into damage limitation?

As with any form of risk, there are measures that we can take to manage each element of the threat we face. We know we cannot alleviate all risks. The reality is that every one of us is likely to be a victim of some form of cyber crime, probably on numerous occasions.

What we can do is identify cyber risk in different guises, consider the range of measures to deal with those risks and draw up a comprehensive plan to deal with them.

A couple of decades ago, cyber security may have meant little more than ensuring that your business had a firewall and ran regular virus checks. Many organisations probably still have little more than this in place. However, most of us now recognise that cyber security is not a simple, quick fix.

Undertaken properly, implementing cyber security measures will involve all of the following:

- Assessing which aspects of your business are most at risk, including identifying any areas of weakness and calculating their value.
- Assessing what resources, systems and procedures you will need to deal with those risks.
- On the basis of those assessments, devising and implementing a comprehensive plan to manage the risks.
- Backing up the plan with training and regular reviews.

- Refining and reformulating the plan from time to time.
- Investing both time and money.

## Who should be responsible for cyber security?

The main overall responsibility for the process naturally falls to the chief technology officer (CTO) or, if the organisation has one, the chief information officer (CIO). Or does it? In actuality, responsibility for cyber security lies with everyone in an organisation.

There is little point in spending a small fortune on the latest software if your organisation's staff fail to appreciate the basics, if key teams fail to work together or if your plan does not have everyone's full support. An effective cyber security plan needs input from all of the following within the organisation:

- IT team;
- HR team;
- legal team;
- management team/board;
- employees.

It may also need input from outsiders:

- regulators;
- insurers;
- professional bodies;
- suppliers and customers;
- government policy.

### CASE STUDY: WHOSE RESPONSIBILITY IS IT?

**Question**

In the following scenario, identify the potential security risks and who is responsible for them:

- Sarah works in a marketing agency. She is issued a work smartphone, laptop and tablet. She uses a different password on each device, which she is careful to ensure includes both letters and characters. She diarises to change passwords regularly as required by the firm's IT policy.
- Her work involves using specific image-editing software but, as the IT policy prohibits the direct installation of third-party applications, she uses a cloud-based system via a client program on her laptop. She stores new contact

details on her smartphone, and transfers them to the firm's customer relationship management (CRM) system. Her tablet is used primarily for background reading of internal information on clients for new deals.

- Sarah sometimes works from home and is able to connect her laptop remotely using the firm's virtual private network (VPN) system; she can also access this from her own PC using a web-based platform. She occasionally checks her emails on her own smartphone at the weekend and when away on holiday.

- Much of Sarah's work is international and is conducted using videoconferencing or conference calls via a Voice over Internet Protocol (VoIP) connection.

**Answer**

1. Passwords are the most common cyber security measure, but creating and using them ineffectively can in itself give rise to potential risks; and further problems can be created by ill-thought-through corporate password policies. Password best practice is easily implemented, but this should be by way of an approach that does not overburden the user. Changing passwords too frequently may in fact hinder rather than help the problem (as we will see later in this chapter). It is the organisation's responsibility to formulate a sensible and balanced policy, but also Sarah's responsibility to follow it.

2. The firm's VPN offers the potential for eavesdropping. The risk is that users will unwittingly supply sensitive information to the eavesdropper, such as account numbers, passwords and private/confidential/sensitive information. It is the organisation's responsibility to secure its networks and devices, but also Sarah's responsibility to access them in the right way.

3. Applications that rely on installing a client program on an office computer can create a potential tunnel through an organisation's firewall. Employees should be prevented from doing this and should certainly not do so on their own initiative. It is the organisation's responsibility to ensure that administrator settings are applied to systems to control which programs are used and how they are installed. Ultimately, Sarah is responsible for her actions.

4. Conference calls and videoconferencing sessions provide opportunities for the cyber criminal. Anyone with the dial-in and access details can join in. This may be obtained simply by seeing the diary invitation/entry; or it might take place by means of spyware. Both the organisation and its employees need to be aware of this risk.

5. VoIP connections also offer a risk of eavesdropping, since VoIP works over public internet connections. A conventional landline is not immune from eavesdroppers either. Fortunately, the era of the crossed line seems to have passed. The organisation is responsible for the infrastructure, but, as the employee, Sarah also needs to be aware of the potential security risks.

6. Bring your own device (BYOD) policies that allow employees to use their own devices offer many attractions. The main downside is that there are further points of potential access to the prospective hacker. Any system is only as strong as its weakest link – so, again, the responsibility is a shared one. BYOD is discussed in more detail later in this chapter.

7. There are numerous other potential risks in this scenario. All of these, together with the risks outlined above, should be addressed with cyber security training. Any such training programme should demonstrate the perils of failing to follow cyber security common sense, and advise on the practical steps that everyone in the organisation can take. The provision of, and attendance at, training are the joint responsibility of both the organisation and its employees. All too often cyber security training is overlooked or added on as an afterthought to more technical measures, but in reality it is an essential part of risk management.

## WHAT ARE THE MAIN FORMS OF CYBER ATTACK?

### Cyber crime

Cyber crime, as the name suggests, is the collective term for nefarious activities that involve a computer, the internet or both. It generally takes the form of unauthorised computer penetration with the intention of immediate financial gain, often through some form of fraud or blackmail. The attack itself usually focuses on obtaining specific information about individuals or a corporation.

### *The main forms of cyber crime*
Cyber crime takes a wide range of forms, and these are constantly evolving as criminals exploit new technologies or refine their existing practices to counter improvements in security and awareness. Some of the most common forms are as follows:

- **Malware** – malicious software – written with the intent of doing harm to data, devices or people. It comes in many forms with varying degrees of severity ranging from activities that simply cause annoyance to those that are designed to extort and threaten. Examples are viruses, Trojans, spyware and ransomware.

**JARGON-BUSTER: TROJAN**

A Trojan is a computer program that gains access to a computer, system or network by appearing to be harmless, but is designed to do something damaging. (It comes from the expression 'Trojan horse'.)

- **Ransomware** – a relatively simple form of malware. Having entered your computer network it proceeds to threaten the user with harm, generally by denying access to data. It often encrypts the user's files, using an encryption key that remains on the hacker's server. The user is then asked to pay a ransom to receive this private key.

- **Identity theft** – one of the most common types of cyber crime. The term describes a wide range of activities that involve a person purporting to be someone else for financial gain or fraud. The ICO warns that name, address and date of birth all provide enough information to create another 'you' (ICO n.d.). The identity thief can use various methods to find out personal information, and then use it for a variety of purposes.

- **Distributed denial of service (DDoS) attacks** – target multiple compromised systems by flooding the victim with traffic from many different sources and locations. It is used to make an online service unavailable and to bring the relevant network down. It commonly starts by planting malware on the victim's computers. This serves as a diversion tactic. The malware draws the attention of system operators to the attack. The hacker then undertakes a second attack to enter the victim's system and take control.

- **Denial of service (DoS) attack** – whereas a DDoS attack uses multiple computers and internet connections, a DoS attack typically uses one computer and one internet connection to flood a targeted system or resource.

- **Spam** – we are all familiar with spam. In its simplest form, spam consists simply of unwanted emails and messages generated by spambots. However, these communications range from seemingly benign marketing emails (which may in themselves breach many data protection laws) to more sinister criminal techniques such as phishing. (The term's origin stems from a skit from the 1970s comedy series *Monty Python's Flying Circus*, which featured a group of Vikings singing relentlessly 'Spam, Spam, Spam, Spam, Spam, Spam, Spam, Spam, lovely Spam! Wonderful Spam!'.)

**JARGON-BUSTER: SPAMBOT**

A spambot is a program designed to send unsolicited emails. It automatically collects (or 'harvests') email addresses from the internet, which form mailing lists for sending spam.

- **Phishing** – a particularly sinister form of spam. A target is contacted by email, telephone or text message by someone pretending to be a legitimate institution. The aim is usually to lure individuals into providing sensitive data such as personally identifiable information, banking and credit card details, and passwords. It is so named as the activity offers a bait so that the victim takes it and provides information in return.

- **Botnets** – a group of computers that are connected together for a particular task. The term botnet derives from 'robot' and 'network'. A botnet may be used by a hacker to access a computer, often using malware or by exploiting some other security vulnerability. The hacked user is then tricked into installing software that allows the hacker to take control of entire networks of compromised computers. The hacker can then use the controlled network for illicit activity such as a DoS attack or other malicious task.

- **Other forms of cyber crime** – there is an increasingly long list of illegal, illicit and unpleasant activities, all of which are designed to prey on an individual user's or entire system's vulnerabilities. Many of these involve transaction-based crimes, such as fraud, money laundering and counterfeiting. Fake news also ranks as another modern threat that is faced not only by today's businesses but also by some of the most powerful governments, so it seems. The modern cyber criminal may in fact adopt a variety of different methods in a multipronged attack on an unsuspecting victim (e.g. an email that contains malware but which also serves as a phishing attempt).

## Hacktivisim

Hacktivism involves hacking (breaking into) a computer system to achieve a politically or socially motivated end. This could be, for example, pushing for some form of social change.

### Examples of hacktivism

The whistle-blowers' website WikiLeaks has been accused of hacktivism on a number of occasions. Most notably, it was reported in 2010 to have obtained and leaked to newspapers some 90,000 records of incidents and intelligence reports about the Afghanistan conflict (IT Pro Team 2018). These records showed unreported civilian casualties. The Ashley Madison data breach represents a high-profile example of hacktivism of an altogether different nature (Lord 2017). A group calling itself Impact Team hacked into the network and appropriated the personal information of 37 million members who had enrolled with a view to engaging in extra-marital affairs. Personal data including names and email addresses were stolen in an attack that reports speculated was at least partially motivated by moral attitudes. However, Impact Team itself stated that the purpose of the attack was to demonstrate the untruth of Ashley Madison's promise that subscriber details would be kept completely secure and confidential, to show the impossibility of achieving complete impenetrability for any computer or network and to raise awareness of the worthlessness of bland corporate promises to do so.

## Cyber espionage

Cyber espionage involves obtaining information/secrets without the owner's permission or knowledge. The target may be an individual's or a company's competitors or rivals; it might be some other group or enemy; it might be a government. The aim may be personal, economic, political or even military. It is also known as 'cyber spying'.

### Examples of cyber espionage

Gh0st RAT is a form of malware that targets the Windows platform. It was used in 2009 to hack into some of the most sensitive networks, to take screenshots of the computer desktops and access their webcams and microphones. The virus was released when targets opened email attachments. Reports suggest that nearly 1,300 computers in 103 countries were infected, with some belonging to high-profile leaders including the Dalai Lama's office. Computers in foreign affairs ministries and embassies of various countries were also reported to be affected (Markoff 2009).

## Cyber warfare

Will the next world war be a cyber one? In cyber warfare, the battleground involves computers, online control systems and networks. Information systems are targeted for strategic or military purposes, the aim being to disrupt the activities of a state or organisation.

### Examples of cyber warfare

A cyber attack took place in Myanmar just before the elections in 2010 (BBC 2010). It took out most of the internet, and restricted the flow of information to individuals. Reports speculated that the military was behind the attack, using it to prevent the flow of information. Another widely reported act of cyber warfare was the group known as the 'Cyber Caliphate'. A number of sources suggested that, while the group claimed to be affiliated to ISIS, it was in fact an operation alleged to be run by the Russian state-sponsored hacking group APT 28. The US retaliation involved not just attacks on cyber communication channels but also drone strikes against human targets in Syria (McCallion 2020).

## WHAT ARE THE RISK AREAS?

Weaknesses in cybersecurity can threaten a business in many ways. Corporate systems such as email, accounts, sales and HR packages might become unavailable. Sensitive commercial information, financial details or customer data might be deleted or stolen. Industrial control systems might be put out of operation, forcing a costly and time-consuming 'revert to manual' if the business is going to survive at all. With all these threats comes reputational risk, and the risk of civil and criminal liability as well. Some of the principal threats are outlined in this section.

### The main threats to corporate systems

### Loss of files

A primary cyber threat is that a user will lose (or lose access to) files. This could be temporary, but frequently will involve permanent loss or corruption of data.

The impact of a cyber breach is likely to extend far beyond simple data loss. For example:

- Software or systems may become corrupted.
- Access to important third-party systems may be lost.
- Websites may be slowed or taken down entirely.
- Databases may be infiltrated or altered.
- Search engine metadata may be hijacked.

### Email attacks and theft

Emails contain all sorts of data. Private messages, contact details and sensitive data can all be found lurking in our email folders. Hackers are aware of this and that these emails have potentially great value. Not only do criminals seek the business information they hold, but they also target personal data, which may be equally valuable for the purposes of extortion, theft or fraud.

The cyber thief may be looking for, and in the majority of cases will find, some or all of the following in an email folder:

- names and addresses;
- telephone numbers and email addresses;
- credit card and bank account information;
- employment details and history;
- online account details, including passwords;
- potentially any other form of private, business or sensitive information.

The potential knock-on effect of email theft is huge. Accessing a user's emails may unlock the combination to every aspect of the user's world, or that of the organisation for which the user works. This includes access to systems and software, bank accounts, social networks and contacts. It also sets up the hacked user perfectly for identity theft.

Email attacks are one of the easiest forms of cyber breach. On an individual basis, an unlocked work computer may be an invitation for a nosy colleague to have a snoop; as a broad corporate risk, email accounts that are not sufficiently secure may be the hacker's simplest route into your network.

**The breaches most likely to put an organisation at risk**

In its latest survey of cyber security breaches (DDCMS 2020), the UK government highlighted that:

- The most common breaches/attacks by a significant margin were via fraudulent emails. This remains consistent with the findings of its 2017 cyber breach study. It includes activities such as tricking staff into revealing passwords or financial information, plus the old chestnut of opening dangerous email attachments causing the release of viruses and malware.
- Medium and large businesses reported that they have greater exposure to a wide range of attacks. In particular, compared to small businesses, they are more likely to experience: impersonation, viruses or malware, ransomware and unauthorised use of computers or networks by staff.

The survey reported that – no surprise here – cyber attacks have both evolved and become more frequent. One positive finding was that organisations are now more resilient to breaches and attacks. Although less inclined to report negative outcomes or impacts from breaches, they are more likely to make a faster recovery. Those breaches that do result in negative outcomes, though, still come at a substantial cost. The report stresses that there is a lot more that organisations can do – specifically in terms of audits, cyber insurance, supplier risks and breach reporting.

## The threats to industrial control systems

The term 'industrial control system' (ICS) describes the integration of hardware and software in a network to support critical infrastructure. Systems of this kind control industrial processes across every kind of industry. They range from machinery and engineering components used in manufacturing to the operation of entire power plants. ICS technologies include a wide variety of applications such as control servers and industrial automation systems.

### What are the risks to industrial control systems?
The growth of the industrial IoT has increased the risk to ICSs. An ICS can be a desirable target for a terrorist because it may regulate the operation of key elements of critical national infrastructure such as:

- telecommunications networks;
- transport networks (including railways, airports and traffic controls);
- utilities such as power stations, energy distribution and water;
- hospitals and healthcare systems.

### What measures can be taken to protect industrial control systems?
Specific measures are required to deal with this sort of risk, including:

- Protection of infrastructure from potentially harmful programming.
- Configuration and patch management to keep control systems secure.
- The requirement of multi-factor authentication (MFA).
- Time limits and operator controls on remote access.

> **JARGON-BUSTER: MULTI-FACTOR AUTHENTICATION**
>
> MFA is a method of confirming a user-claimed identity that relies upon the user supplying multiple pieces of information. These are the factors by which the system authenticates the validity of the user. The authentication mechanism may be based on a number of different factors, such as the user's knowledge and/or something only they possess, know or are.

Industrial cyber security firm Dragos reported in 2017 a significant increase in ICS threat activity groups armed with new capabilities (Dragos 2017). The report also highlighted a new piece of malware that represents a more alarming concern: Trisis.

Trisis specifically targets and disrupts safety instrumented systems (SIS), systems that are designed to avoid dangerous situations. The Dragos report explains that a SIS attack involves multiple, potentially dangerous, impacts. These include taking systems down, false safety alarms, physical damage and destruction. The risk Trisis introduces is considerable, as it represents the first piece of malware to specifically target human lives.

## The threat of exposing confidential information

There will be both legal and practical implications of exposing confidential information.

### *The legal implications of exposing confidential information*
From the purely legal point of view, loss of confidential information may expose an organisation to a range of sanctions. Many of these will be regulatory, but the possibility of civil action should not be discounted.

The leaking of data is likely to do more than simply breach a user's rights under data protection legislation. In many cases the loss or theft of confidential information, or unauthorised access to it, will also be a breach of a third-party's rights to have that confidential information protected.

This potentially puts the party suffering the data loss in breach of a duty of confidence owed to the third party. That duty might arise simply as a result of the relationship between the parties; or it may be set out under a contract that includes financial or other remedies, such as termination.

### *The practical implications of exposing confidential information*
There may be significant reputational and operational implications of exposing confidential information that belongs to you or to a third party. The most obvious impact is that, once your confidential information is out there and exposed to the public, there is little you can do. The confidential information genie cannot be put back in the bottle.

## The other commercial risks of cyber breach

### *Operational impact*
Loss of your data may represent merely the start of a hacked organisation's problems. The ultimate impact on your organisation of a cyber breach is potentially limitless and includes:

- losses of market and financial value;
- loss of competitiveness;
- damage to facilities;
- damage to reputation and goodwill;
- exposure to investigation;
- possible litigation;
- loss of custom.

## THE SNOWBALLING NATURE OF A DATA BREACH

1. A short email from your IT director contains an attachment that instructs you immediately to install important security upgrades.
2. You click on the attachment, which is in fact an executable file. This allows a hacker to access your email account.
3. The hacker is now able to pretend they are you, and to obtain a new system password.
4. Having obtained access to your system, the hacker proceeds to steal data from your organisation and gain access to the network servers and databases.
5. The hacker releases a bot that destroys some of your organisation's key systems so that no one is able to send emails, book meeting rooms, access documents from the document management system or use key applications.
6. Your sales website has also been taken down as a result, and you are now losing significant business.
7. Of more concern is the risk that your customers' payment details may have been accessed.
8. Employees' personal data and key client data has also been stolen.
9. Key information is leaked into the public domain, including to your competitors.
10. You need to pay for emergency IT support to tide you over while your systems are not working and to help fix/stop the escalating problems.
11. News of the breach makes the national newspapers and their websites, which convey unfavourable reports on your organisation, including criticism of its weak procedures and poor security.
12. The ICO decides to investigate this as a serious breach of data protection laws; your organisation faces the possibility of a large fine and further negative publicity.
13. Other regulators consider investigating and may impose their own fines.
14. Of those who remain, a number of clients, customers and employees are considering litigation.
15. Both your organisation's profitability and morale have dipped significantly – all of which is the result of your failure to identify a suspicious email.

### *The potential for large fines*
Topping the long list of significant financial losses caused by a cyber breach is the potential for a hefty fine.

The UK government has issued stern warnings to organisations of the financial risks of failing to put in place effective cyber security measures. In particular, organisations in the energy, transport, water and health industries face potential fines of up to £17 million if they do not have in place effective cyber security measures (GOV.UK 2018). These fines form a key part of measures introduced by the Cyber Security Directive (see 'Specific cyber security and related legislation' section).

The potential fines under the General Data Protection Regulation (GDPR) have been well publicised. In case you missed the headlines, organisations now face significant penalties for data breach. There are two levels of administrative fines (European Union 2016: Article 83):

- Certain contraventions will attract fines up to €10 million or 2 per cent of global annual turnover, whichever is higher.
- Particularly serious breaches may attract an even more severe sanction of up to €20 million or 4 per cent of global annual turnover, whichever is higher.

## Cyber breach can destroy your business

There are numerous examples of businesses that have been devastated by a cyber breach. It does not take much to bring a business to a halt; any business that relies on the internet for its trade cannot make money if its website has been held hostage or taken down by a cyber attack.

Similar but less evident damage can also be caused by search engine hacking. One day your retail website is ranked on the first page of the major search engines. The next day the same listings are sabotaged by unscrupulous traders pushing their men's lifestyle medications through your well-ranked listings. Even if a cyber breach falls short of wiping out your business, it may have a significant long-term or even permanent impact. A joint study by IT consultant CGI and Oxford Economics in 2017 found that, following a severe breach (CGI 2017):

- An organisation's share price falls by an average of 1.8 per cent. This is the equivalent to a loss of £120 million of a FTSE 100 company's value.
- In extreme cases, cyber breaches have reduced a company's value by 15 per cent.
- Two-thirds of companies suffered a negative impact on their share price after a cyber breach.

## The main vulnerabilities

### Password and policy issues

How many passwords are you required to enter each day? Today alone you have probably signed on to your work computer, accessed at least one mobile device and visited a number of secure sites, all of which require a password. Passwords are a primary measure designed to deal with cyber risk. However, the proliferation of their use brings with it a number of problems:

- Password requirements are becoming increasingly complex, requiring sophisticated combinations of letters, numbers, upper case, lower case, symbols and minimum character lengths.
- The requirement of complex passwords makes passwords difficult to remember.
- Most best-practice guides suggest having a different password for each system or device.
- Users are suffering from password overload.

How might a user cope with the above problems, which collectively are the cause of the modern malady known as 'password-fatigue'? Perhaps by writing down passwords; or by reusing the same password across devices or systems; or by making only very minor changes each time a password needs to be updated. This is a potential gift to the cyber criminal, who accesses your organisation's passwords using a variety of methods. These include:

- Accessing a password stored in a written document, logged electronically or held within a database in an organisation's IT infrastructure.
- Observing a password entry, either physically or by use of software such as a keylogger.
- Interception of transmission of the password over a network.
- Phishing and fraud.
- Automated systems that try to determine large numbers of passwords.

**JARGON-BUSTER: KEYLOGGER**

A keylogger or keystroke logger is software that tracks or logs the keystrokes made on a user's keyboard, typically in a covert manner.

### *BYOD and shadow IT*

Your organisation may allow employees to bring to the workplace their personally owned devices, including smartphones, tablets and laptops. It may also allow them to use these devices to access your organisation's applications, systems and networks. This is known as 'bring your own device' or BYOD.

Increasingly, organisations are both encouraging BYOD and implementing BYOD policies. Despite the obvious cyber risks, there are clear benefits of allowing users to have access to systems, networks, applications and social networks on their own devices. If your organisation has authorised this activity, it should consider putting in place systems, policies and controls to manage it. Even if such BYOD activity is not officially approved by the organisation, the fact is that staff will often use their own devices anyway, so it makes sense to recognise this and to manage it effectively. This is a better approach than outright denial and punishment after a breach has taken place.

Similar issues are raised by the use of shadow IT. Overly restrictive IT policies are often met with disdain by employees, who may be likely to disregard important controls such as prohibitions on visiting certain websites or using (or, worse still, installing) certain applications or software.

> **JARGON-BUSTER: SHADOW IT**
>
> Shadow IT is the use of IT systems within an organisation without the approval, or even the knowledge, of that organisation's IT department.

We may need to accept that certain risks are inevitable and will need to be managed as a part of our cyber security plans. This is generally better than trying to avoid such risks altogether and then, when this fails, having to put in place repair and sanction measures.

### Loss or theft of devices

We have all read stories about hapless politicians who left on the train unsecured laptops that contained highly sensitive information putting the nation's security at risk. The reality is we all carry a number of devices and all of us face a risk that these may be stolen or lost.

### MitM

MitM stands for man in the middle. It refers to a form of cyber attack that takes place when a communication between two systems is intercepted by an outside entity. It may take the form of email or website hijacking, Wi-Fi eavesdropping or any other form of hacking into a communication between two other parties.

### Technical flaws (backdoors, applications)

A backdoor is a means to access a computer system or encrypted data that bypasses the system's standard security mechanisms. Backdoor programs are often intentionally put in place by network administrators (NAs) to assist troubleshooting or other official uses. Backdoors clearly also present a great opportunity to the cyber criminal.

Your network is only as secure as the least secure application installed on it. Each application may offer its own vulnerabilities – a system flaw or weakness that could be exploited by a cyber attacker. Of particular risk are the confidentiality, integrity and availability of resources possessed by an application, its creators and its users.

The application layer is the hardest to defend, due to its complexity. Firewalls and intrusion prevention may be ineffective as these can often be bypassed. The best form of defence is to use or develop applications that are themselves secure.

### Out-of-date applications

A significant number of the world's PC users still use Windows XP as their operating system (NetMarketShare 2018). Incredibly, it is estimated that over 25 million PCs continue to run on Windows XP,[1] despite the fact that it first went on sale in 2001 and Microsoft stopped supporting the platform many years ago.

---

1 https://www.techradar.com/uk/news/if-you-can-believe-it-millions-of-people-are-still-using-windows-xp.

The older the application, the more likely it is that it is no longer secure or requires regular software patches.

### Insider threats

The main cyber risk to your business may in fact be your own staff. Insider threats do not need to be hostile or mischievous. Employees routinely cause unintentional corporate data breaches and leaks all the time. This may take place through a variety of methods: opening executable files in an email that allow malware into a system; keeping a written record of passwords; using an infected device on the organisation's network; or honest mistakes.

Particular insider threats to look out for include:

- **Outsiders inside your organisation** – including subcontractors, agents, partners and anyone with remote or direct access to your system.
- **Privileged users** – individuals who have additional rights or access beyond those available to the majority of employees. They will often be members of the IT support team, but sometimes also include senior management outside the IT department (who may be less aware than the experts about cyber security and hence represent a greater vulnerability).
- **Employees who have left the organisation** – who may still have access to data or certain systems after termination, either through oversight or by design.

### Data storage issues (SQL injections, cryptographic flaws)

The greater the amount of data your organisation stores, the greater the attraction to the cyber criminal and the greater the risk.

A structured query language (SQL) injection is a code technique that sets out to alter or destroy a database. It is a very common form of hacking. The malicious code usually makes its way to your database by a process that inputs data through a web page.

Websites that interact with users are particularly at risk. Contact forms, message boards, blog pages and chatrooms all offer opportunities for an SQL injection.

> **JARGON-BUSTER: SQL**
>
> SQL – structured query language – is a standard language for storing, manipulating and retrieving data in databases.

Cryptography enables the storing and transmitting of data in a particular form so that only those for whom it is intended can read and process them. It generally uses a form of encryption that converts ordinary plain text into unintelligible text, and vice versa. This protects data from theft or alteration. It can also be used for user authentication.

This all sounds wonderful from the cyber security point of view, but there are many ways that cryptographic software can fail. This may be due to poor design or bugs in the system or implementation, hardware issues, misconfigurations or as a result of a range of other issues. A hacker who finds a way to use one of your encrypted channels may have a virtually undetectable pathway into your business.

## Cloud-based storage and systems

Where an organisation uses cloud computing, the very fact that its data are stored 'in the cloud' indicates that the data are stored remotely, at the data centre run by the cloud service provider. The actual security risks of cloud storage depend on many factors. First, what kind of cloud computing are you using? Is it public, private or a hybrid? Is it used for data storage, for applications (SaaS), for platforms (PaaS) or for some other purpose?

The reality is that 'cloud computing' these days essentially just means computing. As with any element of your IT infrastructure, the type of cloud you choose and the level of risk it presents are determined by the specific applications, servers and databases that underpin your cloud solution. For example, if you use a public cloud service provider for data, the likelihood is that it has spent millions on the latest, most robust servers and systems to try and ensure that security is maintained at all times.

The downside is that any major public cloud service provider presents to hackers a highly valuable prize with a big target on its back. Even the largest cloud provider of them all, Amazon, has not been totally immune from attack. In 2018, hackers hijacked Tesla's public cloud environment and gained access to non-public Tesla data. These resources were stored within a Tesla-owned Amazon cloud account (DeNisco Rayome 2018).

## WHAT LAWS GOVERN CYBER SECURITY?

### EU cyber security policy

The EU has put a number of policies and other activities in place to deal with cyber threats. The key initiatives are detailed below (European Commission 2017).

### EU Cybersecurity Strategy (2013)

The EU formally launched its Cybersecurity Strategy in 2013. This set the agenda, framework and priorities for cyber security and focused on the following areas:

- increasing cyber resilience;
- drastically reducing cyber crime;
- developing EU cyber defence policy and capabilities;
- developing the industrial and technological resources for cyber security;
- establishing a coherent international cyberspace policy for the EU.

### European Agenda on Security (2015)

The EU's plan for 2015–2020 expanded its strategy to include additional aspects, including:

- measures for specific systems;
- policies to combat child sexual exploitation;
- measures to defeat fraud and counterfeiting of non-cash means of payments, taking into account newer forms of crime/counterfeiting in financial instruments;
- review of obstacles to the criminal investigation of cyber crime;
- policies to increase access to evidence and information.

### Digital Single Market Strategy (2015)
One of the EU's most comprehensive initiatives is the Digital Single Market Strategy. This encompasses a broad range of practical measures, legislation and other proposals in a wide variety of digital areas. These include the creation of a public–private partnership on cyber security. This was created in part to help structure and coordinate resources to deal with cyber security in Europe.

### Other EU measures
A number of other European measures have been initiated, in particular to increase cooperation across Europe and support the emerging single market for cyber security products and services in the EU (European Commission 2016). For example:

- Europe has its own security agency, namely the European Union Agency for Network and Information Security (ENISA).
- The European Commission's lofty plans for a single cyber security market include an ENISA-backed EU certification framework.
- The Commission is also planning to introduce measures to reduce product and software vulnerabilities and the promotion of a 'security by design' approach for all connected devices (European Commission 2020).

## Specific cyber security and related legislation

### NIS/Cyber Security Directive (EU legislation)
The Directive on security of network and information systems 2016 (known as the 'NIS Directive' or the 'Cyber Security Directive') provides a wide range of legal measures to help network and information systems to deal with cyber security in the EU.

The NIS Directive applies to:

- Operators of Essential Services (OESs) that are established in the EU.
- Digital Service Providers (DSPs) that offer services to persons within the EU.

It does not apply to DSPs that are considered small and micro businesses, meaning companies employing fewer than 50 people whose annual turnover and/or balance sheet total is less than €10 million.

Who are OESs? OESs include public and private entities in the fields of energy, transport, banking, financial market infrastructures, health, drinking water supply and distribution, and digital infrastructure that fulfil the following criteria:

- The entity provides a service that is essential for the maintenance of critical societal and/or economic activities.
- The provision of that service depends on network and information systems.
- An incident affecting the network and information systems of that service would have significant disruptive effects on its provision.

### Network and Information Systems Regulations 2018 (UK legislation)

The UK government implemented the NIS Directive by way of the Network and Information Systems Regulations 2018 (NIS Regulations). The NIS Regulations came into effect on 10 May 2018 and apply to:

- OESs in the UK;
- Relevant Digital Service Providers (RDSPs) that are established in the UK.

**Who are OESs under the NIS Regulations?** OESs are operators of services deemed critical to the economy and wider society. They include public and private entities in the following fields:

- energy – electricity, oil and gas;
- transport – air, water, rail and road;
- healthcare – including hospitals, private clinics and online settings;
- drinking water supply and distribution;
- digital infrastructure.

An OES must also:

- meet certain subsector and threshold requirements (Schedule 2);
- rely on network and information systems (Regulation 8(1)).

Even if a person does not meet the relevant threshold requirement, a competent authority may designate that person as an OES for the subsector if certain conditions are met, including the competent authority concluding that an incident affecting the provision of that essential service by that person is likely to have significant disruptive effects on the provision of the essential service (Regulation 8(3)).

**Why do banking and financial markets not appear as OESs in the NIS Regulations?** The NIS Regulations do not include the banking and financial market infrastructure sectors as OESs. The reason why no criteria for identifying and regulating those in the banking sector and the financial market infrastructures sector is included is that equivalent EU legislation (such as the Revised Payment Services Directive[2]) already applies.

**What do the NIS Regulations require of OESs?** OESs are required to implement appropriate and proportionate:

---

[2] https://eur-lex.europa.eu/legal-content/en/TXT/?uri=CELEX%3A32015L2366.

- Technical and organisational measures to manage risks posed to the security of the network and information systems on which their essential service relies.
- Measures to prevent and minimise the impact of incidents affecting the security of the network and information systems used for the provision of an essential service, with a view to ensuring the continuity of those services.

**Who are RDSPs?** RDSPs are organisations that provide the following specific types of digital services:

- online search engines;
- online marketplaces;
- cloud computing services.

An RDSP must:

- Provide one or more of these services.
- Have its head office in the UK (or have nominated a UK representative).
- Not be a micro or small enterprise (i.e. not apply to RDSPs employing fewer than 50 people whose annual turnover and/or balance sheet total is less than €10 million).

**What do the NIS Regulations require of RDSPs?** RDSPs are required to identify and take appropriate and proportionate measures to manage the risks posed to the security of network and information systems on which they rely to provide their digital service. RDSPs must ensure a level of security of network and information systems appropriate to the risk posed to:

- Prevent and minimise the impact of incidents affecting their network and information systems with a view to ensuring the continuity of those services.
- Take into account the following:
  - security of systems and facilities;
  - incident handling;
  - business continuity management;
  - monitoring, auditing and testing;
  - compliance with international standards.

An RDSP must also notify the Information Commissioner about any incident that has substantial impact on the provision of the digital services it provides.

### *Cybersecurity Act (EU legislation)*
The Cybersecurity Act (or Regulation on ENISA and on information and communications technology cybersecurity certification), as the full name suggests, does two things. It revamps and strengthens ENISA. It also establishes an EU-wide cyber security

certification framework for digital products, services and processes. The framework enables the creation of EU certification schemes for products and services.[3]

### Computer Misuse Act 1990 (UK legislation)
The Computer Misuse Act protects computer users against wilful attacks and theft of information.[4] The Act deals with offences such as hacking, unauthorised access to computer systems and purposely spreading malicious and damaging software (such as viruses). It makes it an offence to access (or attempt to access) a computer system without the appropriate authorisation. The legislation also covers unauthorised access to different parts of a computer system.

The following categories are all criminal offences under the 1990 Act:

- Unauthorised access to computer material.
- Unauthorised access with intent to commit or facilitate a crime.
- Unauthorised modification of computer material.
- Making, supplying or obtaining anything that can be used in computer misuse offences.

### Regulation of Investigatory Powers Act 2000 (UK legislation, replaced by Investigatory Powers Act 2016, known as the 'snoopers' charter')
The investigatory powers legislation deals with law enforcement investigative powers, covering interception of communications, acquisition of communications data, surveillance, covert human intelligence and protected data.

The 2016 Act brings together all of the powers available to law enforcement and the security and intelligence agencies to acquire communications and communications data. It makes security/intelligence agencies subject to enhanced, consistent safeguards. It also makes provision for the retention of internet connection records for law enforcement, to identify the communications service to which a device has connected.

The legislation in this area has been the subject of much controversy, including a successful legal challenge over certain aspects of the legislation that were declared unenforceable.

### Counter-Terrorism and Security Act 2015 (UK legislation)
The Counter-Terrorism and Security Act 2015 sets out specific measures to deal with security and terrorism issues. In particular, it enhances law enforcement agencies' ability to investigate terrorism and serious crime. It does so by extending the retention of relevant communications data to include data that will help to identify who is responsible for sending a communication on the internet or accessing an internet communications service.

---

3   https://ec.europa.eu/digital-single-market/en/cyber-security.
4   https://www.legislation.gov.uk/ukpga/1990/18/contents.

## Data protection legislation

### GDPR (EU legislation)
The GDPR[5] (covered in detail in Chapter 6) imposes extensive obligations relating to the security of data handled by an organisation. Organisations should be introducing measures to prevent threats to personal data that will affect data subjects, such as loss of access to data (whether temporary or permanent), damage or corruption of the data or loss of control such as through unauthorised access in a cyber attack.

Specific provisions of the GDPR that deal with cyber security include:

- **Security of processing** – data processors and controllers must put in place measures to ensure a level of security appropriate to the risk (Article 32).
- **Breach of personal data** – the controller must notify the supervisory authority within 72 hours (Article 33). If there is a personal data breach, then the controller must notify the data subject without undue delay (Article 34).
- **Data Protection Impact Assessments (DPIAs)** – where an organisation carries out processing that is likely to result in a high risk to data subjects, it is obliged to carry out a DPIA prior to the processing and potentially consult with the supervisory authority (Article 35).
- **Data protection by design** – an organisation needs to take measures that are actually designed to implement the data protection principles. Factors that the controller should take into account when considering design include the state of the art, the prevailing best practice and technology and the costs of implementation.

### Data Protection Act 2018 (UK legislation)
The new Data Protection Act replaces the Data Protection Act of 1998 as the primary piece of data protection legislation in the UK. The main aim is to ensure that the UK and EU data protection regimes are aligned post-Brexit (not least of all increasing the maximum level of fines in the UK so that it is consistent with the GDPR).

### Privacy and Electronic Communications Regulations 2003 (UK legislation, known as 'e-Privacy Regs' or 'PECRs')
The PECRs provide individuals with specific privacy rights in relation to electronic communications. They set out rules on a broad range of areas such as:

- marketing calls;
- emails;
- text messages and faxes;
- cookies and similar technologies;
- keeping communications services secure;
- customer privacy regarding traffic and location data, itemised billing, line identification and directory listings.

---

5  http://eur-lex.europa.eu/legal-content/EN/TXT/PDF/?uri=CELEX:32016R0679&from=EN.

They operate alongside the Data Protection Act 2018 and are due to be replaced by updated regulations (see below).

### Privacy and Electronic Communications Regulation (EU legislation that will replace the 2003 PECRs)

The replacement of the current European e-Privacy Directive/Regulations will establish a new privacy legal framework for electronic communications. It is aimed at enhancing the protection of privacy and personal data in the electronic communications sector. The scope of the Regulation will be extended to all electronic communication service providers. It is likely that many UK businesses will need to comply with the Regulation even after the UK ceases to be a member of the EU.

## WHAT PRACTICAL STEPS SHOULD YOU CONSIDER?

### Planning for risk

Dealing with any form of risk in an organisation requires careful planning. As we have seen in this chapter, the risk of cyber attack is high, the scope is comprehensive and the effect is potentially devastating. Simply installing antivirus software and a firewall are far from the solution.

The plan for your cyber security strategy should include all of the following six steps.

---

**THE SIX STEPS TO A SUCCESSFUL CYBER SECURITY PLAN**

**Step 1: review your current situation**

- Assess what cyber security measures you already have in place.
- Work out which individuals within and outside your organisation you need to involve.
- Consider what infrastructure and information needs protecting, including databases, documents, software and hardware.

**Step 2: fact find**

- Speak to all relevant individuals.
- Research potential measures to protect your assets.
- Find out what budgets are available.
- Assess vulnerabilities in your current cyber security protection.

**Step 3: formulate your plan**

- Draw up a list of priorities.
- Devise your procedures and policies. These should deal with how to:

- Identify an issue.
- Prevent occurrence or recurrence.
- Respond to security threats.
- Achieve full compliance.
- Set specific objectives and map out a realistic timeframe for achieving them.
- Schedule a flexible programme for review, maintenance and upgrades for systems, software and backups.

**Step 4: assign responsibilities**

- Assign responsibility to relevant persons for:
  - Implementing technical measures.
  - Implementing staff policies.
  - Monitoring of the plan.
  - Providing training.
  - Implementing other aspects of your plan.

**Step 5: implement the plan**

- Monitor progress.
- Record achievements, omissions and failures.

**Step 6: regularly revisit and refine the plan**

- Consider/research new threats.
- Adapt for changes in your organisation's infrastructure, information and personnel.
- Review at regular stages.
- At end of plan, go back and review/repeat earlier stages.

### What areas does my plan need to cover?

The specific areas that your plan should cover depend on the size, nature and complexity of your business. For example, a regulated business such as a financial institution will have specific procedures that it must follow and sensitivities that it needs to address, and will probably have significant resources to devote to cyber security planning. By contrast, a small organisation in an unregulated sector will face different risks, and may not have the same resources available to deal with risk as those of a large corporation.

The following 20 key questions are some of the areas to consider in your cyber security plan.

**20 KEY QUESTIONS TO ASK WHEN FORMULATING YOUR CYBER SECURITY PLAN**

1. What is the attitude towards risk in your organisation?
2. Are there risk management, business continuity, disaster recovery or information security plans or procedures in place?
3. Has your organisation conducted a Data Protection Impact Assessment? Is it GDPR compliant?
4. Does your organisation need to comply with any standards such as:
   - International Organization for Standardization (ISO)/International Electrotechnical Commission (IEC)?
   - Consortium for IT Software Quality (CISQ)?
   - Payment Card Industry Data Security Standard (PCI DSS)?
   - National Institute of Standards and Technology (NIST)?
   - Information Assurance for Small and Medium Enterprises (IASME)?
   - Cyber Essentials?
5. Does your organisation need to comply with any specific regulatory requirements?
6. What information is stored and where is it stored (document management system, client relationship management system, other databases)? How is it classified (private, public, confidential)?
7. Does your organisation keep backups of data? Where are these stored?
8. What systems are in place for network security and encryption?
9. What security procedures/systems have been implemented for both applications and hardware, including malware/firewall/virus/spam detection and protection?
10. Who has enhanced/administrator access rights and to what information, applications and systems?
11. What IT systems, software and applications does your organisation use? How up to date are they? Have all upgrades and patches been installed?
12. Are systems developed internally or by third parties?
13. Who is responsible for your organisation's website? Is it used for sales, two-way communication or just information?
14. What can system/network users access? How are users monitored?
15. What policies are in place for employees, agents and subcontractors?
16. What do IT/staff policies allow users to do?
17. Does your organisation permit BYOD and is there a policy for this?

18. Do users work remotely? What devices do they use?
19. Is there a staff training programme? Does it cover cyber security?
20. How are cyber issues dealt with? Is there an incident log?

## Testing for weaknesses

At various stages of your cyber security plan your system should be tested for weaknesses and vulnerabilities (GOV.UK 2017). There are two main methods that can be applied:

- **Vulnerability assessments** – designed to identify, quantify and prioritise the potential vulnerabilities in a system.
- **Penetration tests** – designed to replicate an attack on a system to find its weaknesses and understand how easy they are to exploit.

Issues to consider include:

- Who should conduct the tests?
- When should the tests take place? How often?
- Should testing routinely take place following upgrades or new software and hardware installations?
- What is the scope of your testing? Ideally this should cover the whole system rather than specific software or applications.
- Do you need consent from any third-party suppliers to use their software in your tests?

## Technological and practical solutions

The specific solutions that flow from your cyber security plan will depend on the findings of your research and should be tailored to the specific needs of your organisation. Some general considerations are set out below.

## Backups

- **Identify what needs to be backed up** – it may not be practical or necessary to backup all of your data, but a duplicate should be made of anything that is essential to your organisation. Consider what would happen if you lost all of your organisation's data, and plan to mitigate the exposure to losing anything that is irreplaceable.
- **Ensure backups are secure and accessible** – make sure backups are password-protected and accessible at all times by authorised users.
- **Schedule regular backups** – backups can be scheduled to take place at whatever frequency you choose. Alternatively, backups of key information may take place as information is generated.

CYBER SECURITY

- **Store the backup somewhere sensible** – backing up your holiday photographs to an external hard drive seems like a good idea, but offers limited protection if you keep your hard drive in the same cupboard as your laptop. A thief will take both. A fire will destroy both. It is no different in a business context. Consider backing up your data to a different location.
- **Consider cloud options** – an external cloud solution may be the best option for storing backups of data and applications. Public cloud generally offers cost advantages, excellent accessibility and first-rate security. Certain industries and professions (such as financial services) have been reluctant to use public cloud for various operational reasons. Some of these are justifiable, but others may be based on misplaced fears regarding the security of public cloud. See below for more on this topic.

## Passwords (and password policy)

- **Change all default passwords** – default passwords are easily exploited because they provide a simple means for the cyber criminal to access a system or a service (as the *News of the World* phone hacking scandal showed in 2011). If possible, scan your systems to identify when/if default passwords (and indeed other passwords) were last changed.
- **Consider the benefits of a regular schedule for changing passwords** – it may seem obvious to require users to change their passwords at regular intervals. In reality this may offer limited benefits, because passwords are generally exploited by hackers immediately at the time of password entry into a system. A password change interval that is too frequent only increases the likelihood of a user writing it down. Consider instead only requiring the change of a password when a particular type of event requires this, such as a breach or unusual activity on an account.
- **Monitor logins** – monitoring can be used to detect unusual or unsuccessful login attempts. Make sure that users know when, how and to whom to report suspicious activity.
- **Establish a sensible password policy** – the password policy should prohibit password sharing between users. If passwords need to be shared (such as for emergency access), consider using MFA or some other form of authentication, such as a unique token or a code sent to the user's smartphone, which must be entered in addition to the password.
- **Balance complexity with practicality** – clearly a simple password that can easily be guessed or determined is to be avoided. Equally, a password policy that insists on a complex combination of numbers, symbols, upper case and the middle letter from the name of your first pet is not ideal. A sensible balance needs to be achieved.
- **Consider alternatives to passwords** – increasingly devices now include fingerprint recognition to lock a device with no need for a password.

## Cloud

- **Work out what cloud solutions you need** – the plan for cloud depends on what type of cloud solution your organisation implements and what it is used for. Is it only for backups? What other databases are stored in the cloud? Does your organisation have its own private solution, use a hybrid solution or is it entirely reliant on someone else's (public cloud) servers? Will it be used more broadly for other purposes, such as SaaS or PaaS?

- **Do your homework** – if you plan to use public cloud, find out as much information as possible about the provider. Do they adhere to any standards? At which data centre/server will your data be stored? What security measures are in place? Are data encrypted?
- **Follow cloud standards** – various industry-specific standards have been developed for cloud and these are discussed below.
- **Test for vulnerabilities** – use appropriate vulnerability and penetration techniques to test your cloud solution's security measures.
- **Consider what information to store in the cloud** – your organisation may have restrictions on or concerns about storing certain information on a cloud server, for example data that are sensitive or confidential such as trade secrets. Many of these will be based on rigid misconceptions regarding cloud security. Even so, you do not want fingers pointing at you if the worst-case scenario occurs and there is a security breach involving key data that you had chosen to store on a public cloud server.

## *Social media*

- **Educate your users** – social media can represent a big threat to an organisation. Social media services provide the perfect hunting ground for cyber attackers, because of the volume of information that users share. You can reduce the risks by education and training that demonstrates the perils of social media. Consider also offering help and guidance on the use of privacy settings on devices and applications.
- **Implement staff policies?** – policies are rarely the complete answer to any risk issue. The strongest policy in the world will not prevent a disgruntled employee posting confidential or inflammatory information online. Most large organisations will have extensive IT usage policies and the recently added paragraph relating to social media can easily be hidden in the policy's small print. If you choose to implement a social media policy, make sure it is a sensible, standalone one that contains more than a long list of rules. Consider implementing a best-practice guide for social media users containing useful information that is regularly updated and presented in a user-friendly format.
- **Turn it off?** – blocking websites is often seen as too draconian a measure for many organisations, and can have unintended consequences. Canny employees may find a way around any controls or limits on social media use, for example by frequenting similar but less popular websites that you have overlooked and that have weaker security measures in place. Certain social media sites might also be an important business tool that you want users to be able to access.
- **Take care with corporate accounts** – many organisations operate corporate social media accounts. These should be monitored closely for suspicious activity and threats, in particular any that relate to specific marketing initiatives and campaigns.
- **Test** – random tests on employees' susceptibility to social media cyber attacks might be advisable, if only to serve as a warning of the risks presented.

## Email

- **Configure user accounts carefully** – phishing is a real threat to any organisation. One way of minimising the impact is to configure user accounts so that access to applications and certain databases is only given to those, and to the extent, required.
- **Implement software for spam and phishing** – software solutions are one of the most effective ways to remove cyber attacks that attempt to enter a network through the email system, by identifying and then quarantining or neutralising any spam or phishing emails.
- **Educate and train** – regular training sessions using case studies will help to educate users on email best practice. Having staff who are aware of what a phishing scam might look like and who know what – and what not – to do might help to avoid malware making its way into your organisation's systems.

## Mobile device management

- **Keep devices up to date** – older devices tend to offer weaker resistance to cyber attacks. Make sure all devices have the latest software patches and the most recent firmware/operating systems.
- **Ensure PINs and passwords are used** – mobile devices should all be protected by at least a unique personal identification number (PIN).
- **Install a layer of organisational control software** – all devices need to be protected by security software. This should be routinely updated and the user prevented from disabling it. Consider also installing security software that locates the device if lost or stolen or disables its functionality.
- **Assign responsibility to the user** – ensure that anyone in your organisation who uses a mobile device that connects to your organisation's network is made fully responsible for their behaviour and actions and clearly understands that this is the case. This is something that can be addressed from the outset as part of new joiner induction programmes, as well as by 'business as usual' cyber security training.

## Home working and BYOD

- **Include a clear BYOD policy in your staff handbook** – as discussed earlier in this chapter, allowing employees to use their own devices for work purposes can offer many benefits. You can, however, reduce the associated risks by ensuring that employees follow certain protocols. These should include implementing the correct applications and software, and following the correct password conventions on their devices.
- **Consider where information is stored** – it may be important to ensure that minimal data are stored locally on the device itself and the majority are only accessible remotely. Data that are stored on the device should ideally be encrypted. It is also advisable to limit the number of actual copies of a piece of information across different devices. This can be achieved by sourcing the information from one single cloud-based server (one of the security benefits of cloud computing).
- **Limit the range of systems and devices** – set minimum requirements for operating systems and particular types of device. Restrictions on the ability to transfer data should also be considered.

- **Give yourself the ability to control devices** – the same control and security software should be installed on a user's own device as is installed on any of the corporation's devices. In particular, this should include software that allows your organisation the ability to remotely locate a device and delete all data as necessary.
- **Use tokens and MFA** – devices or apps that create unique tokens are a common method of authenticating users who access systems remotely.

## Strategic, technical and operational solutions

The practical solutions suggested above should all be incorporated into your organisation's overall cyber security strategy. In addition, key technical and operational considerations and solutions should form the core of your plan.

### *Governance*

There are important decisions to be made on cyber security. Some of these will necessarily involve significant initial expenditure; others may have costly implications further along your plan.

Budgets will need to be agreed. Individuals across many functions in your organisation will need to be involved. Policies will need to be created and implemented. Compliance with and the effectiveness of your cyber security measures will require regular monitoring and measurement.

All of these issues can be set out in a cyber security governance framework. This can be used to ensure that information security activities are properly managed, that plans are implemented according to your timetable and that policies are prepared and updated as required.

The framework should be reviewed and updated on a regular basis. Consider also whether a dedicated chief security officer (CSO) should be appointed to manage your organisation's security issues.

### *Staff policies and technical capability*

Specific policies relating to data and security should be formulated for a range of circumstances and users. Aspects to consider include:

- IT usage policy for staff;
- IT usage policy for subcontractors and agents;
- social media policy;
- internet acceptable use policy;
- email policy;
- document management/filing policy;
- disaster recovery plan (see below).

In regulated industries or professions, additional requirements (or even policies) may need to be specified.

### Crisis management/communications/disaster recovery

Your organisation's cyber security plan and governance framework should make provision for a comprehensive business continuity/disaster recovery plan. What the plan covers depends on a number of factors. These include the nature of your industry or profession, the size and complexity of your organisation and the systems that need to be maintained or protected.

A typical disaster recovery plan will include details of:

- potential threats to the business;
- procedures to follow in the event of a disaster;
- roles and responsibilities;
- triggers that activate particular aspects of the plan;
- practice drills;
- other key information, such as contact details, insurance, key contracts and inventories.

### Training and awareness

To give any policy within an organisation the best chance of success it needs to be backed up with an appropriate programme of training and education. Highlighting not just the risk and issues but also the consequences of a security breach or other attack is one of the most effective methods of protection – or, rather, prevention.

Regular education programmes should cover all staff. In particular, training should be provided to new employees as part of their induction into your organisation. The training should be supported with best-practice guides, top tips and checklists – all of which must be easily accessible.

### Insurance

Specific insurance that deals with cyber risks is increasingly being offered by insurers. Standard insurance policies may cover some aspects of disaster recovery, but only to a limited degree. To be confident that the risk of cyber breach is covered, dedicated cyber insurance policies may be required. Policies are available that cover a range of cyber risks, including:

- damage caused by hacking;
- loss of data;
- costs of dealing with a security breach;
- ransomware demands;
- impact of viruses;
- business interruption;
- data protection breaches, including amounts payable to others for such breaches (including some regulatory penalties).

The main downside is the same as for any form of insurance. The better the protection you require, the more it will cost you. Remember also that insurance is not really **protection**, it is merely compensation for some of your financial losses.

## Software and configuration

Many organisations will rely on specialists to implement sophisticated solutions to protect their networks, applications and data. The software, its deployment and configuration involve a complex process, which can be very costly. You may wish to enlist specialist advice to provide the best software solution for your organisation.

Antivirus software needs to be considered for all devices your organisation uses. This may require a range of different approaches to suit each device type.

Network security most commonly relies on some form of firewall. Other intrusion prevention devices and systems can also be deployed.

Neither firewalls nor antivirus software are infallible, but they remain a primary defence mechanism against cyber threats. The National Cyber Security Centre (NCSC) and Cyber Essentials guides stress the importance of these devices as primary means of protection against cyber threats.[6]

Some of the fundamental principles are easy to overlook. Make sure your software is set to 'on' for all users, up to date and appropriate, and test it regularly to see it is effective. Out-of-date and expired cyber security software is probably as risky as having no protection at all.

The physical security of your systems should also be considered. There is no benefit in having the most sophisticated systems on your network if someone has stolen your server.

## Future-proofing your plan

How can you ensure you keep fully on top of cyber security? The answer is you can't: **none** of us can keep all the cyber threats fully at bay.

Information is one of the keys to ensuring your plan remains as effective as possible. In particular:

- Understanding behaviour patterns will help you to identify where issues lie.
- Knowing when your operating systems will be in need of upgrade allows you to remain a step ahead.
- Discovering a service or solution is no longer required allows you to decommission potentially troublesome older applications.
- Keeping an eye on legal and industry developments will help you to remain informed about the latest cyber security threats and strategies for dealing with them.

---

[6] https://www.cyberessentials.ncsc.gov.uk/advice/.

Like any good plan it will need to be reviewed and revitalised frequently. This should be an ongoing process, not just scheduled for an annual date that can all too easily be disregarded or pushed back.

Your plan can only be future-proofed to the extent that you feed into it the knowledge and information that it needs. The more you can systematise the process, the easier, more efficient and effective it will become.

## WHAT GUIDES, FRAMEWORKS AND STANDARDS ARE AVAILABLE?

### Cyber Essentials

Cyber Essentials is a UK government-backed, industry-supported programme to help organisations protect themselves against common online threats.

It operates by way of a certification scheme. This is designed to ensure participants have taken measures that have been assessed as the best way to protect against the majority of common cyber attacks.

The Cyber Essentials scheme is suitable for all organisations, of any size and in any sector.

### *What are the certification levels?*
The scheme offers two levels of certification, each of which comes with its own special badge:

- **The basic (entry level) Cyber Essentials certification** – this option involves self-assessment/certification (details of how this works are set out below). It provides/demonstrates protection against a wide variety of the most common cyber attacks. It also educates participants on the basics and recommends prevention against the most common attacks.

- **Cyber Essentials Plus** – this option differs from the basic certification in its method of verification. In place of the standard questionnaire, independent verification of the participant's cyber security is undertaken by a Cyber Essentials certification body. The certification is more stringent and additional support may need to be purchased from the certification body.

---

**CYBER ESSENTIALS BODIES**

- **Cyber Essentials certification body** – these are organisations that are trained and licensed to certify conformity with the Cyber Essentials Scheme. Certification bodies utilise a standard questionnaire when certifying an organisation. The questionnaire is produced by the accreditation bodies.

- **Cyber Essentials accreditation body** – these are organisations selected by the NCSC to oversee Cyber Essentials. The accreditation bodies recruit and manage the certification bodies and ensure the standards for the scheme are met. They also audit the certification bodies at least once every 12 months and verify that they meet the NCSC's level of technical competence.

## How do I get a Cyber Essentials certification/badge?

The self-certification process for the standard Cyber Essentials scheme requires a participant organisation to follow these steps:

- Select a certification body through one of the accreditation bodies. The Cyber Essentials website maintains a list of these.
- Verify that your IT is suitably secure and meets the standards set by Cyber Essentials. Cyber Essentials sets out in detail the requirements for the participant organisation's IT (see below).
- Complete the questionnaire provided by the certification body, and submit this back to them.
- The certification body then verifies your answers. If your organisation has passed, it will be awarded a Cyber Essentials certificate.

## What are the IT requirements for Cyber Essentials?

The primary requirement of Cyber Essentials is that an organisation meets all the stipulations it sets for the participant organisation's IT systems and procedures. The scheme recommends that, to achieve the best possible protection, it should cover the whole IT infrastructure if this is possible.

A summary of **some** of the key Cyber Essentials requirements for IT is set out below. These represent best-practice advice generally and should form the basis of any organisation's cyber security plan.

## Cyber Essentials 1: Use a firewall

Every device that is in scope must be protected by a correctly configured firewall (or equivalent network device). In addition, organisations must carry out specific measures, including:

- Changing any default administrative password to an alternative that is difficult to guess, or disable remote administrative access entirely.
- Preventing access to the administrative interface from the internet, unless there is a clear and documented business need and the interface is adequately protected.
- Blocking unauthenticated inbound connections by default.

## Cyber Essentials 2: Select the most secure configurations

The configurations for hardware and software should be checked and altered as required. This means you will need to consider: email, web and application servers; desktop computers; laptop computers; tablets; mobile phones; firewalls; and routers.

**Accounts and software:** General measures that organisations must carry out include:

- Checking for, removing and disabling any unnecessary user accounts.
- Changing any default or guessable account passwords to something non-obvious.
- Removing or disabling unnecessary software.
- Disabling any auto-run feature that allows file execution without user authorisation.

- Authenticating users before allowing internet-based access to commercially or personally sensitive data or to data that are critical to the running of the organisation.

**Passwords:** Organisations must make good use of the technical controls available to them on password-protected systems, including:

- Protecting against brute-force password guessing.
- Setting a minimum password length of at least eight characters but no maximum password length.
- Changing passwords promptly when there is suspicion they have been compromised.
- Having a sensible password policy in place, covering issues such as: how to avoid choosing obvious passwords; not using the same password anywhere else, at work or at home; where and how to record passwords; whether password management software can be used; and which passwords must be memorised and not recorded anywhere.

Note that the scheme advises **against** regular password expiry for any account (for similar reasons to those explained earlier in this chapter). It also does not set out specific password complexity requirements.

### *Cyber Essentials 3: Control who has access*

User access should be controlled for: email, web and application servers; desktop computers; laptop computers; tablets; and mobile phones.

An organisation must be in control of all user accounts and the access privileges granted to each user account. Measures that an organisation must put in place include:

- Having a user account creation and approval process.
- Authenticating users before granting access to applications or devices.
- Removing or disabling user accounts when no longer required.
- Implementing two-factor authentication, where available.
- Using administrative accounts to perform administrative activities only.

### *Cyber Essentials 4: Implement malware protection*

Measures to protect against malware should be maintained on: desktop computers; laptop computers; tablets; and mobile phones.

Organisations must use at least one of the following mechanisms:

- **Anti-malware software** – the software must be kept up to date, with relevant files updated at least daily. It needs to be configured to scan files automatically upon access. It must also scan web pages automatically and prevent connections to malicious websites on the internet (unless there is a clear, documented business need not to do so).

- **Application whitelisting** – only approved applications should be allowed. These require active approval before being deployed to devices. A current list of approved applications must be maintained. Users must not be able to install any application that is unsigned or has an invalid signature.

> **JARGON-BUSTER: CODE SIGNATURE**
>
> Code signature is the process of digitally signing key aspects of the code (executables and scripts) to confirm the software author and to guarantee that the code has not been altered or corrupted since it was signed.

- **Application sandboxing** – all code of unknown origin must be run within a 'sandbox' (testing environment) that prevents access to other resources unless permission is explicitly granted by the user. This includes other sandboxed applications, data stores, sensitive peripherals and local network access.

*Cyber Essentials 5: Patch management*
An organisation must keep all of its software up to date. Software must be:

- licensed and supported;
- removed from devices when no longer supported;
- patched within 14 days of an update being released, where the patch fixes a vulnerability with a severity the product vendor describes as 'critical' or 'high risk'.

> **JARGON-BUSTER: PATCH**
>
> A patch is a software update comprising code that is inserted – or 'patched' – into the code of an executable program, typically being an existing software program. Patches are often temporary fixes between full releases of a software package.

**NIST cyber security framework (US)**

In the US the National Institute of Standards and Technology (NIST) has established a voluntary framework for cyber security-related risk. It consists of standards, guidelines and best practices.[7]

*What are the components of the NIST framework?*

- **Framework Core** – provides a set of desired cyber security activities and outcomes. It is intended as a guide for organisations in managing and reducing their cyber

---

[7] https://www.nist.gov/cyberframework.

security risks. One of its selling points is that it is designed to complement an organisation's existing cyber security and risk management processes.

- **Framework Implementation** – is undertaken by tiers. These are designed to provide context on how an organisation views cyber security risk management.
- **Framework Profiles** – map an organisation's unique organisational requirements and objectives, risk appetite and resources against the desired outcomes of the Framework Core. They are primarily used to identify and prioritise opportunities for improving cyber security.

## Security standards

### ISO/IEC

> **WHO ARE THE ISO/IEC?**
>
> **ISO**
>
> ISO is the International Organization for Standardization. As the name suggests, ISO provides standards and specifications for products, services and systems. It maintains more than 23,000 international standards covering almost all aspects of technology and manufacturing.[8]
>
> **IEC**
>
> IEC is the International Electrotechnical Commission, which focuses on the publication of international standards for all electrical, electronic and related technologies.

The ISO/IEC have developed standards for information management.[9] These are the ISO/IEC 27000 series (also known as the 'ISO/IEC 27000 family').

The best known of the ISO/IEC 27000 series is ISO/IEC 27001. This sets out the requirements against which an organisation's information security management system (ISMS) can be audited and certified. The 27001 standard specifies the requirements for:

- establishing an ISMS;
- implementation;
- maintaining and continually improving an organisation's ISMS;
- assessment and treatment of a range of information security risks.

The 27001 standard is supported by ISO/IEC 27002, a code of practice for information security management.

---

8  23,439 at time of publication. https://www.iso.org/about-us.html.

9  https://www.iso.org/about-us.html.

Why would an organisation want to attain an ISO/IEC 27001 accredited certification? Many consider the rigorous process offers significant benefits in terms of:

- demonstrating that your organisation adheres to information security best practice;
- providing verification that information security is managed in line with independent, industry-recognised best practice.

### Information Assurance for Small and Medium Enterprises (IASME) governance standard

The IASME governance standard is a cyber security standard for small and medium businesses. The standard is based on ISO 27001, but is tailored for small and medium businesses.[10]

IASME is a certification body for Cyber Essentials. If an organisation uses an IASME body, the IASME standard is provided alongside Cyber Essentials certification. As with Cyber Essentials, IASME provides a self-assessment version and a higher standard, which requires an on-site verification. It also offers its own set of badges.

### CISQ

CISQ is the Consortium for IT Software Quality.[11] The group produces international standards for evaluating software, in terms of both the size and the structural quality of the code. It also provides specifications for automated measures.

A key element of evaluation involves assessing cyber resilience. CISQ defines this as the ability to architect and build software that can withstand malicious attacks and continue to operate in unexpected circumstances.

The group stresses that cyber-resilient systems are less likely to suffer unauthorised penetrations, outages, data corruption, slow recovery times and other operational problems. CISQ claims that cyber-resilient coding practices are critical for the safe, confidential and sustained operation of software systems.

These CISQ standards are used in assessing the cyber resilience of existing systems, and are also included in contracts as a means of specifying the cyber resilience of delivered source code. It is a common standard used in financial services outsourcing contracts.

> **KNOW YOUR CODE**
>
> **Source code** is the version of a computer program as it is originally written by a human in a programming language.
>
> **Object code** is the output of a compiler after it processes source code. It is usually machine code or machine language that can be recognised by a type of computer.

---

[10] https://www.iasme.co.uk/the-iasme-standard/.

[11] http://it-cisq.org/standards/.

> **Compiler** is the program that converts source code into object code. It reads the source code and translates it into computer language.
>
> **Executable code** is code that can be run on a computer.

## *PCI DSS*

'PCI DSS' stands for Payment Card Industry Data Security Standard. It is a set of guidelines that regulate card transactions to protect customer data. The guidelines ensure that all card payments are accepted, processed, stored and transmitted securely.

Any business that processes card payments needs to be fully compliant with the PCI framework.

PCI DSSs regulate both the use of software and hardware and certain aspects of personal behaviour in relation to payment cards. Firewalls and up-to-date antivirus software must be in place to protect data stored on computers. Any customer data that are shared across open networks must be encrypted.

There are 12 security standards that businesses accepting card payments must adhere to. These fall under six categories:

- Build and maintain a secure network.
- Protect cardholder data.
- Maintain a vulnerability management programme.
- Implement strong access control measures.
- Regularly monitor and test networks.
- Maintain an information security policy.

The latest version is PCI DSS 3.2.1[12] All of its requirements became effective in 2018.

## *Cloud standards*

A number of specific standards for cloud exist or are under development. These include:

- **Cloud Industry Forum (CIF)** – the CIF is an industry body that offers certification to its own code of practice. The code enables service providers to benchmark their operations against standards developed by their peers. The CIF claims this provides a checklist for best practice in the provision of cloud services.[13]
- **Institute of Electrical and Electronics Engineers (IEEE) Standards Association** – the IEEE Standards Association is a collaborative industry group that has been developing global cloud standards.[14]

---

12 https://www.pcisecuritystandards.org/document_library.

13 https://www.cloudindustryforum.org/content/code-practice-cloud-service-providers.

14 https://cloudcomputing.ieee.org/standards.

- **International Telecommunication Union (ITU)** – the ITU has released various reports and recommendations on cloud standards.[15]
- **Cloud Standards Customer Council (CSCC)** – the Cloud Standards Customer Council is an end-user advocacy group that has issued various white papers on cloud standards covering numerous topics, one of which is security for cloud computing.[16]

## SUMMARY

Here is a cyber security checklist for you:

### A. Identify and assess the internal and external threats to your organisation

- Assess which aspects of your business might be at risk:
  - infrastructure;
  - software;
  - hardware and devices;
  - databases;
  - documents;
  - other information.
- Identify areas of weakness.
- Assess the value of risk areas.
- Determine the measures you have in place to deal with cyber risks.
- Assess what other resources, systems and procedures you will need.
- Conduct a Data Protection Impact Assessment.

### B. Prepare for your cyber security plan

- Identify key individuals you need to involve within your organisation:
  - IT team;
  - HR team;
  - legal team;
  - management team/board;
  - employees.

---

[15] https://www.itu.int/en/Pages/default.aspx.

[16] https://www.omg.org/hot-topics/cybersecurity-initiatives.htm.

- Identify key individuals you need to involve from outside your organisation:
  - regulators;
  - insurers;
  - professional bodies;
  - suppliers and customers.
- Fact find:
  - Speak to all relevant individuals.
  - Research potential measures to protect your assets.
  - Find out what budgets are available.
  - Assess vulnerabilities of current protection.
- Test for vulnerabilities:
  - Run vulnerability assessments.
  - Run penetration tests.

## C. Draw up your cyber security plan

- Consider the 20 key questions to ask when formulating your cyber security plan (see 'What areas does my plan need to cover?' section).
- Draw up your list of priorities.
- Devise your procedures and policies.
- Set specific objectives.
- Set the timeframe.
- Schedule the programme for review, maintenance and upgrades.
- Assign responsibilities.
- Consider viability of available guides, frameworks and standards:
  - Cyber Essentials?
  - NIST framework?
  - security/cloud standards?

## D. Implement technological and practical solutions for all areas

- backups;
- passwords;
- cloud;
- social media;
- email;

- mobile device management;
- home working and BYOD.

## E. Implement strategic, technical and operational solutions

- governance;
- staff policies and technical capability;
- crisis management/communications/disaster recovery;
- training and awareness;
- insurance;
- software and configuration.

## F. Back up and strengthen your plan

- Back up the plan with training and regular reviews.
- Consider/research new threats.
- Adapt for changes in your organisation's infrastructure, information and personnel.
- Review constantly and at regular stages.
- At end of plan, go back and review/repeat earlier stages.
- Refine and reformulate the plan.

## REFERENCES

BBC (2010) 'Burma hit by massive net attach ahead of election'. *BBC News*. www.bbc.co.uk/news/technology-11693214.

Cabinet Office (2011) *Security Strategy: Protecting and promoting the UK in a digital world*. https://assets.publishing.service.gov.uk/government/uploads/system/uploads/attachment_data/file/60961/uk-cyber-security-strategy-final.pdf.

CGI (2017) *White Paper: The cyber value-connection*. CGI. https://www.cgi-group.co.uk/en-gb/white-paper/cyber-value-connection.

DDCMS (2020) *Cyber Security Breaches Survey*. Department for Digital, Culture, Media & Sport. https://www.gov.uk/government/publications/cyber-security-breaches-survey-2020/cyber-security-breaches-survey-2020.

DeNisco Rayome, A. (2018) 'Tesla public cloud environment hacked, attackers accessed "non-public" company data'. TechRepublic. https://www.techrepublic.com/article/tesla-public-cloud-environment-hacked-attackers-accessed-non-public-company-data/.

Donnelly, L. (2017) 'Security breach fears over 26 million NHS patients'. *The Telegraph*. https://www.telegraph.co.uk/news/2017/03/17/security-breach-fears-26-million-nhs-patients/.

Dragos (2017) *2017 Vulnerabilities: Meaningful metrics and insights into the ICS vulnerabilities of 2017*. Dragos. https://www.dragos.com/year-in-review/.

European Commission (2016) 'Press release: Commission signs agreement with industry on cybersecurity and steps up efforts to tackle cyber-threats'. Europa. http://europa.eu/rapid/press-release_IP-16-2321_en.htm.

European Commission (2017) *EU Cybersecurity Initiatives*. Europa. https://ec.europa.eu/information_society/newsroom/image/document/2017-3/factsheet_cybersecurity_update_january_2017_41543.pdf.

European Commission (2020) 'Cybersecurity'. Europa. https://ec.europa.eu/digital-single-market/en/cyber-security.

European Union (2016) *Regulation (EU) 2016/679 of the European Parliament and of the Council of 27 April 2016: On the Protection of Natural Persons With Regard to the Processing of Personal Data and on the Free Movement of Such Data, And Repealing Directive 95/46/EC (General Data Protection Regulation)*. European Parliament and Council of the European Union. http://eur-lex.europa.eu/legal-content/EN/TXT/PDF/?uri=CELEX:32016R0679&from=EN.

GOV.UK (2017) 'Vulnerability and penetration testing'. GOV. UK, Crown copyright. https://www.gov.uk/service-manual/technology/vulnerability-and-penetration-testing.

GOV.UK (2018) 'Press release: Government acts to protect essential services from cyber attack'. GOV. UK, Crown copyright. https://www.gov.uk/government/news/government-acts-to-protect-essential-services-from-cyber-attack.

ICO (n.d.) 'Identity theft'. Information Commissioners Office. https://ico.org.uk/for-the-public/identity-theft/.

IT Pro Team (2018) 'What is hactivism? From Anonymous to Omega, here's everything you need to know about hackers with a conscience'. ITPro, In-Depth. https://www.itpro.co.uk/hacking/30203/what-is-hacktivism.

Lord, N. (2017) 'A timeline of the Ashley Madison hack'. Digital Guardian's Blog. https://digitalguardian.com/blog/timeline-ashley-madison-hack.

Markoff, J. (2009) 'Vast spy system loots computers in 103 countries'. *The New York Times*. https://www.nytimes.com/2009/03/29/technology/29spy.html.

McCallion, J. (2020) 'What is cyber warfare?'. IT Pro, In-Depth. www.itpro.co.uk/security/28170/what-is-cyber-warfare.

National Cyber Security Centre (2018) *Cyber Security Small Business Guide*. National Cyber Security Centre. https://www.ncsc.gov.uk/collection/small-business-guide.

NetMarketShare (2018) *Operating System Market Share*. Market Share Statistics for Internet Technologies, April. https://netmarketshare.com.

Ponemon Institute (2018) *2018 Study on Global Megatrends in Cybersecurity*. Raytheon Technologies. https://www.raytheon.com/cyber/cyber_megatrends.

Symantec Security Response Team (2017) 'What you need to know about the WannaCry Ransomware'. Broadcom, Symantec Enterprise Blogs. https://symantec-enterprise-blogs.security.com/blogs/threat-intelligence/wannacry-ransomware-attack.

Tech Advisor (2019) 'The biggest data breaches: the most notorious data breaches around the world, from BA to the Bundestag'. Tech Advisor from IDG, Small Business. https://www.techworld.com/security/uks-most-infamous-data-breaches-3604586/.

# 6 GDPR AND DATA PROTECTION: THE LAW

Victoria Hordern

## INTRODUCTION

Data protection law has been around in the UK since 1984. However, the requirements around data protection have been given greater prominence due to the advent of the EU General Data Protection Regulation 2016/679 ('GDPR') and the Data Protection Act 2018.

The GDPR is based on its previous incarnation – the Data Protection Directive 1995/46/EC ('the Directive') – but is more prescriptive and comprehensive. The GDPR has applied across the EU (and in the UK as a member of the EU) since 25 May 2018.

Data protection law is a complicated area and this chapter will not cover all aspects of data protection law (see also Chapter 7). However, this chapter aims to give you an overview of the framework of data protection law. It is primarily focused on the GDPR, but you should be aware of other law regulating electronic communications set out in the Privacy and Electronic Communications (EC Directive) Regulations 2003. These regulations implement the E-Privacy Directive 2002/58/EC, which is itself due to be replaced by an E-Privacy Regulation that, at the time of writing, is still being debated within the EU.

Organisations that decide to collect and process personal data for their own purposes are known as controllers. A controller may engage a service provider or processor to process personal data on behalf of the controller. A processor is an individual or legal person or other body that processes personal data on behalf of the controller (but is not an employee of the controller). Both controllers and processors are subject to obligations under the GDPR, although the processor's obligations are more limited.

## WHAT DATA ARE COVERED?

The GDPR regulates the processing of personal data. Anonymous data are not personal data and fall outside the scope of the GDPR. Therefore, it's vital that we understand what personal data means. The GDPR states that:

> 'personal data' means any information relating to an identified or identifiable natural person ('data subject'); an identifiable natural person is one who can be identified, directly or indirectly, in particular by reference to an identifier such as a name, an identification number, location data, an online identifier or to one or more factors specific to the physical, physiological, genetic, mental, economic, cultural or social identity of that natural person.

Over the years there has been much debate about the parameters of personal data – where do personal data end and anonymous data begin? The definition under the previous data protection legislation added to the uncertainty, as did particular decisions by UK courts (see *Durant v. Financial Services Authority* (2003) EWCA Civ 1746).[1] The definition provided under the GDPR is broader than the definition set out in previous data protection legislation. In particular, the GDPR expects organisations to consider the means reasonably likely to be used to identify an individual directly or indirectly taking into account all objective factors such as the cost and amount of time required for identification, available technology and technological developments.

The GDPR makes clear that pseudonymous data are a subset of personal data. Additionally, online identifiers such as Internet Protocol (IP) addresses, cookies or radio-frequency identifications (RFIDs) can also be personal data.

While some data are clearly personal data – a person's name, an email address or twitter handle – other data are not necessarily so (e.g. info@bbc.co.uk). Information about George V, for example, is not personal data because he is dead. Data protection law only protects the information of living individuals. By the same token, data protection law does not regulate information about legal entities or businesses (e.g. companies) except for where an individual is inextricably linked to the activities of that business (such as a sole trader or certain partnerships).

The GDPR refers to information that relates to an identified or identifiable individual. An identifiable individual can be someone whose name is unknown but who is tracked online through an identifier – such as an IP or media access control (MAC) address – so that an organisation builds a profile of the device to which the IP address or MAC address is assigned. If a device is used by multiple people, then it is harder to argue that the identifier is personal data. However, if a device is only used by a single person, it is more likely the identifier will be personal data.

Images of individuals can also be personal data. This means that closed-circuit television (CCTV) or cameras recording images of individuals are regulated by the GDPR.

The GDPR primarily impacts the processing of personal data by automated means, given how widely technology is now used, but the GDPR also regulates all manual processing of personal data contained in a structured filing system.

## SPECIAL CATEGORIES OF PERSONAL DATA

The GDPR identifies a subset of personal data known as special categories of personal data. These data are subject to a stricter regime. Special categories of data consist of personal data that reveal:

- racial or ethnic origin;
- political opinions;

---

[1] https://www.bailii.org/ew/cases/EWCA/Civ/2003/1746.html.

- religious or philosophical beliefs;
- trade union membership.

As well as:

- genetic data;
- biometric data for the purpose of uniquely identifying a natural person;
- data concerning health;
- data concerning a natural person's sex life or sexual orientation.

In general, the controller has to take particular care when dealing with special categories of data. The controller has to rely on two lawful grounds (or, strictly speaking, one lawful ground and one exception from a prohibition) when processing special categories of personal data rather than one lawful ground when processing non-special categories of personal data.

## DATA PROTECTION PRINCIPLES

The GDPR sets out six (or seven if you count accountability) principles relating to the processing of personal data. These are:

1. lawfulness, fairness and transparency;
2. purpose limitation;
3. data minimisation;
4. accuracy;
5. storage limitation;
6. integrity and confidentiality;
7. accountability.

### Lawfulness, fairness and transparency

This principle is arguably the most important of the principles. It concerns three related aspects: (1) ensuring that the processing of personal data relies on a lawful basis/bases, (2) ensuring that the processing is fair and in line with the individual's reasonable expectations, and (3) ensuring that a privacy notice is provided. All three aspects must be satisfied in order for the first principle to be met.

#### *Lawful basis*
Any and all processing of personal data must be able to rely on at least one of the bases set out under Article 6. These are:

- The individual has given consent to the processing of their personal data for one or more specific purpose(s).

- Processing is necessary for performance of a contract to which the individual is party or in order to take steps at the request of the individual prior to entering into a contract.
- Processing is necessary for compliance with a legal obligation to which the controller is subject.
- Processing is necessary in order to protect the vital interests of the individual or other natural persons.
- Processing is necessary for the performance of a task carried out in the public interest or in the exercise of official authority vested in the controller.
- Processing is necessary for the purposes of the legitimate interests pursued by the controller or by a third party, except where such interests are overridden by the interests or fundamental rights and freedoms of the individual that require protection of personal data, in particular where the individual is a child.

There are other aspects to consider in order to rely on one of these bases. So, for example, Article 6 makes clear that for compliance with a legal obligation and the performance of a task carried out in the public interest, the basis for the processing must be laid down in EU or the Member State law to which the controller is subject. In other words, you cannot rely on a legal obligation under a foreign law.

If a controller is processing a special category of data, it must not only meet a basis under Article 6 but also rely on an exception under Article 9. Article 9 states that the processing of special categories of data is prohibited unless a controller can rely on an exception. The exceptions are:

- The individual has given explicit consent to the processing of personal data for one or more specific purposes except where EU or Member State law provides that the prohibition cannot be lifted by the individual.
- Processing is necessary for the obligations and exercising specific rights of the controller or of the individual in the field of employment, social security and social protection law in so far as it is authorised by EU or Member State law or a collective agreement pursuant to Member State law providing for appropriate safeguards for the fundamental rights and interests of the individual.
- Processing is necessary to protect the vital interests of the individual or another natural person where the individual is physically or legally incapable of giving consent.
- Processing is carried out in the course of its legitimate activities with appropriate safeguards by a foundation, association or any other not-for-profit body with a political, philosophical, religious or trade union aim and on condition that the processing relates solely to the members or former members of the body or to persons who have regular contact with it in connection with its purposes and the personal data are not disclosed outside that body without the consent of individuals.
- Processing relates to personal data that are manifestly made public by the individual.

- Processing is necessary for the establishment, exercise or defence of legal claims or whenever courts are acting in their judicial capacity.
- Processing is necessary for reasons of substantial public interest on the basis of EU or Member State law that shall be proportionate to the aim pursued, respect the essence of the right to data protection and provide for suitable and specific measures to safeguard the fundamental rights and interests of the individual.
- Processing is necessary for the purposes of preventive or occupational medicine, for the assessment of the working capacity of the employee, medical diagnosis, the provision of health or social care or treatment or the management of health or social care systems and services on the basis of EU or Member State law or pursuant to a contract with a health professional and subject to additional conditions and safeguards around confidentiality.
- Processing is necessary for reasons of public interest in the area of public health, such as protecting against serious cross-border threats to health or ensuring high standards of quality and safety of healthcare and of medicinal products or medical devices, on the basis of EU or Member State law that provides for suitable and specific measures to safeguard the rights and freedoms of the individual, in particular professional secrecy.
- Processing is necessary for archiving purposes in the public interest, scientific or historical research purposes or statistical purposes in accordance with Article 89(1) based on EU or Member State law that shall be proportionate to the aim pursued, respect the essence of the right to data protection and provide for suitable and specific measures to safeguard the fundamental rights and interests of the individual.

## IS CONSENT THE ANSWER?

While many could think that consent should always be the first choice basis to rely on, and is a preferred basis, there are certain weaknesses with relying on consent.

Under the GDPR, demonstrating that consent is valid requires a high standard. Consent of the individual is defined as any freely given, specific, informed and unambiguous indication of the individual's wishes by which they, by a statement or by a clear affirmative action, signify agreement to the processing of personal data about them.

In order to rely on consent, a controller must be able to prove all these respective elements and additionally allow an individual to withdraw consent at any time (since if an individual can't withdraw their consent, the original consent was not freely given). If an individual withdraws their consent, strictly speaking the controller no longer has a lawful basis to process their personal data.

The Article 29 Working Party (now known under the GDPR as the European Data Protection Board) has produced guidance on consent indicating that 'consent can only be an appropriate lawful basis if a data subject is offered control and is offered a genuine choice with regard to accepting or declining the terms offered or declining them without detriment' (WP 259).

It is important to note that there may be other reasons why a controller **must** rely on consent regardless of the options under the GDPR. For instance, because another legal requirement, such as the forthcoming E-Privacy Regulation, stipulates that consent is the only legal basis available in certain circumstances.

### *Fairness*

Once lawful basis or bases have been identified, a controller must be able to demonstrate that the processing is fair to the individual(s) concerned. Fairness is directly linked to transparency. If the controller clearly sets out in a privacy notice how personal data will be used, this helps to set the expectations of an individual and demonstrate fairness. But fairness is a broader concept than this – unfairness can also arise if a controller expects an individual to be responsible for continuing to review any changes in a privacy notice without any obligation on the controller to notify the individual directly of the changes. The requirement for fairness can also require a controller to provide a greater degree of transparency in the privacy notice where the processing is considered to be intrusive.

### *Privacy notice*

Privacy notices must be provided to individuals when personal data are directly collected from individuals. The GDPR sets out in Article 13 the specific information that must be provided to the individual. This builds on the requirements under the Directive but are much more specific. They are:

- the identity and contact details of the controller and, where applicable, the controller's representative;
- the contact details of the data protection officer, where applicable;
- the purposes of the processing as well as the legal basis for the processing;
- where the processing is based on legitimate interests, the specific interest must be identified;
- the recipients or categories of recipients of the personal data; and
- where applicable, the fact that the controller intends to transfer personal data to a third country or international organisation and the existence or absence of an adequacy decision by the European Commission, or in the case of transfers under appropriate safeguards or Binding Corporate Rules, or for one-off exceptional transfers permitted under Article 49 (second paragraph), reference to the appropriate or suitable safeguards and the means by which to obtain a copy of them.

Additionally, the controller should provide the following information as is necessary to ensure fair and transparent processing:

- The period for which the personal data will be stored, or if that is not possible, the criteria used to determine the period.

- The existence of the right to request from the controller access to and rectification or erasure of personal data or restriction of processing concerning the individual or to object to the processing as well as the right to data portability.
- Where the processing is based on consent or explicit consent, the existence of the right to withdraw consent at any time, without affecting the lawfulness of processing based on consent before its withdrawal.
- The right to lodge a complaint with a data protection authority.
- Whether the provision of personal data is a statutory or contractual requirement, or a requirement necessary to enter into a contract, as well as whether the individual is obliged to provide the personal data and the possible consequences of failure to provide such data.
- The existence of automated decision-making, including profiling, referred to in Article 22(1) and (4) and, at least in those cases, meaningful information about the logic involved, as well as the significance and the envisaged consequences of such processing for the individual.

Where the personal data are not obtained directly from individuals, a controller is required to provide individuals with broadly the same information plus:

- the categories of personal data concerned; and
- from which source the personal data originate.

A privacy notice must be provided to these individuals, although there are certain exceptions where no notice must be provided. These are:

- where the individual already has the information;
- where the provision of the information proves impossible or would involve disproportionate effort;
- where obtaining or disclosing the personal data is expressly laid down in EU or Member State law to which the controller is subject and which provides appropriate measures to protect the individual's legitimate interests; or
- where the personal data must remain confidential subject to an obligation of professional secrecy regulated by EU or Member State law, including a statutory obligation of secrecy.

**Purpose limitation**

As under the Directive, personal data must be collected for specified, explicit and legitimate purposes and not further processed in a manner that is incompatible with those purposes.

This means that a controller should have identified the purpose for the collection of personal data before collecting the data. This principle is to ensure that a controller cannot decide later to use the personal data collected for a completely different purpose that the individual would not have been aware of.

However, the principle does allow for a test of compatibility for any further processing. Unless the processing is based on consent or on EU or Member State law, a controller is required to ascertain whether processing for another purpose is compatible with the original purpose for which the personal data were collected by taking into account:

- any link between the purposes for which the personal data have been collected and the purposes of the intended further processing;
- the context in which the personal data have been collected, in particular regarding the relationship between individuals and controllers;
- the nature of the personal data;
- the possible consequences of the intended further processing for individuals; and
- the existence of appropriate safeguards, which may include encryption or pseudonymisation.

The GDPR gives special status to further processing for archiving purposes in the public interest, scientific or historical research purposes or statistical purposes, which, if processed in accordance with Article 89 of the GDPR, are not considered incompatible.

## Data minimisation

The data minimisation principle is designed to ensure that controllers only collect and process the minimal amount of personal data that are necessary for their purposes. The personal data must be adequate, relevant and limited to what is necessary.

Consequently, controllers should review and securely delete any extraneous personal data that are collected that they cannot justify as necessary for the purposes identified.

## Accuracy

Controllers should ensure that the personal data they collect and use are accurate and, where necessary, kept up to date. Controllers are required to take every reasonable step to ensure that any personal data that are inaccurate is erased or rectified without delay.

## Storage limitation

Personal data should be kept in a form that permits identification of individuals for no longer than is necessary for the purposes for which personal data are processed. To comply with this principle, controllers should deploy anonymisation measures to ensure identification of individuals is not possible or securely delete personal data once the retention period has expired or arrange regular review and deletion of personal data that are no longer required. A controller should implement a Data Retention Policy and Schedule setting out the relevant retention periods for the types of personal data that it processes.

Again, there is recognised special status for personal data processed solely for archiving purposes in the public interest, scientific or historical research purposes or statistical purposes in accordance with Article 89(1), which may be stored for longer periods so long as there are appropriate technical and organisational measures in order to safeguard the rights and freedoms of individuals.

## Integrity and confidentiality

This principle is concerned with data security and the requirement to ensure appropriate security of personal data, including protection against unauthorised or unlawful processing and against accidental loss, destruction or damage, using appropriate technical or organisational measures.

As under the Directive, the GDPR doesn't specify precise security measures that must be taken but requires organisations to determine what is appropriate depending on the circumstances. So, broadly speaking, special categories of data warrant more stringent security measures than non-special categories of data.

## Accountability

The accountability principle is new under the GDPR. Essentially it requires controllers to put in place appropriate and effective measures to ensure that the principles and obligations set out in the GDPR are complied with and to demonstrate as such to data protection authorities upon request.

Compliance with the accountability principle therefore requires a controller to introduce policies and procedures that demonstrate how it complies with the other data protection principles. This should be complemented by a data protection governance framework expressed in staff training, audits to check that policies are complied with and a line of responsibility within the controller, that is, someone who is responsible for ensuring that policies are adhered to and updated where necessary.

However, there is recognition that compliance with this principle is scalable. A controller can tailor the measures required to demonstrate accountability according to its particular processing operations whether high risk or not.

## RIGHTS OF INDIVIDUALS

The GDPR deliberately strengthens the rights that individuals have to control how their personal data are used. The rights are:

- right of access;
- right to rectification;
- right to erasure;
- right to restriction of processing;
- right to data portability;
- right to object;
- right not to be subject to a decision based solely on automated processing, including profiling, which produces legal effects concerning the individual or similarly significantly affects the individual.

A number of these rights existed in the Data Protection Act 1998. For instance, the right of access to personal data and the right to object. However, the GDPR refashions these rights to give greater control to the individuals.

As an example, under the previous data protection legislation, an individual had a right to object to a controller using their personal data if the individual could demonstrate that the use of their personal data was causing or was likely to cause them or another person unwarranted substantial damage and distress. So, the burden was on the individual to prove why the use of their personal data should cease.

In contrast, under the GDPR, an individual has the right to object at any time to the use of their personal data (where the lawful ground the controller is relying on is legitimate interest or performance of a task carried out in the public interest) and now the controller must comply with that objection unless it can demonstrate compelling legitimate grounds to continue processing the personal data that override the interests, rights and freedoms of the individual or to establish, exercise or defend legal claims. In other words, the burden of proof has shifted from the shoulders of the individual to the controller.

This illustrates one of the main objectives behind the reform of the EU data protection framework: to give individuals more control over how their personal data are used.

We'll look at each right in turn.

## Right of access

This is probably the right that most people have heard of and is most commonly used. In the UK, we usually refer to it as a subject access right.

An individual has a right to obtain (from the controller) confirmation of whether the controller is processing their personal data. Where the controller is processing their personal data, the individual has a right to obtain access to their personal data and to information about the:

- purpose of the processing;
- categories of personal data concerned;
- recipients or categories of recipients to whom the personal data have been or will be disclosed;
- where possible, the envisaged period for which the personal data will be stored or the criteria to determine the period;
- existence of the right to request from the controller rectification or erasure of the personal data or restriction of processing or to object to such processing;
- right to lodge a complaint with a data protection authority;
- source of the data (where information is available about the source) where the personal data were not collected from the individual directly; and

- the existence of any automated decision-making that produces a legal effect or similarly significantly affects an individual and meaningful information about the logic involved, as well as the significance and envisaged consequences of such processing for the individual.

The controller must provide a copy of the personal data free of charge. Further copies may be subject to a reasonable administration fee.

If a request is manifestly unfounded or excessive (e.g. repetitive), a controller may either charge a reasonable fee taking into account the administrative costs of providing the information, or may refuse to act on the request. The controller is responsible for demonstrating that a request is manifestly unfounded or excessive.

A controller may still seek additional information where necessary to verify the identity of the individual making the request. A controller is required to respond to a request for access without undue delay and within one month of receipt of the request. This response time may be extended by a further two months where necessary due to the complexity and number of requests. If a controller decides not to take action on the individual's request, it must inform the individual, without delay and within one month of receipt of the request, of the reasons for not taking action and on the possibility of lodging a complaint with a data protection authority and seeking a judicial remedy.

If the individual makes the request electronically, the information should be provided to the individual electronically unless they request otherwise.

The GDPR states that a right to obtain a copy of personal data must not adversely affect the rights and freedoms of others, which indicates that there are circumstances where third-party personal data restricts what personal data can be disclosed in response to an access request.

**Right of rectification**

An individual has the right to ask a controller to rectify inaccurate personal data about them without undue delay. An individual also has a right to have incomplete personal data completed, including through providing a supplementary statement. A controller is bound by the same timing obligations to respond to the individual as for a right of access (see above).

The right to rectification existed under previous data protection legislation but an individual was required to go to court to enforce a right to rectification against a controller whereas now under the GDPR a controller is required to comply with a right to rectification.

**Right to erasure**

Much has been written about the right to erasure (also known as the right to be forgotten) since the European Court of Justice ruled in 2014 that Google was required to remove from the list of search results displayed (following use of Google's search engine to search for a person's name) any links to web pages published by third parties relating to that person. This was required even if the publication of the person's name by those third parties was lawful. The court made clear that this ruling involved a balance between the economic interests of the search engine, the interests of internet users in having access to information and the interests and fundamental rights to privacy of the individual affected.

The GDPR seeks to reflect this balance, since the right to erasure is not automatic. An individual has a right to obtain erasure of their personal data without undue delay where one of the following grounds applies:

- The personal data are no longer necessary for the purpose for which they were collected or used.
- The individual withdraws consent (when consent was the lawful ground relied upon) and no other lawful ground is available.
- The individual objects to the processing (where legitimate interests or performance of a task in the public interest was the lawful ground) and there are no overriding legitimate grounds for processing the personal data.
- The personal data have been unlawfully processed.
- The personal data have to be erased for compliance with a legal obligation in EU or Member State law to which the controller is subject.
- The personal data have been collected in relation to the offer of information society services offered directly to a child and consent is the lawful ground.

It is only if one of the above grounds applies that an individual can seek a right to erasure.

However, the right to erasure does not apply if the processing of the personal data are necessary for:

- exercising the right of freedom of expression and information;
- compliance with a legal obligation, which requires processing by EU or Member State law to which the controller is subject or for the performance of a task carried out in the public interest or in the exercise of official authority vested in the controller;
- for reasons of public interest in the area of public health;
- for archiving purposes in the public interest, scientific or historical research purposes or statistical purposes in so far as the right to erasure is likely to render impossible or seriously impair the achievement of the objectives of that processing; or
- for the establishment, exercise or defence of legal claims.

However, if the right to erasure does apply and the controller must erase the data, then the controller is required to take further steps if it has made the personal data public. In such circumstances, the controller must take reasonable steps, including technical measures, to inform controllers processing the personal data that the individual has requested erasure.

A controller is bound by the same timing obligations to respond to the individual as for a right of access (see above).

For completeness, it is worth noting that the right to erasure existed under previous data protection legislation but in a form that was harder for individuals to exercise, given that it was only enforceable by the courts.

## Right to restriction of processing

The GDPR refers to a right for the individual to obtain from the controller restriction of processing in one of the following situations:

- Where the accuracy of the personal data is contested by the individual, the personal data are subject to restricted processing for a period to enable the controller to verify the accuracy of the personal data.
- Where the processing is unlawful and the individual opposes the erasure of the personal data and requests restriction of use instead.
- Where the controller no longer needs the personal data for its purposes but the data are required by the individual for the establishment, exercise or defence of legal claims.
- Where the individual has objected to the processing pending verification of whether the legitimate grounds of the controller override the grounds of the individual.

Where the processing of personal data has been restricted, the personal data can only be processed for storage purposes, on the consent of the individual for the establishment, exercise or defence of legal claims, for the protection of the rights of another individual or legal person or for reasons of important public interest of the EU or a Member State.

A controller must also inform the individual if it intends to lift the restriction of processing.

## Right to data portability

This is a new right under the GDPR. An individual has a right to receive from the controller the personal data that they provided to the controller in a structured, commonly used and machine-readable format and has the right to transmit these data to another controller without hindrance.

But this right only applies where:

- the lawful ground upon which the controller is processing those personal data is either consent or necessary for performance of a contract; and
- the processing is carried out by automated means.

An individual has the right to have their personal data transmitted directly from one controller to another where technically feasible, but this right must not adversely affect the rights and freedoms of others.

## Right to object

An individual can only exercise the right to object if the lawful basis for the processing of their personal data is either:

- the legitimate interest ground; or
- performance of a task carried out in the public interest or in the exercise of official authority vested in the controller.

The controller must comply with a right to object unless the controller demonstrates compelling legitimate grounds for the processing of the personal data that overrides the interests, rights and freedoms of the individual or for the establishment, exercise or defence of legal claims.

An individual also has the right to object to or opt-out from their personal data being used for direct marketing purposes including profiling. In such circumstances, a controller must comply with the individual's rights.

In the context of information society services, an individual may exercise their right to object by automated means using technical specifications.

Where personal data are processed for scientific or historical research purposes or statistical purposes, the individual has the right to object to such processing of their personal data unless the processing is necessary for the performance of a task carried out for reasons of public interest.

## Right not to be subject to a decision based solely on automated processing, including profiling, which produces legal effects concerning the individual or similarly significantly affects the individual

The forerunner of this right existed in the previous data protection legislation but the right in the GDPR is stricter, more complex and has been interpreted by the Article 29 Working Party as a prohibition.

Therefore, in effect and accounting for the Working Party's position, a controller cannot process personal data in a way that an individual is subject to a decision based solely on automated processing where that decision produces legal effects or similarly significantly affects the individual. To fall within this restriction the processing must be:

- wholly automated processing (i.e. no human intervention);
- that produces a decision; and
- which has a legal effect or similarly significantly affects the individual.

There are exceptions so that this restriction does not apply if the decision:

- is necessary for entering into, or performance of, a contract between the individual and a controller;

- is authorised by EU or Member State law to which the controller is subject and which also lays down suitable measures to safeguard the individual's rights, freedoms and legitimate interests; or
- the explicit consent of the individual is obtained.

For reliance on entering into a contract and explicit consent, the controller must implement suitable measures to safeguard the individual's rights and legitimate interests as well as provide the individual with the right to obtain human intervention on the part of the controller and for the individual to express their point of view and to contest the decision.

The ability to process special category data in this context is especially complicated. The only way that a controller can rely on an exception from the restriction, when processing special category data, is where it has explicit consent from the individual or it can argue that the processing is necessary for reasons of substantial public interest and suitable measures are implemented to safeguard the individual's rights, freedom and legitimate interests.

## EXEMPTIONS

The GDPR includes provisions relating to specific processing situations where Member States may set out further rules on how personal data may be processed:

- freedom of expression and information;
- public access to official documentation;
- processing of the national identification number;
- processing in the context of employment;
- processing for archiving purposes in the public interest, scientific or historical research purposes or statistical purposes.

Additionally, EU or Member State law may restrict the scope of certain obligations and rights when such a restriction respects the essence of fundamental rights and freedoms and is a necessary and proportionate measure in a democratic society to safeguard:

- national security;
- defence;
- public security;
- prevention, investigation, detection or prosecution of criminal offences or the execution of criminal penalties, including the safeguarding against and the prevention of threats to public security ('preventing crime');
- other important objectives of general public interest of the EU or a Member State, in particular an important economic or financial interest of the EU or Member State, including monetary, budgetary and taxation matters, public health and social security ('public interest');

- protection of judicial independence and judicial proceedings;
- prevention, investigation, detection and prosecution of breaches of ethics for regulated professions ('ethics');
- a monitoring, inspection or regulatory function connected, even occasionally, to the exercise of official authority in the cases of national security, defence, public security, preventing crime, public interest and ethics;
- protection of the individual or the rights and freedoms of others; and
- enforcement of civil law claims.

## REMEDIES, ENFORCEMENT POWERS AND PENALTIES

The GDPR is concerned with civil remedies, enforcement and penalties. Member States may additionally make it a criminal offence for a person to misuse personal data in some way. For instance, UK law includes a criminal offence of the unlawful obtaining or disclosure of personal data.

### Remedies

One criticism of the previous data protection legislation was that it was very difficult for individuals to be able to enforce their rights and seek a remedy when a controller contravened the law. The GDPR sets out the following specific remedies.

#### Right to lodge a complaint with a data protection authority
Every individual has a right to lodge a complaint with a data protection authority, in the Member State where they live or where their place of work is or the place of the alleged infringement, if the individual considers that the processing of personal data infringes the GDPR.

#### Right to an effective judicial remedy against a data protection authority
Every natural or legal person (so this includes individuals and companies) has a right to an effective judicial remedy against a legally binding decision of a data protection authority that concerns them. This essentially gives parties to a decision a right to appeal the decision given by a data protection authority.

Every individual also has a right to an effective judicial remedy where the data protection authority does not handle their complaint or does not inform the individual within three months of the progress or outcome of any complaint the individual has lodged.

#### Right to an effective judicial remedy against a controller or processor
Each individual has a right to an effective judicial remedy where they consider their rights under the GDPR have been infringed as a result of the processing of their personal data in non-compliance with the GDPR. The individual can bring proceedings against a controller or a processor.

#### Right to compensation
Any person who has suffered material or non-material damage as a result of an infringement of the GDPR has a right to receive compensation from a controller or processor for the damage suffered.

A controller is liable for the damage caused by processing that infringes the GDPR and a processor is liable for damage only where it has not complied with obligations under the GDPR specifically directed at processors or where it has acted outside or contrary to lawful instructions of the controller. A controller or processor is exempt from liability if it can prove that it is not in any way responsible for the event giving rise to the damage.

If a controller or processor has paid full compensation for the damage suffered, that controller or processor is entitled to claim back from the other controllers or processors involved in the processing that part of the compensation corresponding to their part of responsibility for the damage.

## Enforcement powers of data protection authorities

Data protection authorities like the Information Commissioner's Office (ICO) in the UK receive increased powers under the GDPR. Additionally, the Data Protection Act 2018 sets out specific rules about enforcement in certain situations (e.g. issuing Information Notices). Furthermore, UK law is likely to require the ICO to publish guidance about how it proposes to exercise its enforcement and fining powers.

Data protection authorities have investigative and corrective as well as authorisation and advisory powers.

### *Investigative powers*
These are:

- To order the controller and processor and, if relevant, a representative to provide any information the data protection authority requires for the performance of its tasks.
- To carry out data protection audits.
- To carry out a review on certifications issued.
- To notify the controller or processor of an alleged GDPR infringement.
- To obtain access to all personal data and to all information necessary for the performance of its tasks.
- To obtain access to any premises of the controller and processor including to any data processing equipment and means.

### *Corrective powers*
These are:

- To issue warnings to a controller or processor that intended processing operations are likely to infringe the GDPR.
- To issue reprimands to a controller or processor when processing operations have infringed the GDPR.
- To order the controller or processor to comply with an individual's requests to exercise their rights under the GDPR.

- To order the controller or processor to bring processing operations into compliance with the GDPR.
- To order the controller to communicate a personal data breach to the individual.
- To impose a temporary or definitive limitation, including a ban on processing.
- To order the rectification or erasure of personal data or restriction of processing and to notify such actions to recipients to whom the personal data have been disclosed.
- To withdraw a certification or to order a certification body to withdraw a certification.
- To impose an administrative fine.
- To order the suspension of data flows to a recipient in a third country or to an international organisation.

### *Authorisation and advisory powers*

These are:

- To advise the controller in accordance with a prior consultation procedure where the controller consults with the data protection authority.
- To issue opinions to the national parliament, Member State government or other institutions or bodies as well as to the public on any issue related to the protection of personal data.
- To authorise processing that involves a high risk.
- To issue an opinion and approve draft codes of conduct.
- To accredit certification bodies.
- To issue certifications and approve criteria of certification.
- To adopt standard data protection clauses.
- To authorise contractual clauses.
- To authorise administrative arrangements.
- To approve binding corporate rules.

## Fines

One of the most significant changes to the EU data protection enforcement regime is the much higher fines that can be imposed for infringements of the GDPR. Most (but not all) of the fines that have been issued by the ICO under the previous data protection legislation have involved a breach of the principle to implement appropriate security measures to protect personal data.

It is important to note, however, that a data protection authority is required to ensure that when using its power to impose a fine for infringements of the GDPR, such imposition must be effective, proportionate and dissuasive. A fine can be imposed in addition to other measures or instead of such measures, but a data protection authority must, in imposing a fine, have due regard to certain factors such as the nature, gravity and duration of the infringement, the intentional or negligent character of the infringement and the degree of cooperation the controller or processor demonstrates with the data protection authority. In other words, the data protection authority has to be able to justify why imposing a fine and the specific level of the fine was appropriate in the circumstances.

The GDPR establishes that it is only the infringement of specific provisions in the GDPR that can lead to a fine. In addition, there are two tiers of fines so that certain infringements are subject to the lower tier whereas other infringements are subject to the higher tier.

The lower tier sets out that a fine of up to 10 million euros or up to 2 per cent of total worldwide annual turnover of the preceding financial year (whichever is higher) can be imposed upon an organisation due to infringements of the following provisions:

- obligations of the controller and processor under Articles 8, 11, 25 to 39, 42 and 43;
- obligations of the certification body under Articles 42 and 43;
- obligations of the monitoring body under Article 41 (4).

It is important to note that a processor can be subject to a fine if it infringes its obligations to comply with, for instance, implementing appropriate security measures to protect personal data. It is also significant that a controller can be fined for a failure to comply with the requirement to implement data protection by design and by default as well as a failure to carry out a Data Protection Impact Assessment or appoint a data protection officer (if it is required to).

Under the higher tier a data protection authority can impose a fine on an organisation of up to 20 million euros or up to 4 per cent of total worldwide annual turnover of the preceding financial year (whichever is higher) due to infringements of the following provisions:

- basic principles for processing, including conditions for consent, in Articles 5, 6, 7 and 9;
- data subjects' rights in Articles 12 to 22;
- transfers of personal data to a recipient in a third country or an international organisation under Articles 44 to 49;
- any obligations under Member State law adopted under Chapter IX;
- non-compliance with an order or limitation on processing by the data protection authority or failure to provide access to a data protection authority.

For the higher tier, most of the provisions listed involve obligations on controllers only. However, a processor has obligations concerning international data transfers in Articles 44 to 49 and could be subject to the higher tier of fining if it failed to comply with a requirement from the data protection authority.

GDPR AND DATA PROTECTION: THE LAW

## SUMMARY

There are thousands of items of personal data held, about every single reader of this book, by government bodies, by employers, by doctors, by banks and insurers, and by innumerable other organisations. That is not counting the thousands of other items that we knowingly share more widely, when we update our career status on LinkedIn or post family photographs on Facebook.

Businesses will be aware of the huge fines that regulatory authorities have started to impose (or have indicated that they intend to impose) on companies such as British Airways, Marriott Hotels and Google for failing to comply with data protection law in respect of the personal data that they process, and individual citizens are also entitled to claim compensation for data breach in some circumstances.

It is incumbent on all of us, both as data subjects and as people who make use of personal data about others, to ensure that we understand the main principles of data protection law, and that personal data are handled with suitable respect for the privacy of the individual.

# 7 DATA PROTECTION IN PRACTICE

Andrew Katz, Michaela MacDonald, Tim Astley, Usha Guness, Jiri Svorc and Chris McCormick

## INTRODUCTION

While the previous chapter (Chapter 6) looks at data protection legislation and its history, this chapter covers some of the most significant topics in greater depth, examining their practical impact and means of compliance. We suggest that you read Chapter 6 first.

This chapter covers:

- Data protection by design and default
- What amounts to 'processing personal data' under the GDPR?
- Creating a 'record of processing'
- Deciding upon the lawful basis of processing
- Drafting data protection policies
- Data Protection Impact Assessments (DPIAs)
- Requests from data subjects
- Children's personal data
- Controllers and processors
- Sub-processors
- Data protection officers (DPOs)
- International transfers
- Processing data of EU data subjects
- Breach notifications

## DATA PROTECTION BY DESIGN AND DEFAULT

One of the most radical changes to affect organisations as a consequence of the GDPR is the legal requirement that data protection must be 'baked' into an organisation's culture, systems and processes by design and default. To understand how the GDPR works in practice (and to put the rest of this chapter in context) it is vital to understand these concepts.

Data protection **by design** means integrating data protection safeguards into organisations' data processing activities and business practices from the very beginning of a project life cycle. Although this concept is not new, the changes made by the GDPR mean that it is now a **legal** requirement.

Data security is no longer seen as an afterthought, but as a first priority at every stage of the process in order to minimise the risk of harm to individuals. But this philosophy is not just about reducing the risk to individuals, it also reduces the risk to data processing organisations. This is because it is much easier, and therefore cheaper, to put appropriate data security provisions in place from the start, than try to fix them further down the line.

Data protection **by default**, also known as 'data minimisation' or the 'privacy first' approach, concerns data collection. This model focuses on the idea that the amount of data that organisations capture should only ever be the bare minimum that is needed to achieve an objective. For example, data collection processes on an app should automatically be set to collect the minimum amount of data needed for the app to function. The user can then choose if they want to change the privacy settings to allow data to be captured and shared above the minimum level.

Data Protection Impact Assessments (DPIAs), which are described in more detail later in this chapter, must capture and document all the decisions that organisations make relating to 'data privacy by design' and 'data privacy by default' in order to minimise the data protection risks of a project.

## WHAT AMOUNTS TO 'PROCESSING PERSONAL DATA' UNDER THE GDPR?

Understanding what amounts to 'processing personal data' is vital as an organisation cannot be compliant with data protection legislation unless it knows **what** data it is processing, and **how** those data are processed.

Under the GDPR, 'processing' personal data means much more than using individuals' personal data actively. It covers the collecting, inserting, storing, amending, analysing, exploiting, transferring, extracting and even erasing of personal data, and applies to databases of all kinds, including those of existing customers, data suppliers, employees, sales contacts and marketing targets. Likewise, it applies to the use of individuals' biometric data and CCTV footage, as well as pattern-tracking including location and purchasing patterns. It is also worth noting that the regulations are not limited to a particular means of processing – they apply to the processing of paper-based records and information in the same way as they apply to electronic ones.

So, almost every employee of an organisation will find themselves involved in personal data processing at some stage and obligations arising from the GDPR are likely to affect many processes and activities regularly carried out by organisations.

### Who does the GDPR protect? How to recognise personal data within an organisation

It has been established in Chapter 6 that the GDPR protects anyone who can be identified by the information held on a database.

There are two types of identifiable records: a named person and an unnamed person.

If an individual's name is known (named person) as well as their contact details, it is possible to identify them. For example, *Joe Brown of 5 Broadway Avenue, EN2 7PU* is easily identifiable and is covered by the GDPR.

Perhaps surprisingly, it is unnecessary to have someone's name to identify who they are (unnamed person). For example, if we hold a database record for the *Finance Director at Widgets plc*, that person is also covered by the GDPR. That is because it is possible to work out exactly who this person is, even though their name is not known. An unnamed person can be indefinable by number, location data or an online identifier, such as an IP address.

Data can be considered to be personal depending on the size of the data pool and the number of data items held. It is much easier to identify a specific person in a small pool of individuals, because differences between individuals are clearer. For example, if there are three sales managers in the database and only one is female, then the data *Female Sales Manager* becomes personal information. Therefore, organisations should be careful when processing a smaller data pool that they do not inadvertently find themselves in the territory of identifiable individuals. By contrast, if there are 1,000 sales managers in a room, and 500 are women, the data *Female Sales Manager* does not identify a specific individual and will therefore not constitute personal data. However, having a larger number of data items will reduce a seemingly large pool; for example, in a room of 50 sales managers there might only be one who is female, wearing glasses, with long, curly hair. So, having a larger pool is not necessarily a safe position either.

## Anonymisation and pseudonymisation

Having considered the question on identifiable personal records, it is relevant to discuss the question of anonymisation and pseudonymisation of such data. These terms refer to data storage processes that can be adopted to exploit any data an organisation holds, while remaining entirely GDPR compliant.

### *Anonymisation*

An anonymous record relates to an individual whom it is impossible to identify. For example, a supermarket might record data which show that sales of canned lager increase by 25 per cent the day before a rugby international. They might even be able to identify that this spike is largely down to purchases made by 50-year-old Caucasian males. They exploit this information when planning stock levels before future matches. However, they keep no record of the names or identifying information of the individuals who make those purchases. This is anonymous data and therefore falls outside the GDPR.

### *Pseudonymisation*

Pseudonymisation is a technique recognised under the GDPR by which the security of personal data can be increased. This is achieved by setting up two related but disconnected databases: one is designed to contain the bulk of the information held, and the other is designed to contain only the individuals' names or other specifically identifying material. So, the personally identifying parts of the personal data are separated from the parts that are being processed. This means that, in the event of a breach that affects the processing, no personal data can be accessed or released, reducing the danger of any loss or damage caused to data subjects.

The process works by first stripping out the name from each record on the first database and replacing it with a unique key code. The name is transferred into the second database, along with the key code assigned to it. The first database holds no names, and the second database holds no information except for names and keycodes. This second database is often referred to as the index.

The bulk of the data remaining on the first database are still personal data, but they do not need to be kept as securely. Any breach would not allow access to the personal data because they do not include a personal identifier. By contrast, the index database needs stronger security protections.

Essentially, pseudonymisation is 'anonymisation light': it has the same effect as anonymisation but can be reversed.

Since data controllers are required to ensure that their systems and processes are designed, from the outset, to protect data by design and default, pseudonymisation (and full anonymisation) are techniques that must be considered when designing systems to handle personal data.

An organisation's IT department ought to be able to set up a pseudonymised database. External support is also commercially available.

## CREATING A 'RECORD OF PROCESSING'

The GDPR requires organisations to have a written record of procedures by which personal data are processed, referred to as 'a record of processing'. This must hold information about data processing, including data categories, the group of data subjects, the purpose of the processing (discussed in the 'Deciding on the lawful basis of processing' section) and the data recipients. Many organisations use a spreadsheet to do this – there are templates available for download from the Information Commissioner's Office (ICO) website.

Writing a record helps an organisation to identify not only all the types of personal data that it holds but all the departments that process those data, including outsourced processors. It is also important to examine all of an organisation's business functions for data processing activity. This investigation process usually involves an internal audit or data mapping exercise. Organisations use a combination of questionnaires, meetings or interviews with staff from all departments, and analysis of existing policies, procedures or contracts.

Typically, there are at least three types of personal data processed by an organisation:

1. **employee data** – usually found in HR, payroll and staff admin departments;
2. **customer data** – often crop up in sales, marketing, customer management, service provision and order fulfilment departments; and
3. **supplier data** – generally occur in purchasing departments.

Choosing the lawful basis for these common processing activities tends to be relatively straightforward. However, there may be other business functions that carry out data processing, making this more complex – see the 'Deciding on the lawful basis of processing' section for information on lawful bases.

### Identifying special category data within an organisation

As explained in Chapter 6, an organisation must take particular care when dealing with special categories of data. For example, special categories of data may occur in many HR departments, such as records of maternity leave, pay and trade union memberships. As such, organisations must make sure they put additional protections in place for special category data, even if these data are found in unexpected places.

### Updating the record of processing

A record of processing will need to be reviewed and refreshed periodically, and particularly if anything significant changes. Many organisations diarise a regular review date for the record of processing, which can be set to take account of the nature and volume of data processing.

### Exceptions

Organisations with fewer than 250 employees are exempt from keeping a record, provided the processing is not likely to pose a risk to the rights and freedoms of the data subject, no special categories of data are processed or the processing is done only occasionally. However, in practice, this exemption rarely applies and it may be necessary to undertake the exercise to understand the processing activity and whether an exemption might apply.

### Failure to comply

If an organisation does not maintain records of processing activities, they may be subject to fines up to 10 million euros or 2 per cent of their annual turnover (whichever is the greater).

## DECIDING UPON THE LAWFUL BASIS OF PROCESSING

The next step is to categorise the basis on which each category of data is being processed. This is known as determining the lawful basis for processing.

### Lawful basis

Chapter 6 explored the legal framework behind what are known as the six lawful bases. This section examines in detail what that means in practice: selecting one of the six justifications for each and every data processing that the organisation does. This choice must then be justified and documented in the record of processing (see 'What amounts to "processing personal data" under the GDPR?' section).

Each of the six bases will now be considered in turn.

### Legitimate interest
Legitimate interest permits data processing if:

- it is in an organisation's commercial interest; or
- it is in the interests of another individual; or
- it is in the interest of broader society.

Arguably this is a very wide definition, which seems to make any kind of processing lawful if it can be shown that such processing is in the data controller's interests. Because of this, legitimate interest is conditional upon satisfying the most demanding procedural requirements of the decision-making process. These requirements are discussed in detail later in this section. The decision must be documented and defensible.

### Contract
Naturally, it is lawful to process an individual's personal data in order to fulfil a contract that an organisation has with them. For example, if a retailer needs to send a product that a customer has purchased from them, they need to collect and process the customer's name and address.

This basis does not only refer to a completed process, such as a sale. It also includes situations where holding data is also necessary in advance of a contract being executed. For example, processing customers' personal data is permitted in the process of preparing a sales quote.

### Legal obligation
This basis refers to situations when the processing of individuals' personal data is necessary to comply with other legal obligations. For example, an employer may need to process personal data to comply with their legal obligations in relation to the tax authorities and an employee cannot demand that their employer keeps this information private. In practice, legal obligation will almost certainly be the lawful basis for much of the processing carried out in an organisation's HR department.

### Consent
It is lawful to process personal data if an individual has given their consent. This usually happens in the context of sales and marketing databases. Most websites invite users and visitors to tick a box or submit their email address to receive newsletters or information on the latest deals. This is 'GDPR consent' in action. Some websites ask for users' permission to receive information and offers from 'partners' who offer products and services that 'will be of interest to them'. By doing so they ask for users' consent to pass on their personal data to another organisation, or even to sell it on. There are additional rules for sending electronic marketing communications, which are intended to limit the sharing of marketing databases.

### Vital interest
It is possible to rely on the vital interest basis to process personal data in order to protect an individual's life. It should only be used in a life or death situation. For example, health data can be passed to a paramedic in an emergency, even though the individual cannot give their consent and the information falls into a special category of personal data.

### Public task
This basis is relied upon mainly by public authorities. For example, it allows local councils to process personal data in order to charge Council Tax and plan capacity for schools and infrastructure.

### Identifying the most appropriate basis

When deciding on the most appropriate basis for data processing, the organisation must compare the characteristics and requirements of the six lawful bases with the project they have planned, and then select the most suitable one. The decision-making process must be documented in the record of processing (see 'Creating a "record of processing"' section) for each separate data usage.

The following guidelines apply to this decision-making process:

- The decision-making process must be robust and proactive. It must be formal and documented.
- The lawful basis adopted for the project must be identified right at the start; the basis cannot be changed during the project, nor once the project is completed.
- Despite a careful decision-making process, the scope of projects can change. In that situation, 'repurposing' the data held for a compatible purpose may be allowed, but a new Data Protection Impact Assessment (discussed later in this chapter) must be carried out and the lawful basis decision-making process must be rerun from scratch.

### Legitimate interest as the most appropriate basis

Despite the attractions of its very broad definition, legitimate interest is not always the most appropriate basis for establishing whether data processing is lawful. It must be used with care and not as a blanket permission. The GDPR guards against its over-exploitation by requiring organisations to prove (and document) that their interests outweigh the rights of the individual.

There are also several checks and hurdles in place to prevent over-reliance on legitimate interest.

The first of these hurdles is the need to carry out and document a Legitimate Interest Assessment (LIA). As part of the LIA the following questions have to be answered:

- Are personal data used in ways that individuals would reasonably expect?
- Has the organisation made sure that it has formally balanced its interests against the individual's rights?
- Is the processing planned necessary to achieve the specific results required from the legitimate interest? Or, is legitimate interest being used as a blanket permission?
- Will the processing only have a minimal effect on individuals' privacy?

- Have the higher safeguarding standards applicable to children's personal data processing (discussed later in this chapter) been met?
- Have the legitimate interests relied on been specified in the organisation's External Privacy Policy?

If an organisation cannot answer 'yes' to all of these questions, legitimate interest may not be the appropriate basis for a particular purpose.

Second, it is necessary to consider the three-part balancing test recommended by the ICO. As part of this, the organisation must:

1. Identify their interest.
2. Show that the processing is necessary to achieve this interest and that the same result could not be achieved in another, less intrusive way. And
3. Balance the interest against the individual's interests, rights and freedoms.

Finally, if an organisation does decide to use legitimate interest as its basis for lawful processing, it must keep a record of its LIA, to help it demonstrate compliance, and include details of its legitimate interests in its privacy notice.

Therefore, it is highly advisable to use legitimate interest basis with care and document an organisation's decision-making process very thoroughly.

## Consent as the most appropriate basis

There are also important restrictions around using consent as a lawful basis, including:

- **Opting-in** – as opposed to the historic need to 'opt-out', individuals now need to choose to be added to a database.
- **Proof of consent** – organisations must keep a record that people have given their consent.
- **Ease of withdrawing consent** – individuals should be able to get their names taken off organisations' databases with a single click of the 'unsubscribe' button.
- **Plain language** – requests for consent must be easy to understand.
- **Minors** – organisations must be extra careful when obtaining consent from people under the age of 16.
- **Repurposing** – an organisation can only process personal data for the specific purpose identified at the time of collecting those data. For example, if a customer gives consent to a retailer to have their receipt sent by email and provides their email address, the retailer cannot also use it for marketing. Similarly, if an employer uses a swipe card entry system relying on employee consent, they cannot start using the time stamps as a way to check up on employees' punctuality or absence, although in practice it would be difficult to do this relying on any other lawful basis unless the employer makes clear up front that this is what they will be doing.

The remaining four lawful bases are either much less common, or much simpler to apply, so are not protected by additional requirements.

## DRAFTING DATA PROTECTION POLICIES

Determining the lawful basis for processing and creating a record of processing provides the foundation for drafting and implementing appropriate policies. So, an organisation can now draft the policies needed for its business.

Importantly, there must be a meaningful and straightforward link between the policies and their translation into any projects. While having the right paperwork is essential, being able to prove that the paperwork is genuinely connected to the organisation's projects, and that this connection is obvious, is equally important.

Every organisation will need a unique set of policies that reflect the specific needs of their business; however, here is a list of the six basic policies commonly used as a starting point:

1. **External Privacy Policy or Privacy Notice** telling individuals how an organisation will collect and use their personal data.
2. **Data Retention Policy** clarifying how long individuals' personal data will be kept.
3. **Internal Privacy Policy** setting out all the ways in which an organisation exploits data, so that all employees understand their responsibilities.
4. **Individual Rights Policy** clarifying the rights that any individual enjoys under the GDPR.
5. **Data and IT Security Policy** setting out the responsibilities of everyone using the organisation's systems and IT.
6. **Personal Data Breach Policy** setting out in detail what an organisation will do if it suffers a data breach.

Policies can be drafted internally if an organisation has the required skillset. There are model policies available for download from the ICO and other approved sources. The ICO has also produced helpful checklists that can be used as a guide to ensure that the policies drafted are robust enough. If the skillset is not available internally, or if an unusual or unusually complex policy is needed, policies can also be outsourced to specialist firms.

Once the policies have been drafted, they need to be reviewed by senior management, and rigorously implemented. Ultimate responsibility for data security sits at board level under the GDPR.

Next, the policies need testing to ensure that they work in practice. It is also important to check that they all work together as many will be co-dependent. Once all the checks have been completed, and any necessary tweaks made, then the policies are ready to be put into action.

This is a question of driving through changes in corporate culture. This is most effectively achieved through training, which needs to be matched to the skillset and job function of employees.

- Chief executive officers (CEOs) and board members need to understand their own responsibilities under the GDPR – which may well be a new skillset for existing officers. They need to add the risk of a data breach to their ongoing risk management processes.
- Legal departments and IT departments will need detailed technical training.
- HR, sales, marketing and purchasing staff will need less technical training, but all need to be GDPR aware.

## DATA PROTECTION IMPACT ASSESSMENTS

A DPIA is a risk management tool that helps organisations to identify and gauge the data protection risks of a particular project. This allows organisations to make effective decisions and take actions to minimise such risks. In order for these decisions to be most effective, both data processors and data controllers should be involved in the DPIA process.

All analysis and decisions made in response should then be recorded in the DPIA. Therefore, if carried out correctly, a DPIA will demonstrate how each organisation complies with all its data protection obligations. It is the organisation's proof of accountability and the key document reviewed by the ICO in the event of a complaint.

The GDPR dictates that a DPIA must be carried out for any processing where the processing activity is likely to result in a high risk to individuals and the ICO mandates of DPIA is carried out for certain processing activities. Yet, many organisations choose to carry out DPIAs for most (if not all) of their data processing projects, even if the risk to individuals is not as high as the GDPR cut-off point. They do this as a cost- and time-effective way to minimise business risk.

DPIAs are not supposed to be a bureaucratic minefield. They can be flexible and scalable, depending on the complexity or sensitivity of the processing planned. A basic template is available for download from the ICO website.

Advising on DPIAs, carrying them out and monitoring them through the project life cycle are all core elements of the job of an organisation's data protection officer (DPO) – details of the role are discussed later in this chapter.

## REQUESTS FROM DATA SUBJECTS

Chapter 6 provides an insight into the rights of individuals under the GDPR, while this chapter focuses on the practical implications of some of these rights.

### Subject Access Requests (SARs)

Answering the following questions should help an organisation to handle an SAR:

- What timescales must the organisation work within?
  - It must respond to the SAR within one month.

- Can the organisation refuse to respond to an SAR?
  - It can refuse only when the SAR is unfounded, or excessive. This generally means a request that repeatedly asks for the same information. Taking specialist advice should be considered.
- How should the organisation deal with an SAR concerning personal data of other people?
  - The organisation is not obliged to comply with the request if another individual can be identified from that information, except if they have consented to the disclosure or it is reasonable to comply with the request without their consent.
- The organisation is required to respond 'in kind'. What does that mean?
  - This means that the organisation must reply via the same medium used by the SAR. For example, it must respond to an electronic request using a common electronic format.
- How does the organisation know that it is responding to the correct person?
  - It must check identities if necessary.
- How does an organisation deliver an organisation-wide response?
  - It must embed cultural change through policies and training.
- Who has to respond? Controllers or processors?
  - The controller responds. The controller's contract with the processor must contain a clause requiring the processor's assistance.

## Rectification requests

Individuals have the right to demand that controllers take reasonable steps to verify that their data are accurate. 'Reasonable' means proportional to the individual's risk of harm if the data are inaccurate. So, where there is high risk of harm, for example where a database is used for credit scores, extra steps should be taken to ensure accuracy.

The process for dealing with a rectification request is similar to that surrounding an SAR: the controller has one calendar month to respond, and all members of staff need to know how to process a request or who they should route the request to. If any data are discovered to be inaccurate, they must then be deleted or corrected as soon as reasonably possible.

## Restriction requests

If an individual requests the restriction of their personal data, the controller may need to stop processing that individual's data until the issue is resolved. However, they can still store it. Practically, this means temporarily moving the data to another processing system, making it unavailable to users or removing it from a website.

## Erasure requests

If an individual requests for their personal data to be erased, the controller may be required to delete that individual's data. However, this is not an absolute right – an individual cannot ask a bank to erase data about their mortgage, for example.

Just deleting the data that you have may not be enough. If you have shared these data with a third party (such as a processor), you must also ensure that the third party deletes the relevant data – holding a record of processing is important for this reason. Also, if the data have been made public in an online environment, you must ensure that they are removed.

## Objections to processing

If an individual asks a controller to stop processing their personal data for direct marketing, the controller must comply. This includes any data analysis or profiling. However, outside direct marketing, controllers can continue processing if they can demonstrate compelling legitimate grounds that override the individuals' rights and freedoms.

# CHILDREN'S PERSONAL DATA

There are special requirements for dealing with the personal data of vulnerable natural persons, in particular children. This section outlines the practical requirements for situations where the personal data of children could be or are being processed.

## Identifying children

Where a service is aimed directly at children, the data must be processed as if they belong to a child. If a service is not offered to children, then measures (such as age verification) must be taken to mitigate the chances of a child using the service. No method of age verification is infallible. Therefore the security of the measures implemented should be proportionate to the risks inherent in the processing and take into account whether the offering is attractive to children. A good example of a service that is inherently attractive to children is Facebook. It has been reported that half a million children who are 12 or under in the UK have Facebook accounts, despite the site having restrictions intended to prevent those from under 13 holding them.[1]

The term 'child' is not defined by the GDPR. However, the EU does recognise the primacy of treaties, such as the UN Convention on the Rights of a Child, which defines a child as a person under 18 years of age. It would therefore be sensible to treat anyone who is under 18 as a child under the GDPR.

## Lawful basis for processing

The basis for the processing of children's personal data is similar to that of adults. Before processing occurs, one of the six lawful bases must be identified (see 'Deciding

---

1 https://www.telegraph.co.uk/technology/2018/08/28/half-million-british-children-12-use-facebook-despite-underage (paywall)

upon the lawful basis of processing' section). When the data belong to a child, these bases become increasingly strict.

## Consent
When seeking to gain consent from a child, the controller must ensure that the information given is presented in a child-friendly manner (see 'Clarity of communication' section for more information). There must be a real choice provided to the child. The imbalance of power must not be exploited, even inadvertently.

Additional protection is afforded to child consent regarding information society services (see 'Information society services' section for more information).

## Contract
When relying on the fact that processing is necessary for the performance of a contract, the controller must consider the competence of the child in question to agree to the contract and to understand the potential consequences. This basis can only be relied upon for processing where the child has been found to be competent, and this has been evidenced in internal documents.

## Legitimate interests
Where legitimate interests are relied upon for processing, the controller must balance their own legitimate interests for processing against the interests, fundamental rights and freedoms of the child. This involves a judgement as to the nature and purpose of the processing, and the potential risks that it poses to children. Appropriate measures should be taken to safeguard the child against the risks identified.

## Extra protection

The personal data of children must be processed in accordance with all data protection principles. In certain situations, there are extra requirements for the processing of a child's data.

## Marketing and creating user profiles
When considering marketing directed at children, the controller should consider the child's reduced ability to recognise and critically assess the purposes behind the processing and the potential consequences. Any sector-specific guidance on marketing should be considered, and steps must be taken to ensure that children's personal data are not used in a manner that may lead to their exploitation.

## Information society services
An information society service (ISS) is defined as 'any service normally provided for remuneration, at a distance, by means of electronic equipment for processing (including digital compression) and storage of data, and at the individual request of a recipient of a service'.[2] This includes online shops, live or on-demand streaming services and companies providing access to communication networks.

---

[2] Article 1(1) of Directive (EU) 2015/1535 of the European Parliament and of the Council of 9 September 2015 laying down a procedure for the provision of information in the field of technical regulations and of rules on Information Society services (OJ L 241, 17.9.2015, p. 1).

For an ISS to rely on consent from a child, it must first be established that the child is over the age of digital consent; in the UK this is 13. Parental consent must be sought for those under the age of 13 if the processing relies on consent (unless the service is a counselling or preventative service).

Where consent is given by a parent on behalf of a child, reasonable steps should be taken to verify that the person providing parental consent does, in fact, hold parental responsibility for the child. These steps must be proportional to the risks of processing, but verification solutions that involve excessive collection of personal data should be avoided.

When a child reaches the age of digital consent, they have the option to withdraw the consent given by their parents on their behalf. The controller should inform the child about this possibility in accordance with the principles of fairness and transparency.

## Automated decisions and profiling

As a general rule, the controller should avoid making decisions based solely on automated processing where the decisions have a significant effect on the child. For example, one that has health implications or affects access to education.

Any automated processing of a child's data should be justifiable as necessary for the performance of a contract, authorised by law or based on the child's explicit consent. The automated processing should not be used for any purpose other than the purpose specified. In addition, suitable and child appropriate safeguards must be put in place to protect the rights, freedoms and legitimate interests of the child.

## Clarity of communication

Information presented to an individual should always be written in a manner that is clear enough for them to understand. The same is true about information presented to children. The readability can be simply checked by asking a child, of the same age as the target child, to read and explain the information.

Where this is not sufficient, further work may have to be done to ensure readability. To ensure that the information is child friendly, the presentation of information should also be addressed, breaking the information down and adding illustrations or graphics where appropriate.

## Rights to erasure

Data subject requests for erasure of personal data provided as a child should be complied with where possible, especially where it is likely that the data subject gave their personal data without fully understanding the implications of doing so.

An adult can request erasure on behalf of a child. If there is uncertainty, it is acceptable to take reasonable measures to check whether the adult has the right to make that request on behalf of the child. Where the child is competent to exercise their rights, their wishes must be considered, and the best interests of the child should prevail.

The process for requesting erasure must be as simple as the process to give consent. Therefore, if an identity check were not required on collection of information it is disproportionate to require one as a standard condition for erasure.

## CONTROLLERS AND PROCESSORS

Organisations must investigate all of the data controllers and processors that they deal with – for a quick explanation on what controllers and processors are, see the introduction of Chapter 6.

It tends to be relatively easy to identify controllers – they are the organisations that commission work on data and who benefit from the output. The only potential source of confusion is that, in large multi-departmental and multi-site organisations, there will be several different data controllers accessing the same data for different purposes, often without knowing about the other controllers. It is also worth noting that 'controller' does not refer to the person within an organisation, but the organisation itself.

While a controller will typically carry out some data processing themselves, it is very likely that the majority will be carried out by one or more third parties: data processors and sub-processors.

In simple terms, wherever a controller provides personal data to a third party (in order for that third party to provide services to the controller or the controller's customers) and that third party does not make any decisions regarding the means and purpose of the processing (they simply act on the controller's instructions), that third party will be a data **processor**. This means that many of the controller's suppliers are likely to be processors.

Common examples of data processors include:

- third-party service providers, such as a company providing payroll or HR services;
- subsidiaries of a multi-company group that processes data on behalf of another company in the same group;
- delivery companies;
- cloud service providers storing organisations' databases in the cloud; and
- other IT service providers (which could include anything from basic email to full outsourced IT services).

It may be relatively difficult to identify **all** of the data processors that work for your organisation, but it can be even more challenging to recognise that an organisation can be both a controller **and** a processor. For example, a delivery company may hold information about a controller's employees for the purposes of managing the contract as a controller, but may act as a processor for the personal data that it is processing on behalf of the shop to make a delivery.

### The relationship between controllers and processors

One of the major changes introduced by the GDPR was to streamline the relationship between the controller and the processor. Under the 1998 Act, controllers used to try and evade their data protection obligations by pushing them down onto the processor. Under the GDPR, this is no longer possible and it is now compulsory to have a contract in place between the controller and the processor detailing where data protection obligations sit. This is called a data processing agreement (DPA).

If you are a controller, you may have some specific requirements or restrictions that you must place upon your processors. These requirements and restrictions will, or should, be detailed in the DPA you have in place with your processors.

## Who writes the DPA?

In practice, organisations' legal departments should be able to draft the appropriate contracts. External expertise should be sought if there is no internal resource. But which organisation is responsible for doing this? The obligation to have a DPA in place lies with the controller. However, this does **not** prevent processors having their own DPA and asking that it be used.

It is particularly common for processors to write the DPA where they are a large organisation, or the services provided are particularly commoditized or specialised. This is because one of the key changes brought about by the GDPR is that processors are now directly liable to regulators and data subjects. Therefore, it is in the processor's interest to have a DPA that aligns with its own business, so having a draft DPA that you can suggest to a controller is generally a good idea. You should also note that it is common for controller DPAs to go beyond the requirements of the GDPR, which can result in additional obligations for, and risk/liability transfer to, the processor.

If, as a processor, you do not want to go that far, and are generally happy to sign up to the controller's DPA (which should be checked to make sure it fits to what is actually happening and is not transferring liability from the controller), you should still have your organisational and security measures documented so they can easily be added as a schedule to a DPA.

## What does the DPA need to include?

While neither the GDPR nor the ICO provide any template DPAs, there are rules and some guidance as to what the DPA should contain. This section will discuss the areas the DPA should cover in general terms. This is not a substitute for getting advice to suit your particular business needs, as the exact composition of a DPA should be tailored to your business.

In some cases, where there is little or no personal data, the DPA could be quite simple. The complexity of the DPA will increase relative to the amount of processing that will be carried out, particularly if that processing includes sensitive or special category data, or transfers personal data outside the European Economic Area (EEA).

As the controller, you must ensure that the DPA gives you all the rights that you need – see below for examples. If the processor or sub-processor is unwilling to make reasonable concessions, you must consider whether they are suitable. This can be difficult, as there may not be a viable alternative, so you will need to take a risk-based approach in deciding how to proceed. You may also have to be up front with your data subjects that you are dealing on the standard terms of those organisations.

The DPA must set out the following information:

- The **subject matter** of the processing – this should detail, in broad terms, what will take place. For example, ABC Ltd will engage XYZ Ltd to provide HR services to ABC Ltd's employees. This will require ABC Ltd to send personal data relating to its employees to XYZ Ltd.
- The **duration** of the processing – for how long will the processing continue? Often, this will be for the duration of the contract for services.
- The **types of personal data** to be processed – for example, customer names and contact information, or employee records, billing information and so on.
- The **categories of data subjects** – to what type of people will the personal data belong? These are simply broad descriptive categories; for example, customers, employees, potential customers or employees, suppliers.
- The **controller's obligations and rights** – the DPA must specify that all processing is under the effective control of the controller and must address all of the duties that the controller has in respect of the personal data. For example, the controller must ensure that the processing is lawful, and that any necessary consent is in place. Also, the controller must issue instructions on how the data are to be processed. It will also contain provisions setting out the controller's rights, for example the right to audit the processor to ensure compliance with the DPA.
- The **processor's obligations and rights** – setting out the processor's obligations in respect of the personal data is equally important. For example, the processor must:
  - Only process data in accordance with the controller's documented instructions. But, if the processor believes that the controller's instruction would cause it to process data in a manner not compliant with the GDPR, then the processor must immediately inform the controller.
  - Ensure that all personal data are kept secure and confidential.
  - Play a proportionate role in supporting the controller to meet their legal obligations. This includes providing evidence on how they treat personal data, that their security standards are adequate and that their documentation is up to date.
  - Have appropriate technical, organisational and security measures in place.
  - Assist the controller, for example, by responding to or informing them of data SARs.
  
  How a processor may be able to engage a sub-processor is also crucial. The DPA could contain an outright prohibition, set out a procedure for permission to be sought, or list pre-agreed subcontractors. More information about sub-processors can be found in the 'Sub-processor' section of this chapter.
- **Breaches** of the DPA and data protection legislation, including security breaches resulting in the loss or disclosure of personal data – the DPA should contain provisions to deal with breaches properly.
- **End of contract** provisions – there should be a specific clause to clarify what will happen at the end of the contract. For example, will the data be returned or deleted, and how will this be evidenced?

## When to update a DPA

Note that a DPA is not a 'draft and forget' document. Over the course of a relationship it is likely there will be some changes. For example, the nature of the processing, or the data that are being processed may change. If this happens, the DPA will need to be updated to reflect the changes. It is good practice to capture the information relating to the nature of the processing, categories of data subjects and type of personal data in a table located in a schedule to the DPA. This makes it easier to update and are usually contained in a separate schedule.

## SUB-PROCESSORS

What if the processor also uses a processor? This occurs, for example, where an organisation (the controller) outsources its HR functions to a specialist HR services provider (the processor), who then uses an application that is hosted on a cloud platform. Here, the cloud provider will be a processor of the HR service provider **and** a sub-processor of the company.

### When can a sub-processor be engaged?

A processor does not have an unfettered right to engage a sub-processor. They can only do so with written consent, either general or specific, from the controller. Without this permission, the use of a sub-processor will be unlawful. Therefore, it is very important that suppliers obtain permission from their clients to engage a sub-processor, even if they already engage these sub-processors as part of their regular business. This can be addressed in their contracts to ensure security for future dealings, as discussed below.

### Sub-processor DPAs

As explained earlier in this chapter, the GDPR requires data controllers and processors to have a DPA in place. Where a processor then engages a sub-processor, there must be another DPA in place between the processor and the sub-processor.

If you are a controller and one of your processors uses a sub-processor, you need to consider whether the same requirements and restrictions (detailed in the DPA between you and the processor) should also apply to the sub-processor. If they should, then you will need to ensure the DPA between your processor and the sub-processor contains those provisions. However, this may be difficult, or impossible, to monitor in practice. For example, some processors, especially large organisations or those dealing with large multinational cloud providers as sub-processors, may not be willing to accept your provisions and/or flow them down to sub-processors. If this is the case, then you will need to carefully consider how to proceed.

Suppliers who are processors or sub-processors must ensure that any DPA is compatible with the services that they provide. Many controllers use template DPAs, or DPAs that are finely tuned to their business, so some of the provisions are more likely to be unsuitable for suppliers. The more specialised the service is, the more likely the DPA will not 'fit'.

## DATA PROTECTION OFFICERS

The arrival of DPOs is arguably one of the major practical impacts of the GDPR. DPOs monitor all internal compliance procedures within organisations, inform and advise on their data protection obligations, provide advice on DPIAs and act as the point of contact for individuals and also for the ICO. They must be independent, experts in data protection, adequately resourced and report to the highest management level.

### Does an organisation need to have a DPO?

Some organisations do not have a choice in the matter. There are defined categories of organisations that are required to appoint a DPO. Broadly speaking, these organisations carry out large-scale monitoring of individuals (for example online behaviour tracking) or large-scale processing of special categories of data. The requirement to appoint a DPO under these circumstances applies to both controllers and processors.

Even if an organisation is not required to appoint a DPO, it is worth carrying out a thorough analysis of the risks, costs and benefits to an organisation of appointing one in any case. Organisations choose to voluntarily appoint DPOs for two reasons:

1. Because it reduces the risks of a data breach occurring in the first place.
2. Because if a breach does occur, a DPO is ideally placed to deal with it in the least damaging way.

An organisation may decide not to appoint a full DPO, but a data protection lead (DPL) instead. DPLs do not have the same legal status as DPOs, but have to carry out similar functions. They act as the point person within organisations with responsibility for GDPR compliance. They are in post to make sure that the demands of data protection are at the forefront of all business decisions. This is why they are sometimes referred to as 'data champions'.

### Who can be a DPO?

DPOs can be hired or existing employees can be promoted to take up the role. Depending on the organisation size, and the sensitivity and complexity of the data processed, the DPO role can be full or part-time. In order to maximise cost-effectiveness, some organisations appoint external DPOs from specialist providers.

As with the DPOs, DPLs can range from being new hires, a full-time external appointment, through to a part-time post filled internally but supported with appropriate training.

If an organisation does not have a DPO or a DPL to carry out an impact assessment, it will have to identify an overall project leader from within the business function that is piloting the project. It will suffice that the person is qualified to carry out a thorough DPIA. They need to have a good understanding of the GDPR, buy-in at board level and sufficient time and resources to carry out the task diligently. If the project leader does not have the expertise to carry out a DPIA for a higher risk processing project, the organisation should obtain specialist advice.

Remember that it is not just one DPO or DPL that an organisation may need to appoint. It is also necessary to ensure that an organisation has sufficient staff and resources to discharge its obligations under the GDPR. Whatever staffing appointments are made, the decision-making process has to be documented so that the organisation can show that it is GDPR compliant.

## INTERNATIONAL TRANSFERS

Like the Data Protection Act, the GDPR seeks to protect data subjects by restricting the transfer of their data to countries outside the EEA that lack similar protection. In GDPR terms, these external countries are called 'third countries' and transfers made to those third countries are referred to as 'restricted transfers'. To achieve this, constraints are applied to all restricted transfers, no matter the size of transfer or how often you carry them out.

However, it is possible to legally transfer data to third countries. Doing so is a two-step process: the data controller must still ensure that the transfer itself is legitimate (as if it were a transfer within the EU), and that the export of the data is permissible (achieved through one of the gateways).

The gateways include:

- **Adequacy** – where the third country has been found by the European Commission to have an adequate level of protection for data subjects (Article 45(1)).
- **Appropriate safeguards** – where there is an arrangement that fulfils certain criteria, which gives data subjects legally enforceable rights equivalent to the rights they would have in the EEA (Article 46).
- **Derogations** – where specific conditions are met (generally, either consent or necessity) (Article 49).

### Adequacy (Article 45)

Transfers to an 'adequate' country are the simplest way to transfer personal data outside the EEA because they are permitted under the GDPR, so it does not require organisations to obtain individual consent from the ICO.

However, this is not a self-assessment; only the European Commission has the power to determine whether a country outside the EEA has data protection laws that provide adequate protection to data subjects. First, the European Commission must submit a proposal to the European Data Protection Board. The European Data Protection Board then provides an opinion. If positive, it will then pass to the representatives from the EU member states for approval before formal adoption by the Commission.

At the time of writing, Andorra, Argentina, Canada (commercial organisations only), Faroe Islands, Guernsey, Isle of Man, Israel, Japan (private sector organisations only), Jersey, New Zealand, Switzerland and Uruguay have been found to have adequate protection, and official talks are ongoing with South Korea. However, as can be seen from this list, some adequacy decisions, including for Japan and Canada, are subject to certain conditions.

If an adequacy finding is withdrawn for any reason, this will be published in the *Official Journal*.

## Appropriate safeguards (Article 46)

In the absence of an adequacy decision, international data transfers may only take place where organisations have taken appropriate safeguards for the protection of personal data. These generally operate to ensure that the data subject retains the rights they had when their personal data were being processed in the EEA, enforceable through contract rather than through law.

Appropriate safeguards are listed in the GDPR (Article 46) and, if the necessary requirements are met, organisations do not need to seek additional consent from the ICO when transferring personal data to a third country. We look at the most relevant of these in greater detail below.

### *A legally binding agreement between public bodies*
Data transfers can be made from one public body to another public body in a third country by using a legally binding agreement that provides 'appropriate safeguards' for the rights of the individuals whose personal data are being transferred. These 'appropriate safeguards' must include enforceable rights and effective remedies for the individuals whose personal data is transferred.

### *Binding corporate rules (Article 47)*
Binding corporate rules (BCRs) is a safeguarding mechanism whereby an organisation adopts a set of rules that control the international transfer of personal data within that corporate group. As such, it is most relevant to large, multinational organisations with multiple offices or organisations that are engaged in a joint economic activity, such as franchises or joint ventures.

The rules must be legally enforceable and provide the data subjects with appropriate and enforceable protections. Article 47 of the GDPR sets out the required content and criteria in more detail, but, essentially, it requires that every part of the organisation in question submits to legally binding obligations that are equivalent to the obligations imposed on EEA entities by the GDPR. At present, the rules must be approved by the ICO and also by the other supervisory authorities (which are likely to follow the ICO's lead where the ICO has already given an opinion). Therefore, it is a complex, expensive and lengthy process (it is not unusual to take one year). However, it is anticipated that a set of template BCRs may be approved by the European Data Protection Board, which will make this process easier.

Yet, it is important to note that BCRs do not offer a solution for the international transfer of personal data to third parties; they only cover transfers within a corporate group or joint economic activity and should not be considered as an adequate safeguard for international transfers outside the corporate group.

### Standard contractual clauses (Article 93(2))
Small and medium-sized enterprises may be more interested in standard contractual clauses as these involve a smaller investment (both in terms of money and time) than a BCR.

These are a set of clauses approved by the European Commission that contain contractual obligations for the data exporter (based in the EEA) and the data importer (based outside the EEA), and rights for the individuals whose personal data are transferred. Currently, there are two forms of standard contractual clauses: controller to processor and controller to controller. The standard contractual clauses have been subject to repeated legal challenge and it is important for the data exporter and data importer to verify that use of the clauses affords a level of protection broadly equivalent to the GDPR, taking account of any potential access by intelligence or other legal authorities and relevant legal aspects of the importer's legal system.

When adopting these clauses, they must be in their entirety and without amendment. They may be incorporated into other agreements, and additional clauses on business-related issues can be added, provided that they do not contradict or alter the standard contractual clauses. Otherwise, they become **non-standard** contractual clauses and will require ICO approval under Article 46(3)(a).

Sets of standard contractual clauses do already exist, but the Commission is expected to draft a set of new clauses to follow the GDPR standards.

### Transfers subject to an approved code of conduct or certification mechanism (Articles 40, 42 and 43)
Article 40 anticipates the development of codes of conduct that will facilitate the transfer of data between parties in particular sectors. For example, lawyers, through organisations such as the Bar Council or the Law Society, may agree a code of conduct binding on its members that assists both data controllers and data subjects by providing a consistent approach across sectors. Interestingly, this can also potentially be used to permit transfers to organisations in third countries that are required to comply with the approved code of conduct.

Similarly, Articles 42 and 43 anticipate the development of a certification mechanism, which can certify controllers and processors as being compliant. As with codes of conduct, the certification mechanism can be used to allow transfers to certified bodies in third countries.

### Non-standard contractual clauses that have been approved by the ICO (Article 46(3)(a))
It is possible to transfer personal data to a third country where you and the receiver have entered into a bespoke contract (under **non-standard** contractual clauses) governing a specific restricted transfer, provided it has been individually authorised by the ICO. This process is longer than adopting **standard** contractual clauses.

### Derogations (Article 49)

Where none of the above criteria apply, it is still possible to transfer data to a third country, but only where one of the following applies:

- The data subject gives informed and free consent.
- The transfer is necessary for the performance of a contract with the data subject or for the data subject's benefit (or taking steps prior to entry into a contract with the data subject at the data subject's request).
- The transfer is necessary for important reasons of public interest.
- The transfer is necessary for commencing, pursuing or enforcing legal action.
- The transfer is necessary to protect someone's vital interests (i.e. it is a matter of life or death) where the data subject is unable to give consent.
- The transfer arises from a public register subject to various conditions.

Note that all of these, apart from the first and last, require that the transfer is **necessary**. Even if the transfer is very desirable, that is insufficient to trigger the derogation.

## PROCESSING DATA OF EU DATA SUBJECTS

A major addition of the GDPR is its requirement that data controllers based outside the EEA are still required to comply with its principles, even if they have no establishment in the EEA or are not processing data in the EEA. This applies where the personal data of data subjects in the EEA are being processed outside the EEA and the processing activities are related to:

- Offering goods or services (including free-of-charge goods and services) to EEA data subjects.
- Monitoring the behaviour of EEA data subjects, to the extent that monitoring covers their activities within the EEA.

Note that 'data subjects who are within the Union' is potentially a very wide category. It is broader than 'EEA citizens' or 'EEA residents' and covers anyone who is physically present in the EEA.

An obvious question is how the EU intends to enforce the GDPR against organisations in third countries. One answer is that those responsible for breaching the GDPR could find themselves within the EU's jurisdiction when they set foot in a member state, or that the EU could enforce penalties against assets of the organisation that are within the EU. It is also possible that customs on the EEA border could impound any goods sent by the infringing entity, or internet service providers (ISPs) block any online services being provided by the infringer, thus preventing the infringer from dealing with the EEA. At the time of writing, there is no clear guidance on how this might work.

### Actions to take

Those organisations outside the EEA who are processing the data of EU data subjects will have to register with a supervisory authority in the EU (such as the ICO), and appoint an EU-based representative (someone that a data subject and supervisory authority can deal with). This representative (not the same as a DPO), will be legally responsible for the activities of the third country organisation that appointed them.

## Personal data protection after Brexit

One thing is clear: irrespective of the formal relationship between the UK and EU, all UK businesses that interact with EU data subjects will have to comply with the GDPR. Additionally, since distinguishing between EU data subjects and non-EU data subjects is likely to be complicated, most organisations are likely to continue to comply with the GDPR across their whole business. To this effect, the UK Government has accepted that the GDPR will be brought into UK law and the Information Commissioner will remain the country's independent supervisory authority on data protection.

After this, the UK will be regarded as a third country. As such it will no longer automatically benefit from the free flow of data and will need to secure an adequacy decision.

Therefore, until the UK is deemed an adequate country, organisations are advised to review their contracts to make sure that they contain standard contractual clauses (SCCs), or other legal safeguards. This will allow them to continue legally receiving data from EEA countries. If part of a multinational group, they may be able to rely on BCRs to transfer data within their group.

Overall, it is apparent that whatever the politicians might say, after Brexit, in terms of data protection at least, the UK will become a rule taker and not a rule maker.

## BREACH NOTIFICATIONS

This section concerns organisations' data security obligations under the GDPR. In practical terms, data security makes up the large majority of organisations' daily GDPR compliance processes and seeks to secure against data breaches.

A personal data breach occurs when data has been:

- used in an unauthorised manner;
- destroyed or lost;
- altered without a lawful basis; or
- disclosed without a lawful basis.

Breaches can be accidental or deliberate. Examples of accidental data breaches include leaving a laptop containing personal data on a train, accidentally deleting data or sending data to the wrong person. An example of a deliberate data breach would include computer viruses, data hackers or data being deliberately deleted or used for an unauthorised purpose.

In order to guard against data breaches, a strong data protection environment within the whole organisation is needed. This requires having good cyber security (including anti-virus and anti-malware protections, password policies that are stringently implemented) and strong internal physical security (including in the using of external hard drives and other portable devices).

Although the GDPR does not specify what measures data controllers and processors should adopt, it does require these measures to be 'appropriate'. To decide what measures are 'appropriate', organisations must consider the financial cost of the approach and the risks posed to data subjects. For example, if the data are not very sensitive, it may be sufficient to opt for a cheaper, lower-tech security system. This decision-making process must then be documented in the DPIA.

It should be remembered that implementing 'privacy by design' into all data projects (where data protection is integrated into the technology from creation) can reduce the risk, and therefore the cost, of what is appropriate.

It is also worth noting that ensuring data security is a continuous process. The GDPR requires that organisations **regularly** assess and evaluate how effectively their security measures are working. In particular, they should consider the following:

- Are the data available only to the people who need them, or can anyone access them?
- Can staff access the data at home? What security is in place if they are accessing them from home? Is there a VPN in place?
- How are the data stored? Is it processed using cloud-based software? If so, is it accessible to the cloud service provider? Are they encrypted? Are they pseudonymised? Are they analysed?
- What physical security measures are in place? Is a key card needed to enter the premises? Is there CCTV?

Finally, the weakest link in ensuring data security is people. Organisations must embrace a change in corporate culture and facilitate data protection training, so that their staff understand their responsibilities in relation to personal data.

### How to find out that a data breach has happened

Data breaches usually come to light through internal self-reporting. The most common cause of a data breach is human error – for example, accidentally sending an email to the wrong recipient or incorrectly entering data. This is why adopting a 'no-fault' approach within an organisation is so vital. If the internal response is punitive, staff tend to hide accidents or omissions instead of reporting them. This does not provide the desired outcome.

Beyond internal reporting, a third-party data processor may let the controller know that a breach has taken place. Or the controller may find out about a breach through a complaint.

### What to do when a breach has been reported

No matter how they are discovered, all breaches and potential breaches must be taken seriously, and the controller must act quickly. Therefore, any potential data breach should be flagged up urgently with the DPO or DPL, who should then follow the internal policy.

When investigating the breach, the DPO or DPL needs to establish what happened, how it happened, how many people are affected and what the effect of the breach may be.

It is then necessary to gauge the severity of the risk to the affected individual(s). Although **all** breaches must be recorded (no matter the severity), the appropriate responses differ.

### High-risk breaches: what has to be done?

If the risk of harm to the affected individuals is deemed to be high, it might be necessary to report the breach to the Information Commissioner, and to the individuals involved. The controller has 72 hours from discovery of a data breach to report it to the ICO. The controller should aim to be able to supply all data relating to the breach within those 72 hours.

If a breach is likely to cause a high risk to an individual's rights and freedoms, this individual must be notified as well.

### Low-risk breaches: what has to be done?

If the risk of harm to the affected individuals is deemed to be low, it is sufficient to record the breach internally on a dedicated log, investigate how it occurred and fix it.

However, organisations sometimes choose to inform the ICO of a **potential** data breach before they have completed their investigation, to make sure they remain within the 72-hour deadline.

### What happens if an organisation gets its data security obligations wrong? Who will be held accountable?

Ultimately, accountability will be policed and enforced by the ICO. However, GDPR compliance should also be policed by the board of directors (or equivalent senior people in an organisation) as a means of managing significant risk. For many organisations this is a cultural challenge. Board members may not be used to seeing data security as a business-critical risk, but it is.

### What are the implications of a data breach?

First, a data breach may damage an organisation's reputation. For many, this represents the most serious impact of a breach. If an organisation is no longer viewed as a trusted provider of goods or services, existing and future customers may be driven away. Such organisations may also be less desirable to current and prospective employees or suppliers.

Second, organisations may face financial consequences. The GDPR gives the ICO new powers to impose large fines for non-compliance. For example, in 2019 the ICO issued a notice that it would fine British Airways £183 million for poor security arrangements, leaking data of over 400,000 users. The fine was subsequently reduced to £20 million.

In addition, the ICO can issue an Enforcement Action, forcing an organisation to rectify the faults or failings in its data processing systems. This costs organisations resources in terms of time, money and focus.

Finally, the GDPR gives individuals the right to compensation for data breaches.

## SUMMARY

This chapter has addressed some of the main practical measures that organisations need to put in place in order to achieve compliance with data protection law, including drafting suitable data protection policies and procedures, responding to requests from individual data subjects, and dealing with overseas transfers of personal data. However, these practical steps are only the most visible, outward manifestation of what should be a deeper organisational philosophy.

Implementing a culture of 'data protection by design' and 'data protection by default' will help to ensure that data protection issues are properly considered at the start of any new product development or IT project, and that no more personal data are collected or processed than are strictly necessary.

# 8 IT IN THE WORKPLACE: PROTECTING THE EMPLOYER

Jeremy Holt

## INTRODUCTION

This chapter discusses (1) policies for the use of email and computers by employees and (2) policies for the use of social media by employees. Each section ends with a specimen policy.

Employees can cause their employers all manner of problems in their use of computers and email. For example:

- Misuse of computer systems can waste staff time and leave businesses (and their management) exposed to claims for discrimination, harassment, defamation or worse.
- Failure to include proper business information in electronic communications is a criminal offence.

## COMPUTER AND EMAIL USAGE POLICIES

An employer can be held responsible for wrongful actions carried out by employees in the course of their employment. This is the case even if the act is done in a way that has not been authorised by the employer. For example, an employer can be held responsible for employees' acts involving racial and sexual harassment, downloading pornography, defamation of customers or competitors, breach of confidence, copyright infringement, hacking and breaches of data protection legislation.

To provide staff with some guidance and avoid these problems, employers have adopted computer use and email policies. Every business is different and no single policy will suit all.

Employers should also remember that, in certain cases, both the employer and the employee are liable for the employee's wrongful action. It can be useful to remind employees of this in order to encourage them to comply with rules forbidding particular conduct.

### The problem with email

Users adopt a more relaxed manner when using email, similar to a telephone conversation, rather than a letter. However, this form of the communication is much more permanent as it can be stored and passed on very easily. The thoughts of an employee expressed in an email could be critical later when used to defend, or damage, their employer in legal proceedings.

Two graphic examples of what can go wrong come from large law firms in London (who should really know better). In one, a male solicitor received an email from his (then) girlfriend commenting favourably on their most recent sexual encounter. Misguidedly he shared the email with a friend. The explicit content of the email ensured that copies of it were passed on in a chain reaction to millions of people within weeks. In another case, which involved a race discrimination claim, a throwaway comment from the employer about the ideal physical attributes of any new secretary (which was somehow passed on to the claimant, a former secretary, who did not have such attributes) brought a great deal of unwanted publicity to the firm concerned here. Two points should be emphasised. First, if these comments had been spoken (or even expressed in a written letter, which would have been much more difficult to copy and pass on to a large number of people), they would not have caused the trouble they did. Second, the damage to the employer is more likely to be to their public reputation than financial damage, particularly if the comments expressed are sexual or discriminatory in some way.

An email message is stored in a number of places – the sender's machine, the recipient's machine and (because of the technical manner in which email messages are transmitted across the internet) the servers through which it was transmitted in between. As a result, it is extremely difficult to destroy all records of a message sent.

The problem that the storage of emails can cause was highlighted in the renowned Oliver North case in America. Although Oliver North had thought that he could completely delete certain computer data, such data were retrieved by the authorities and used as evidence against him. In another case, a drug dealer was convicted because he had stored details of his drug transactions on his handheld computer and, although he believed that they had been deleted, they were retrieved by the police.

It is surprising how effective a good computer forensic company can be. For this reason, staff should be discouraged from commenting by email on any legal dispute in which their employer is involved, in case such comments are used against the employer later in legal proceedings.

## Monitoring emails and internet use

Employers sometimes wonder whether they have the right to monitor voice calls or email messages, and there are a number of myths about this. For a start, there is no legal distinction between phone calls, faxes and email messages for the purposes of monitoring at work; all telecommunications are treated the same and the same rules apply to each medium.

The basic principle (set out in the Regulation of Investigatory Powers Act 2000) is that telecommunications may not be intercepted by employers unless both the sender and the recipient have consented to the interception. Indeed, it is a criminal offence for employers to carry out unauthorised interception and, if they do, they face up to two years' imprisonment and/or a fine, as well as the possibility of an injunction or damages claim. However, under a separate set of regulations (snappily entitled the

Telecommunications (Lawful Business Practice) (Interception of Communications) Regulations 2000), businesses are allowed to intercept communications without consent for certain limited purposes, as long as the messages relate to the business and are on a system provided in connection with the business. The purposes include:

- establishing the existence of facts (e.g. recording transactions in case there is a contractual dispute);
- compliance with regulatory standards;
- detecting crime (e.g. fraud or corruption);
- investigating unauthorised use of the system (e.g. to check that company rules on emails or internet use are being followed);
- checking on the standards of people using the system (e.g. for quality control or staff training);
- protecting the system from viruses or other threats; and
- backing up or rerouting emails when a member of staff is on holiday or off sick.

Employers are required to take all reasonable steps to notify users that interception may take place. This is relatively easy with employees as it can be stated in a staff policy. However, it is much more difficult with outsiders sending inbound emails. One method of notification is in outbound email and fax disclaimers. Employers should remember that even if interception of messages is carried out by them in a legitimate manner, any use by them of the information gathered must be proportionate and in accordance with data protection legislation.

The Information Commissioner has published a code on monitoring at work. Although this code does not have the force of law, it is used in any enforcement action by the Information Commissioner and may be referred to in employment tribunal proceedings. The code emphasises that:

- Monitoring of messages should only take place when there is a real business need and the methods used should not be unduly intrusive into an employee's privacy.
- Employees have a right to expect that they can keep their personal lives private, which means that they are entitled to some privacy at work.
- Employers should, whenever possible, avoid opening emails, especially ones that clearly show that they are private or personal.
- Employees should be aware that monitoring is taking place and should be told the reasons for it and the means used.
- Covert monitoring will only be legitimate in the most exceptional of circumstances, such as the detection of crime or equivalent wrongdoing.
- It is good practice for the monitoring to be carried out by someone other than the employee's line manager (e.g. security or human resources). In this way, personal information that is picked up can be sifted so that only the most relevant information becomes known to those who work with the employee.

## Laying down a policy for staff

All businesses should draw up a policy for staff on their use of computers and access to the internet and notify all staff of it. Unless it is wildly unreasonable, staff cannot argue about such a policy. Their use of the employer's equipment is conditional upon their following the policy laid down, otherwise they can be in serious trouble. The policy should be emphasised during the induction of new staff. A specimen staff computer use policy is shown at the end of this part of the chapter. Note that this policy should not just be restricted to employees; it should also be given to outside contractors and agency staff.

The policy can be backed up by reminders on computer screens and regular training. Internal audits should check that security policies are being followed and the side should not be let down by senior management (as it frequently is). The aim should be that no user of the firm's computer system could reasonably argue that they were not aware of the rules for the use of it.

### *Private email*
It is unrealistic for employers to ban completely the private use of email by employees. No doubt the same discussions took place when the telephone first started to be used widely within business.

If private email use is allowed, it is critical that such messages be sent in an appropriate format and that they do not appear to be official messages from the company. The best way to do this is in the signature section of the message.

There should be two different formats for the employee to use depending on whether the message is official or private, and private messages should be accompanied by a heading or signature block that states, for example, 'This message is from Jeremy Holt and is sent in a private capacity.' Legal requirements for information on business emails are shown later in this chapter.

Some employers allow employees to set up private web-based email accounts for private emails. In this case, the employer cannot monitor such messages and the messages sent do not use the employer's return address.

### *Website access*
The policy prohibiting staff visits to unauthorised websites (e.g. pornographic or recruitment agency sites) can be reinforced by the use of filtering systems and blocking software (which is surprisingly inexpensive). In my experience, just the knowledge by the staff that such blocking software is being used is enough to reduce significantly visits to unauthorised sites during work time. Obviously, staff may visit them from their home computers, but this does not waste valuable working time.

It is surprising how tough employment tribunals are prepared to be about the dismissal of employees for downloading of pornography, particularly if there is a policy in force forbidding this. One question that is often asked in these circumstances is whether employers are required to notify the police. Generally, the police are not interested unless the pornography is being sold by the employee or it involves children.

There is no doubt that employers can dismiss staff for excessive surfing of the web during working hours. For example, a computer manager at a firm of management consultants was dismissed fairly for using the office computer to do 150 searches for cheap holiday deals. While it may not be practical for employers to check what sites employees have been visiting, peer pressure does work. If other employees are having to work harder because one is surfing the web, the employer is soon likely to hear about it from the other employees.

### Hacking

Some astute employers give new employees a copy of the Computer Misuse Act 1990 when they start. The Computer Misuse Act makes it a criminal offence to use, access or alter another person's computer without prior permission, and providing a copy of it underlines to the employee that the company's systems should not be used other than as permitted in the course of the employment.

### Disclaimers on business emails

Businesses sometimes believe that all their ills can be cured by a well-drafted disclaimer at the foot of an email. Email disclaimers are of little value, other than to notify the recipient that the contents of the email are confidential and to offer a method of reporting any misdirection and to warn that they may be monitored. Such disclaimers are not a substitute either for a proper staff email policy or for the legal information that must be shown in an email, which is the same as must be shown on a business letter.

---

**INFORMATION REQUIRED ON BUSINESS EMAILS AND LETTERS**

The following information must appear on company emails and letters:

- the full name of the company;
- the registered number of the company;
- the address of the registered office and an indication that that address is the registered office;
- the country of registration of the company.

For partnerships of 20 or fewer partners, the names of the partners and an address for service must appear. Partnerships of more than 20 may simply say that a list of the partners is available at a particular address.

Sole traders must have their real name (i.e. not just a trading name) and a geographical address on their business letters.

Businesses who do not abide by these rules risk looking amateur or newly started (or both).

There is no reason to differentiate between a letter sent by post and a letter sent by email. Some businesses still fail to follow these rules fully in relation to emails at the moment. This is all the more surprising when the vast majority of business messages are now sent by email rather than by formal business letter. There are a number of consequences of failing to abide by the law in providing the required information in company letters or emails:

- It is a criminal offence both by the company concerned and by the person who authorises the communication on behalf of the company.
- If the communication relates to an order for goods and the company's name is not mentioned in the email, the individual who sent it can be personally liable for the order.
- Difficulties can arise in bringing legal proceedings to enforce a contract made where the appropriate information has not appeared on the company's notepaper or in the company's email.

## Action plan on computer use

- Introduce a computer use and email policy. If there is no policy, an employer cannot monitor what is happening except in very limited circumstances.
- Make sure that such a policy is notified to all employees and contractors and that they are reminded of it from time to time (e.g. by banner warnings when logging on to the system), otherwise it will not be possible to rely on it later just when it is most needed.
- Ensure that all emails contain the correct business information.
- Devise a system whereby personal emails from members of staff are clearly differentiated from emails on company business. (This might be as simple as requiring the employee to put the word 'Personal' in the subject line of any outbound emails that are of a private nature.)

### SPECIMEN POLICY FOR COMPUTER AND EMAIL USE

We do not wish to restrict in any way your use of our computer system – indeed we encourage it. However, we regard the integrity of our computer system as key to the success of our business. To avoid misunderstanding and confusion, all employees must abide by the following rules. Breaches of this policy will be taken seriously and could amount to gross misconduct. You should direct any queries about this policy to the Human Resources Department.

**Licensed software**

Only properly licensed software may be loaded onto our system. You are not allowed to use within the company any material that you either know or suspect to be in breach of copyright. In addition, you are not allowed to pass such material on to anyone else. It is important to bear in mind that breach of copyright for business purposes can be a criminal offence both by the company and by the individual concerned. No software may be loaded onto our system without first obtaining the express permission of the IT Department. Software includes business applications, shareware, entertainment software, games, screensavers and demonstration software. If you are unsure whether a piece of software requires a licence, please contact the IT Department. The copying of software media and manuals is also prohibited.

**Networks**

You are not allowed to make any change to the connection or configuration of your PC. None of our PCs may be connected to a customer's network without our permission and written permission from the customer concerned. In addition, none of our PCs may be connected to a public network (e.g. the internet) without specific permission.

**Disks, memory sticks or other storage devices**

You must not use disks, memory sticks or other storage devices from unknown sources or from home computers. All such storage devices must be virus-checked before they may be used on our computer system.

**Viruses**

Generally, more damage to files is cause by inappropriate corrective action than by viruses themselves. If a virus is suspected, you should do nothing more until instructed. The matter must be reported immediately. The most likely way that our computer system will be infected by a virus is from an external message. Any outside material must be properly virus-checked before being loaded on to our computer system. Many viruses are now spread by email messages and use the address book of the recipient to pass it on to other people. Some of these viruses are activated when an attachment to the message is opened. Creators of these viruses frequently encourage the user to open the attachment simply by using a header such as 'You must read this!' You should not open any attachment of this type and must generally be suspicious of any message that is received from an unknown source. In other words, only open mail when you know it is from a reliable source. If you receive email warnings about viruses, please ignore the instructions they contain. In the majority of cases they are hoaxes and the instructions, if followed, will damage our computer system.

**Customer procedures**

If you use a customer's computer system you must observe the customer's rules relating to their computers. In the absence of any such rules, our rules should be followed.

### Access

You are only allowed access to those parts of our computer system that you need in order to carry out your normal duties.

### Inappropriate material

You must not view or download or pass on any pornographic material on our computer system or place obscene or offensive screensavers on your PC. In line with the normal rules that apply to you as an employee, you are not allowed to send racist, sexist, blasphemous, defamatory, obscene, indecent or abusive messages on our computer system, either internally or externally. Do think carefully before sending any questionable messages that could reflect badly on us as a company.

### Use of the internet at work

The primary reason for our providing you with access to the internet and/or email is to assist you in your work for us. You are allowed to send personal emails in a similar way to the way that minor incidental personal telephone use is allowed. Such activity should not be excessive and must not affect your ability to work properly for us during normal working hours. Personal emails should be kept to a minimum and the company's footer MUST NOT be shown on a personal email.

You are not allowed to send unsolicited emails or emails to multiple recipients or to use email for personal gain. You are also not allowed to use the company's internet access and email system to sign up for online shopping, internet membership schemes or chat rooms.

### Business emails

You must not order anything on our behalf by email without proper authorisation. You should always bear in mind that an email from the company has the same legal effect as a letter from the company on the company's notepaper. This underlines the importance of being careful with what you say in an email in case it is misunderstood. All company emails must contain our standard footer, which will be notified to you from time to time. As stated above, personal emails must not contain our standard footer.

### Confidentiality

Before sending any confidential information by email consider carefully whether appropriate steps have been taken to maintain such confidentiality. Email is not inherently a more secure medium of communication than traditional means, and emails can be easily copied, forward and stored.

### Security

Do not give internal passwords to anyone outside the company. In addition, you must not give any customer-related security information to anyone other than the customer unless specifically authorised in writing by the customer in advance.

### Inappropriate material

You could be disciplined or even dismissed for forwarding inappropriate emails or accessing inappropriate websites at work. In severe cases it could also be a criminal offence.

### Records

Keep proper records of our dealings with outsiders. It is always possible that what appears to be a relatively trivial point could be of immense significance later. It is not possible to foresee what will subsequently need to be checked, so keep a complete record of all transactions.

### Data protection

If you have access to data about individuals, you must bear in mind at all times the requirements of data protection legislation.

### Passwords

Use passwords at all times and change them at the intervals notified to you. Do not select obvious passwords. All passwords must be kept confidential.

### Backups

Regular backups must be carried out in accordance with the rules laid down from time to time. Critical information should not be stored solely on the hard disk of your workstation in case it is lost.

### Misuse

Misuse of computers is a serious disciplinary offence. The following are examples of misuse:

- fraud and theft;
- system sabotage;
- introducing viruses and time bombs;
- using unauthorised software;
- obtaining unauthorised access;
- using the system for unauthorised private work or game playing;

- breaches of data protection legislation;
- sending abusive, rude or defamatory messages via email;
- hacking;
- breach of the company's security procedures or this policy.

This list is not exhaustive. Depending on the circumstances of each case, misuse of the computer system may be considered gross misconduct, punishable by dismissal without notice. Misuse amounting to criminal conduct may be reported by us to the police.

### Breaches

All breaches of computer security must be reported. If you suspect that a fellow employee (of whatever seniority) is abusing our computer system you may speak in confidence to management. You are responsible for any actions that are taken against us by a third party arising from restricted and/or offensive material being displayed by you on, or sent by you through, our computer system.

### Monitoring

We reserve the right to intercept and monitor your communications, including email, internet and telephone calls. This right to monitor may be exercised, for example, to decide whether communications are relevant to the business, to prevent or detect crime or to ensure the effective operation of the system. In addition, we reserve the right to monitor communications in order to determine the existence of facts, to detect unauthorised use of the system and to decide the standards that ought to be achieved by employees using the system.

### Improvements

We welcome suggestions from you for the improvement of this policy.

## SOCIAL MEDIA

When social media first started it must have appeared to marketing departments as an answer to many of their prayers. The opportunity to raise the company's profile, market new products and expand market research must have seemed irresistible. However, when employees started posting unsuitable material and criticising their employers, the legal risks for employers started to appear. The answer, as with so many other issues on employment law, is to lay down a policy for the acceptable use of social media by employees. The hand of the employer is considerably strengthened by the introduction of such a policy. A specimen social media policy is shown below. Such a policy should warn staff about the risks of social media. It should set down practical guidelines for the use of social media and warn of the consequences of breaching such guidelines.

One question that I am often asked by clients is whether it is acceptable to 'vet' prospective employees by looking to see what they have said publicly on social media. There is no law preventing employers from doing this, provided that the rules prohibiting discrimination are respected and the vetting does not intrude into the applicant's private life. Business is a jungle, and in a jungle it is wise to use all your senses.

> **SPECIMEN POLICY FOR SOCIAL MEDIA USE**
>
> This policy highlights the risks all employees should be aware of when using social media and what their responsibilities are.
>
> **What is social media?**
>
> We define social media as websites and applications that allow users to create and share content and/or take part in online networking. The most popular sites include:
>
> - Facebook
> - Twitter
> - LinkedIn
> - YouTube
> - Google+
> - Instagram
> - Pinterest
> - Flickr
> - Tumblr
> - Reddit
>
> **What could go wrong?**
>
> - What you write on social media could seriously damage your own, another person's or our organisation's reputation.
> - You could lose your job with us. You and we could be sued or fined, or you could even be imprisoned.
>
> **Stop and think before you click**
>
> - It is your duty as an employee to **protect our interests** and you must not publish anything that could directly or indirectly damage such interests or compromise our reputation.
> - You must never speak on our behalf on social media unless you are authorised to do so, and you must always make sure anything you do post is accurate and lawful.

- Always get your colleagues' permission before posting images of them or any of their personal details.
- Failing to take care about what you write can have serious personal, disciplinary and financial implications.
- Even if you are using social media in your own time, if you refer to people at work or work-related matters, you and we could get into trouble.

**Social media postings can be used in legal proceedings**

- Social media postings can be used against you or us in legal proceedings, disciplinary meetings or other regulatory investigations.
- You should never make any postings about a legal dispute or investigation or potential dispute or investigation.

**It is very difficult to permanently remove social media postings**

- Simply deleting social media postings will not necessarily solve the problem. Forensic IT equipment can still find supposedly 'deleted' messages.
- What you publish online will likely be available for a long time, to be read by anyone, including us, future employers and colleagues.

**Do not be hurtful or spread rumours**

- Never make postings that could be thought of as obscene, racist, sexist, bullying or hurtful.
- Never lie, exaggerate or make false or inaccurate statements about another company or person.

**Do not copy someone else's work**

- Only use or attach other people's work to your social media postings if you have permission or you know it is not protected by copyright or other intellectual property rights (for example, trade mark rights). This includes photographs and music.
- Do not assume that work you find on the internet is free to use.

**Avoid unproductive usage**

- We allow light social media usage as long as it does not interfere with your duties. However, excessive, unproductive usage is not permitted and may be treated as gross misconduct.

**Improvements**

We welcome suggestions from you for the improvement of this policy.

IT IN THE WORKPLACE: PROTECTING THE EMPLOYER

## SUMMARY

Employers can be held legally liable for the actions of their staff, even if those actions are done without the employer's approval or permission.

When one considers the damaging ways in which a company's IT systems might be misused by almost any member of staff – to access illegal material, to harass colleagues, to access and circulate confidential information or to commit fraud, to name just a few – it becomes clear that any prudent business should implement policies and staff training to convey precisely what may and may not be done using the company's systems. At the same time, the organisation itself has to stay on the right side of the law relating to privacy, and to ensure that any measures that it puts in place to monitor use by staff are both proportionate and consistent with data protection law.

# 9 IT IN THE WORKPLACE: AVOIDING EMPLOYMENT PROBLEMS

## Nicola Cordell

### INTRODUCTION

This chapter discusses best practice in health and safety and employment law as it applies to an office environment. This is an important topic for IT managers who need to be aware of their responsibilities to the employees they manage. Details regarding the risk assessment of the work environment required under health and safety law, and related regulations that apply in an office environment, are covered in this chapter. It then goes on to explore the requirement under the disability provisions of the Equality Act 2010 to provide reasonable adjustments and best practice dictates consideration of accessibility issues for employees.

### HEALTH AND SAFETY RESPONSIBILITIES

Employers have a duty under the Health and Safety at Work etc. Act 1974 to 'ensure, so far as is reasonably practicable, the health, safety and welfare at work of all his employees'.

Employees, under the same Act,

> have to take reasonable care for the health and safety of himself and of other persons who may be affected by his acts or omissions at work; and as regards any duty or requirement imposed on his employer or any other person by or under any of the relevant statutory provisions, to co-operate with him so far as is necessary to enable that duty or requirement to be performed or complied with.

Related to this Act there are a number of regulations that apply to employers in certain circumstances, and organisations should be aware of their responsibilities.

Why is it important? Health and safety legislation rears its head in relation to all aspects of work, not just those tasks that people consider safety critical. Therefore, having a good knowledge of health and safety law as it pertains to the business and its employees is essential if a business wants to avoid potential prosecution. Prosecutions under the Health and Safety at Work etc. Act 1974 are of a criminal rather than civil nature and proven failure to abide by the legislation can lead to imprisonment or a fine, in addition to the inevitable bad publicity. It also leaves the door open for personal injury claims from past, and in some cases present, employees.

## Management of Health and Safety at Work Regulations 1999

The Management Regulations 1999 are more explicit in informing employers of their responsibilities in managing health and safety. In accordance with the Health and Safety at Work etc. Act 1974, they apply to every work activity whether safety critical or not, including working in an office environment, and require that risks to health that may be associated with work are addressed.

The main requirement is to undertake a risk assessment and, if you have five or more employees, any significant findings are to be recorded and control measures considered to reduce any potential harm to employees from the risks identified.

The HSE five-step approach to risk assessment is:

Step 1: Identify the hazards.

Step 2: Decide who might be harmed and how.

Step 3: Evaluate the risks and decide on precautions.

Step 4: Record your findings and implement them.

Step 5: Review your risk assessment and update if necessary.

Further advice on how to conduct a risk assessment for different work environments can be found at www.hse.gov.uk.

## The Workplace (Health, Safety and Welfare) Regulations 1992

The Workplace Regulations 1992 require certain conditions in the workplace. This includes the following general workplace factors:

- Ventilation by a sufficient quantity of fresh or purified air.
- Temperature that may influence thermal comfort (usually at least 16 degrees Celsius).
- Lighting sufficient to enable people to work without experiencing eye strain (office environment 500 lux with minimal flicker).
- Cleanliness of the environment.
- Appropriate management of waste materials.

When assessing workspaces employers are also expected to consider:

- Room dimensions and space (11 cubic metres per person).
- Floors and traffic routes, considering any slip or trip hazards.
- Windows, doors, escalators and so on.
- Workstation set up with appropriate seating.
- Maintenance of electrical and other types of equipment.

- Sanitary conveniences and washing facilities.
- Drinking water, and places for rest and to eat meals.
- Facilities for changing and accommodation for clothing if there is a requirement to change clothing.

Further advice on environmental factors and assessments can be found at https://www.hse.gov.uk/pUbns/priced/l24.pdf.

## Health and Safety (Display Screen Equipment) Regulations 1992 as amended by the Health and Safety (Miscellaneous Amendments) Regulations 2002

The DSE Regulations define a user or operator as 'employees or self-employed who habitually use DSE for the purposes of an employer's undertaking or as a significant part of their normal work'. Display screen equipment includes screens that display text, numbers or graphics, whether at the work site, offsite or in a home-based office. Where workstations are shared, the assessor will need to ensure the equipment is suitable for all users and in such cases will need equipment that can be adjustable, as it is unlikely the workers will all be the same dimensions.

For all DSE users, there is a requirement for an evaluation of display-screen use to be carried out to assess and reduce risks. An assessment should be repeated if it is no longer considered valid. This would occur in cases where there is a significant change to DSE worker or equipment. Events such as a desk or office move, a change in the health of the employee, a change in the equipment or to assess potential wear and tear of equipment that may no longer be effective at managing risk would require a new assessment.

An assessment should be undertaken by a suitably trained person, which is appropriately recorded and supported by a reporting procedure to deal with any actions required. Having DSE assessors trained within the organisation to undertake DSE assessments can be useful in troubleshooting problems early before they become a significant issue rather than routinely outsourcing these services. Educating users and encouraging them to report issues when they occur should be part of the assessment. More specialist assessments can be undertaken by occupational health professionals where there are significant health problems.

An assessment should consider reducing the following risks:

- Postural problems.
- Visual problems, including informing staff of their rights concerning eye tests and the provision of glasses or contact lenses for DSE use.
- Fatigue and stress, including consideration of software being fit for the tasks required. Varying work activities and ensuring adequate breaks from work and between tasks is advised.

The requirements are in the form of general targets rather than technical specifications:

- Screens should be flicker-free as far as is possible; brightness and contrast should be adjustable. The screen height and angle should also be adjustable allowing operators to avoid glare and to allow a comfortable head posture and to maintain a natural and relaxed position.
- The keyboard should be designed to allow operators to locate and use keys quickly, accurately and without discomfort with space in front to support hands and wrists with wrists not excessively bent. (Some employers offer staff a choice of keyboards such as the Microsoft® ergonomic or 'Cherry' styles.)
- The height of the work surface should allow forearms to be approximately horizontal. If users suffer from back issues, there may be some benefit in a work surface that is height adjustable to allow working from seated and standing positions.
- There should be sufficient space for postural change with no obstacles under the desk.
- Lighting should be appropriate for the tasks performed and reflections and glare reduced to a minimum.
- Background noise should be kept at a level that does not impair normal conversation. Normal conversation is regarded as the ability to hold a conversation up to two metres apart without raising voices.
- Ventilation and humidity should be maintained at levels that prevent discomfort and problems of sore eyes.
- Software must be suitable for the task, easy to use and display information in a format and at a pace that are adapted to users.
- Software must not contain quantitative or qualitative checking facilities of which the user is unaware.
- Seats should have an adjustable back, good lumbar support, adjustable seat height, no excess pressure under the thigh with foot support if needed.

The regulations give users the right to eye tests for display screen work, at the cost of the employer. A user can request a test when they first become a user and at regular intervals afterwards. 'Normal' corrective appliances are at the employee's expense. However, if 'special' corrective appliances are needed specifically for use of display screen work, then the employer is expected to meet the costs of a basic frame and prescribed lenses.

Training is also required by the regulations, which should include the user's responsibilities in using the equipment appropriately and reporting any issues, an explanation of the potential risks and how poor posture and work practice can result in harm due to the static loading on the musculoskeletal system. They should be made aware of the contents of the regulations.

Training should include:

- The importance of comfortable posture and that a user should have frequent breaks/changes of position to help maintain comfort levels.

- The user should understand how to adjust their DSE equipment to suit them and minimise stress and fatigue.
- The user should understand how the set-up of the equipment can facilitate good posture, prevent overreaching of the arms and avoid glare/reflections on the screen.
- The user has a responsibility to ensure that their equipment is regularly cleaned and that it is regularly inspected to pick up any issues that need maintenance.
- The user should be advised of the benefits of breaks and changes of activity and the organisational arrangements by which they can alert management to any issues.

For employees with a disability, there are a variety of different adjustments that can be made to assist them as a DSE user, from ergonomic equipment to Bluetooth headsets and voice activated software. For such cases, it is beneficial to engage an occupational health professional with appropriate experience and training to advise on adjustments.

Further information can be found at https://www.hse.gov.uk/pubns/priced/l26.pdf and https://www.hse.gov.uk/pubns/ck1.pdf.

## Additional health and safety regulations

It is important to at least be aware of the other health and safety regulations that may apply to a workplace depending on the size of the business and the work it undertakes.

### The Health and Safety (First-Aid) Regulations 1981
These regulations require employers to provide 'adequate and appropriate equipment, facilities and personnel to ensure their employees receive immediate attention if they are injured or taken ill at work'. These regulations apply even if an employer has fewer than five employees and to people who are self-employed. Further guidance can be found at https://www.hse.gov.uk/pubns/books/l74.htm.

### Manual Handling Operations Regulations 1992
While many office roles do not have significant manual handling, there may be the need to move equipment, lift boxes of paper, move stock in and out of storage areas and so on. If there is a requirement to lift objects manually, it is important to follow the guidelines for undertaking lifting activities, which can be found at https://www.hse.gov.uk/toolbox/manual.htm.

### Provision and Use of Work Equipment Regulations 1998
The requirement of these regulations is to ensure that equipment is suitable for purpose, maintained to be safe and not a health and safety risk. This covers **any** equipment used by an employee at work, including computer equipment, photocopiers, printers, lifts, motor vehicles and kitchen equipment. In certain circumstances inspection by a competent person is required and a record kept until the next inspection is due.

Further guidance can be found at https://www.hse.gov.uk/pubns/indg291.pdf.

***Reporting of Injuries, Diseases and Dangerous Occurrences Regulations 2013***
There are specific diseases and injuries to workers that are reportable under these regulations. These include deaths, specified injuries to workers and over-seven-day injuries (where an employee is away from work or been unable to perform their normal work duties for more than seven consecutive days) that are work-related. Of note, diseases that may be relevant in the office environment are:

- Severe cramp of the hand or forearm where the person's work involves significant or prolonged periods of repetitive movement of the fingers, hand or arm.
- Tendonitis or tenosynovitis of the hand or forearm where the person's work is physically demanding and involves frequent, repetitive movements.

Further guidance can be found at https://www.hse.gov.uk/pubns/indg453.pdf.

## EMPLOYMENT LAW

There are a number of key points in an employee's time with a business when a good understanding of employment law is important – from recruiting and selection to managing an employee with issues, whether this be conduct/performance or sickness absence, to when they exit the business.

At each stage of this employment journey, you need to understand your role and responsibilities and, where necessary, take advice from HR.

### Recruitment and pre-placement screening

It is important when recruiting new staff that good practice recommendations of the code of practice and other guidance issued by the Equality Commission is followed, that there is no unlawful discrimination and that the best person is selected in terms of qualifications and abilities. To ensure the recruitment process is demonstrated as fair, it is also important that evidence of recruitment against a specific job specification and description is undertaken. A job analysis can help to ensure that the job description and specification are appropriate for the job role.

Processes for pre-shortlisting, shortlisting, interviewing and making or recommending an appointment should be followed in accordance with company policy and each stage appropriately recorded.

Of note, Section 60(1) of the Equality Act 2010 generally prohibits pre-employment health screening (i.e. before a job offer is made). Once a job offer has been made, employment can be conditional with regard to their health as long as it relates to their fitness to undertake the role.

The Act defines some circumstances in which health and disability questions can be legitimately asked prior to a selection interview:

- To establish whether an applicant can take part in an assessment to test their ability to do the job or decide whether any reasonable adjustments need to be made to the assessment process for the applicant.
- To decide whether an applicant can carry out a function that is intrinsic to the job.
- To monitor diversity among applicants.
- To take positive action in relation to disabled people.
- To confirm that a candidate has the disability where having that disability is an occupational requirement of the job.
- If there is another legal requirement that requires an employer to ask health or disability-related questions (e.g. if there is a specific medical standard that applies to the role).

Pre-placement screening can be undertaken after a job offer has been made, and this is usually done to identify any adjustments that may be needed under the Equality Act 2010. This may also be an appropriate time to consider DSE assessments and identify anyone who might need a specialist assessment at the start of the job rather than when they complain of problems.

Further guidance can be found at https://www.cipd.co.uk/knowledge/fundamentals/emp-law/recruitment.

## The Equality Act 2010

The Equality Act 2010 replaced the Disability Discrimination Act 1995, Sex Discrimination Act 1975 and Race Relations Act 1976. It was passed to legally protect people from discrimination in the workplace and also in society and provides protection against direct and indirect discrimination, harassment and victimisation. Further guidance can be found at https://www.gov.uk/guidance/equality-act-2010-guidance.

In summary, under the disability provisions of the Act there is a requirement to make reasonable adjustments in the workplace for anyone who meets the criteria of disabled. A court will consider four specific questions to decide whether an employee meets the criteria of disabled under the Act:

- Is the employee suffering from an impairment – either physical or mental?
- Does the impairment have an adverse effect on their ability to carry out normal day to day activities?
  - Is the effect substantial?
  - Is the effect long term?

There is considerable guidance available to help employers and managers interpret these specific questions, but it can still be difficult and it is often prudent with employees with long-term health conditions to either consider they are covered by the Act or take professional advice from an occupational health professional.

It is often relatively straightforward to assess whether an employee is suffering from an impairment, but the other tests can be more difficult. The definition of normal day-to-day activities is quite wide. Substantial is defined as more than minor or trivial, which can also be difficult to interpret. Long term means 12 months or more, or likely to last for 12 months and the impairment does **not** have to be affecting them every day.

Reasonable adjustments relate to adjustments that are practicable for an organisation to implement given the size of the organisation, how much money and resources are available and the cost of making the changes. The adjustments assist with overcoming the disadvantage of the disability.

In some cases, this may require a change in the way the work is undertaken, which is known as a provision, criteria or practice; however, there is no requirement to establish a new job if the individual is unfit for the key aspects of the current job role.

It is important, when considering disciplinary action for someone who is not performing at work, that underlying health causes are considered and, if there is a possibility of an underlying disability, further advice should be taken prior to disciplinary action being progressed. However, this doesn't mean that, once further advice from an appropriate adviser has been sought, someone with a disability cannot be disciplined for wrongdoing in accordance with usual company policy and procedures once all the facts have been taken into account.

## FURTHER ADVICE

There are a variety of professionals you can engage on a consultancy basis to help you ensure you are meeting your responsibilities and to help avoid employment problems:

> **Human resources professionals** can advise on your policies and procedures to ensure these are fully addressed.
>
> **Health and safety advisers** can support you in undertaking risk assessments to meet the requirements of the Management of Health and Safety at Work Regulations.
>
> **Occupational health professionals** can assist with ergonomics, DSE training and assessments and adjustments for employees with a disability. Safe and effective quality occupational health service (SEQOHS) accredited companies are listed at https://www.seqohs.org/Accreditedunits.aspx.

## SUMMARY

The relationship of employer and employee creates obligations on both sides. For example, there is a mutual duty for both employers and employees to conduct themselves in such a way as to maintain trust and confidence in the employment relationship.

Employers are also subject to onerous obligations under general law, which may expose them not only to direct claims by staff, but also to potential liability under laws relating to health and safety, equality and other matters. IT managers need to be familiar with these rules in order to keep within the law.

The need for sound recruitment practices goes without saying; and although workplace assessments and similar measures are sometimes regarded as an inconvenient nuisance – not least by the employees themselves – these steps are also necessary to protect employee wellbeing. By understanding these risks and obligations, and implementing measures to address them, companies can mitigate the potentially serious consequences of non-compliance, which in the worst instances can involve not only criminal liability and fines but also reputational risks to the business.

# 10 OPEN SOURCE SOFTWARE

## Andrew Katz and Michaela MacDonald

### INTRODUCTION

Open source software is software that is made available under a form of licence that ensures any recipient is free to use, modify and distribute it.

Over the last 30 years, and despite early fears that using open source would expose organisations to vulnerabilities and claims for intellectual property infringement, open source software has become mainstream and now makes up the majority of the software currently being created around the world. It provides the operating system for computers of all sizes, from mobile phones to laptops to games consoles and smart home gadgets, right through to supercomputers. The leading technology platform companies of the moment – Apple, Amazon, Facebook, Google and Microsoft – all make significant use of open source software. The French tax system and Transport for London's Oyster Card system rely on it.

This chapter explains what 'open source software' is, how and why it developed as a business model, and the principal types of open source licence that IT managers are likely to come across.

### WHAT IS OPEN SOURCE?

'Source code' is software's blueprint. A programmer writes **source code** in a computer language, which more-or-less resembles instructions in English, and then uses software tools (compilers and linkers) to generate **object code** from the source. Source code is the form of software created by humans; object code is the form of software run by computers.

However, the distinction is becoming blurred as many modern programming languages (such as JavaScript and Python) run the source code directly, although the version run by the computer has had comments and other attributes helpful to the programmer stripped out. For this reason, it is often better to refer to the source code as 'the preferred form of the code for making modifications'.

Traditional (proprietary) software is supplied solely as object code. For example, a copy of Microsoft Office purchased from Microsoft Corporation will include the object code of Word, Excel and so on, but none of the source code, which is a closely guarded Microsoft secret. The source code is not needed to run the software, but it is (in practice) needed to correct bugs or change the program.

With access to the source code, users can change the software (including changing its functionality, as well as fixing bugs) and more easily examine how it works. In reality, relatively few users have either the desire or the ability to do any of these things, but the very availability of the source code have both commercial and legal consequences, as discussed below.

Source code access is far from the whole story. Each licence of open source software also grants the user other freedoms. As well as access to the source, the user must be able to run and adapt the software for any purpose, to correct bugs and also to pass the software (including any changes to it) to anyone else, under licence terms that confer similar rights, and without that transfer being subject to royalties or any other charge.

Although this chapter generally uses the term 'open source' (a term coined by an organisation called the Open Source Initiative), the freedoms just described are those freedoms that form the philosophy of another (older) organisation, the Free Software Foundation (FSF),[1] which exists to promote **free software**. There are some philosophical differences between the organisations. In a nutshell, the FSF believes non-free software is immoral on the principle that software is a form of knowledge and that knowledge should be common to all mankind, whereas the Open Source Initiative (OSI) (see below) believes that open source is simply a better way of developing software from a technical point of view and takes less of a moral stance. The OSI plays down this distinction. Simon Phipps, who served as a president of the OSI for two terms, often refers to the OSI as 'a marketing program for free software' (meaning that the Open Source Initiative's aims are an alternative way of promoting and supporting free software, as defined by the Free Software Foundation) (Erlang Solutions 2018).

The FSF's four freedoms are:

- The freedom to run the program, for any purpose (freedom 0).
- The freedom to study how the program works, and change it to make it do what you wish (freedom 1). Access to the source code is a precondition for this.
- The freedom to redistribute copies so you can help your neighbour (freedom 2).
- The freedom to distribute copies of your modified versions to others (freedom 3). By doing this you can give the whole community a chance to benefit from your changes. Access to the source code is a precondition for this.

The OSI has developed its own more descriptive criteria, which can be found in The Open Source Definition (Open Source Initiative 2007).

The OSI was established some years after the formation of the FSF, with a view to making free software more business friendly. The restrictive rights of use in traditional contracts and associated licence fees are often perceived, from an enterprise computing perspective, as major obstacles to exploitation, innovation and growth (MacDonald 2014).

In practice, the respective definitions of **open source** and **free software** have very similar effects and, although they can generate lively debate, the differences rarely cause a problem from a legal or business point of view.

---

1 https://www.fsf.org/.

The word 'free' in 'free software' relates to 'freedom', as in the freedoms described above, as opposed to 'zero-price' – think 'free speech' rather than 'free beer'. (As it happens, free software is frequently zero-price as well, but this is not an essential feature of the concept.) The terms 'FOSS' (free and open source software) and 'FLOSS' (free, libre and open source software) are also occasionally used in order to avoid alignment with either the open source or free software camps.

These freedoms (whether FSF or OSI) are guaranteed through the legal mechanism of licensing.

## The legal context

Computer software is protected in the UK mainly by the law of copyright (see Chapter 4). In addition, it can attract protection of other intellectual property rights, such as patents or trade secrets. Open source software is no different from proprietary software in this regard. Use and reproduction of software without a licence is generally an infringement of copyright, and open source licences, in common with proprietary software licences, grant certain permissions to use the software so that, by complying with the conditions attached to those permissions, the user is no longer in breach of copyright. In the case of free and open source software, those permissions are much broader than the permissions granted by proprietary software licences.

### Open source licences

The two most common categories of open source licence are **permissive** licences (which allow the code to be released under different licence terms, including a proprietary licence, and do not require provision of the source code) and **copyleft** licences (which require that the source code and any modifications are made available to the recipient of the object code, and under the same licence terms). We explore these two types of licences in more detail later.

Table 10.1 compares typical open source licences with typical proprietary software licences.

**Table 10.1 Comparison of typical open source licences with typical proprietary software licences**

| Issue | Free/open source | Proprietary software licence |
| --- | --- | --- |
| Payment required for exercise of licence rights | No | Yes (usually) |
| Software can be used for any purpose | Yes (note: cannot be restricted to non-commercial use, for example) | Licences frequently prohibit use for certain purposes (e.g. creating a competing product, use in safety-critical circumstances, use for outsourcing to another business), or restrict use to specific activities (e.g. to academic use only) |

*(Continued)*

## Table 10.1 (Continued)

| Issue | Free/open source | Proprietary software licence |
| --- | --- | --- |
| Access to source code | Yes | No (although possibly through an escrow arrangement, or a shared source licence) |
| Reverse engineering/decompiling | Permitted (although decompiling is not necessary, as the source code is available) | Usually prohibited (to the extent that prohibition is permitted by law) |
| Assignment | Permitted without restriction | Usually restricted (to the extent that restriction is permitted by law) |
| Sub-licensing | May be restricted, because sub-licensing is not normally necessary | Usually prohibited |
| Number of users | No restriction | Usually restricted (although may be a site licence, or an enterprise-wide licence) |
| Territory/location | Usually worldwide (although, with some licences, may be restricted to certain jurisdictions if there are patent concerns) | Usually limited to specific territories. May be limited to a specific location, or even licensed for use only on a specific central processing unit (CPU) |
| Right to copy/to take backups | Unrestricted | May be restricted to the extent permitted by law (perhaps to a certain number of copies) |
| Perpetual | Yes (may be subject to termination for breach) | May be restricted in duration, or automatically renewable (will be subject to termination for breach) |
| Contractual licence | Not usually* | Yes (i.e. places contractual obligations, such as the obligation to pay licence fees, on the licensee) |
| Modification | Permitted | Generally prohibited (subject to some limited rights in the Copyright, Designs and Patents Act 1988) |

(Continued)

**Table 10.1 (Continued)**

| Issue | Free/open source | Proprietary software licence |
|---|---|---|
| Redistribution | Unrestricted (but may be subject to conditions on retaining notices, and (for copyleft) retaining the same licence terms making the source code available) | Generally prohibited (subject to the right to redistribute the original copy placed into circulation with the consent of the right holder) |

\* This is quite a subtle legal distinction specific to common law. A 'bare licence' is a licence that defines the parameters within which you may deal with a copyright work. If you deal with it outside those parameters, you are in breach of copyright: it's as if the licence did not exist at all. A contract is a two-way agreement where two parties have rights (e.g. to use the software) and obligations (to pay a fee, in the case of a typical proprietary software licence). The distinction can be significant from a legal perspective, as courts will have different remedies available, depending on whether the issue relates to a bare licence or a contract. The situation is complicated because civil law (most European jurisdictions) does not recognise this distinction between bare licences and contracts.

## Choice of open source licence

Open source software authors choose to release their code under one or more open source/free software licences. The choice of licence will depend on whether:

- The software is dependent on or combined with other open source software released under a particular licence.
- The software is intended to be part of, or be used in conjunction with, a project that traditionally uses a particular licence.
- The author wants to restrict the code from being incorporated in a non-free project (this is allowed by permissive licences).
- There are software patent concerns.
- The author wants to maximise the number of potential licensees (licensees may be inhibited by copyleft licences).
- The author wishes to use a particular licence because potential licensees are likely to be familiar with it or it is perceived to be more business friendly or community friendly (as the case may be).
- There are specific issues that the author wishes addressed (e.g. whether the software can be amended and used as part of a software as a service offering, without the source code being made available).

## BENEFITS AND RISKS OF OPEN SOURCE SOFTWARE

**Benefits**

- Providing quality software and software-based services.
- Reducing vendor lock-in.
- Reducing the likelihood of security issues.
- Reducing development time.
- Granting access to developer communities.
- Aiding the attraction and retention of quality staff.

**Risks**

- Open source code is not necessarily high quality.
- Open source licensing is complex, and compliance with the licensing terms needs careful consideration, documentation and following of processes.
- Incorrect deployment and distribution of open source software can lead to breaches of intellectual property rights, which, if they can be remedied at all, may only be remediable by the release of your trade secrets, including source code.
- It can be difficult to find warranty cover for open source code and its performance.

Sometimes, the same open source software is made available under more than one licence simultaneously (dual licensing), and the licensee can choose which of the dual licences to adopt. This issue is explored later in 'Dual licensing models' section.

Note also that a licence that restricts the licensee from making commercial use of the software, or for charging for services supplied in connection with it, cannot, by definition, be a free software or open source licence. Much open source software is written and used (and exploited for profit) for commercial purposes, so it is important not to confuse free and open source software with 'trialware' or 'freeware'. When referring to software that is not free or open source software, the preferred terms are 'non-free' or 'proprietary', but not 'commercial'.

The text of such a licence determines whether particular software can be used for commercial purposes or not.

## OPEN SOURCE AND COMMUNITIES

The open source licensing model, together with free software development tools (in both senses of the word 'free') and the existence of the internet to facilitate communication, have led to the emergence of communities of developers and users around certain software projects. This phenomenon (contrasted with the proprietary development model) was explored by Eric S. Raymond in his influential 1997 paper 'The cathedral and the bazaar' (Raymond 2018).

Theoretically, the Bazaar model works like this: when a programmer writes a piece of code to solve a specific problem, they make it publicly available so that other programmers with a similar problem can find the code and adopt it. They in turn adapt it to their needs, correcting bugs and adding features. As they do this, they feed the changes back to the project (which is typically hosted on a service such as GitHub). The internet (usually through a website or mailing list) enables the contributors to discuss with each other the requirements of the software, what the bugs are, which features need adding and in what priority, and so on. This Bazaar model is contrasted with the Cathedral model, in which remote programmers develop and hand down code as if they are high priests endowed with some arcane and sacred knowledge.

The relationship has been described as one of pure meritocracy: the only criterion for code's inclusion into the project is whether it is effective and of suitably high quality. The idea is that those submitting the most and highest quality code become more respected in the project discussions, and greater weight is given to their contribution in any debate. All the contributors are also aware of the possibility of 'forking', which means that anyone within the project community (or even outside it) can take all of the code and use it as the basis of their own competing project. In practice, this rarely happens (and if it does happen, it is unlikely that both branches of the fork will thrive).

This development model sounds utopian, but has in fact been shown to work (reasonably[2]) effectively. The classic example is the development of Linux itself (more diplomatically, and accurately, called GNU/Linux), which was started by Finnish student Linus Torvalds as a project to develop an operating system kernel (for the complete story, see Moody 2002). It has led to the complete Linux operating system that now competes head-to-head with Microsoft's suite of operating systems (among others) and is used to power Amazon, Google, Facebook and every one of the world's 500 most powerful supercomputers, as well as devices such as satnavs and mobile phones.

This model contrasts with traditional software development methodology (sometimes called 'waterfall') that involves a hierarchical top-down approach, whereby requirements are determined and increasingly abstracted until they reach the level of code. This approach to engineering is in turn reflected in the management model, with the coders working under line managers, working under project managers and so on.

Unfortunately, as effective as the Bazaar model has been, it is by no means universal, and gives the misleading impression that open source code is largely written by loosely

---

2  Projects are becoming increasingly aware that issues such as discrimination and harassment have emerged and need to be addressed. One initiative is the contributor covenant: https://www.contributor-covenant.org.

knit groups of students and hackers who do it for the love of coding and the kudos, but without payment. There are, equally, many open source projects that have been closely controlled, or developed, by commercial organisations, and the programmers working on those projects are paid a wage for the job – and are just as likely to work in a sleek modern office as they are in their bedroom. For example, Open Office (now an Apache Foundation project) was a development project of Sun Microsystems, before Sun was acquired by Oracle. Firefox was originally spun out of Netscape in a similar way, and MySQL (also acquired by Oracle through the Sun acquisition) was developed through a professional software development process.

Corporates such as IBM, which are heavily involved in open source, have modified their project management arrangements so that both open source and proprietary projects more closely approximate the classic open source development model, both because it has been shown to work and because it is more likely to attract external contributors. When the methodology is used on proprietary code, it is typically called 'inner source', and is frequently employed as a stepping-stone to releasing the code in question as open source.

Much open source code is developed using public repositories hosted on online services such as GitHub. As a result, the identity of the author and their contributions can be accessed by anyone, including potential employers. Open source programmers frequently refer to their contribution history in their résumés.

From a purely legal perspective, the way that open source is developed raises a number of questions, mainly with regard to liability and code ownership. We deal with these issues later in the chapter, but first, we need to put open source code in a commercial context.

## OPEN SOURCE SOFTWARE BUSINESS MODELS

Companies such as IBM spend vast sums on the coders, testers, documentation authors and other contributors who work on their open source projects. The open source code they write will become available to their competitors. In late 2018, Microsoft purchased GitHub for $7.5 billion (Microsoft News Center 2018), suggesting that there is huge value in the communities that coalesce around code, as opposed to, potentially, the code itself.

There remains the question why a supplier would offer to provide its software on an open source basis (thus foregoing licence income) rather than making it available on a more traditional per-seat licensed basis.

Of course, it may be the case that the supplier has no choice: if a project has to be based on code such as GNU/Linux, which is licensed under a copyleft licence (GPLv2), then the supplier will have no choice but to distribute that project under the same GPLv2 licence, and grant the customer the rights to copy and redistribute the software without limitation. Red Hat, for example, which provides versions of Linux, is a highly successful multi-billion dollar business (Red Hat 2019), which makes all of its revenue by selling services around Linux as opposed to charging for licences of Linux itself.

However, even where the underlying software can in theory be redistributed under a proprietary licence (either because it has been developed in-house, or because it is based on open source software – such as Apache, which is licensed under a permissive licence that does not restrict proprietary relicensing), there may still be good reasons to make the software available under an open source licence.

Typically, licence fees make up a relatively small proportion of the costs of a software project. A (proprietary) software project often involves a large number of activities, including initial requirements definition, functional and technical specification, integration planning, integration, custom programming, configuration, user interface design, staff training, change management, data migration and validation, testing, documentation creation, compliance checking, ongoing maintenance, hosting, connectivity costs and support. All of those elements have to be paid for, in addition to any licence fees.

Those same elements will also exist in an equivalent open source project, with the exception of licence fees. For a large project, the initial licence fees may amount to 20 per cent of the project, so the supplier will still generate 80 per cent of the revenue of the proprietary provider (and will not have to pass back any licence fees to upstream licensors).

Financially, then, the difference between proprietary and open source software is not as great as may first appear.

From an engineering perspective, there are further positive advantages to the open source model. The first is that active participation in (or establishment of) an open source community is likely to lead to greater participation by other people from outside the company, which generates a virtuous circle of increasing quality and functionality in the code, and an increased market share. It also gives the organisation that is actively involved a greater say in the future development path of the software, which will be an advantage when selling the ancillary services to customers (they will more likely buy support services from a company that was engaged in the development project in the first place). The community also creates a pool of potential high-quality and pre-screened recruits.

The second is that the community model essentially allows a company to participate in shared research and development with other companies without any formal collaboration agreement being in place. This works as follows: where a piece of software is providing what is really a commodity service, it becomes difficult to differentiate it from similar pieces of software supplied by other providers. This commoditisation has arguably happened in relation to web servers and relational databases, for example, so there is little point in a company developing a web server from scratch (with all of the developer effort that entails) when there is little likelihood of being able to effectively differentiate it from similar programs in the marketplace. It makes more sense for the company to become part of an existing open source project (such as Apache), to apply a relatively small amount of development effort (and take advantage of the development effort applied by others) and to deploy its programming resource in areas where it can differentiate (and therefore charge a premium). Such areas may include providing customisations for clients, or even providing proprietary extensions to the underlying code (although this latter option, called 'open core', is criticised for being anathema to free software, and, to a slightly lesser extent, open source).

**CASE STUDY: GENIVI ALLIANCE**

GENIVI (https://www.genivi.org/) is a both a collaborative open source project and a standards body driving the adoption of open source in the automotive industry. The 'headunit' is typically the most complex component in a modern vehicle – approximately 70 per cent of the total code in a vehicle can be found in that single device. It provides 'infotainment' services in the vehicle, such as entertainment (radio, including FM and DAB, digital music and video), in-car information (navigation, climate control, car performance information), digitally connected services such as local information, and telephony integration.

The members of the GENIVI alliance recognised that they all needed infotainment systems for their vehicles, but that the vast majority of the coding required for producing the system did not differentiate them from their competitors. The differentiation occurs in the user experience (the user interface: screen display, controls, etc.), so by collaborating with their competitors on the non-differentiating portions of the offering, the benefits of pooled development outweighed the disadvantages of assisting their competitors. (This would not be the case if they collaborated on the user experience, which is why the user interface is not covered by GENIVI.)

Previously, suppliers would develop complete solutions, competing at every level in the architecture to deliver relatively low-volume bespoke devices with a matching price tag, or purchase a more-or-less complete solution from an external supplier.

Currently, more than 140 automakers and their suppliers benefit from a community-based development model, which allows competitors to collaborate around a shared platform without compromising their key differentiator. This ecosystem enables the creation of multiple differentiated products on the basis of a common middleware core.

## BUSINESSES AS CUSTOMERS OF OPEN SOURCE

### Open source and the cloud

Businesses are increasingly customers for cloud applications as opposed to buying software for traditional on-premise software deployment. Although cloud applications typically make extensive use of open source code, the legal implications are quite different.

The wider aspects of cloud computing are covered in Chapter 2. The essence of cloud computing is that the software is running on someone else's computer, and the customer subscribes to access the functionality of the code, rather than running a copy of the code itself.

Cloud applications include services such as Salesforce (customer relationship management), Xero (accounting), and word processing, spreadsheet and other office applications from service providers such as Google Docs and Microsoft 365 (formerly Office 365). These services either run from data centres operated by the service providers (in the case of Microsoft or Google, for example), or they may themselves run on cloud platforms provided by other third-party cloud service providers.

Some of the most well-known cloud services, such as Amazon EC2 and Google Compute Engine, were built on open source software. The most popular cloud management platform is OpenStack, an open source solution.

Because customers for cloud services are accessing the **functionality** of the software, rather than running the software themselves, software in the cloud environment is no longer 'distributed' (distribution here refers to the legal concept of transferring the object code to a user's device or under the user's control), but merely run on the cloud service provider's server. That server makes the functionality of the software available to the customer through a browser or app on the customer's computer or device.

The more onerous clauses of most open source licences (such as those in copyleft licences requiring the source code of the software to be made available) apply when the act of distribution takes place. In contrast, the acts of using, running or making the functionality of the code available do not trigger those clauses. The consequence of this is that cloud service providers can use open source and provide access to its functionality through the cloud for a fee, without being required to disclose the source code of the software, even if heavily modified. While this may be legal within the strict terms of the copyleft licence itself (such as the General Public License (GPL), which Google uses exactly in this way to make available the functionality of a highly modified version of the Linux kernel for its core search services), it is regarded as being a loophole and, by some, against the spirit of open source.

As a response, the FSF introduced a licence – GNU Affero GPL (AGPL). AGPL redefines what a distribution is by expressly stating that interaction over a computer network amounts (in certain circumstances) to a distribution and therefore triggers the copyleft effect. (Affero GPL is not the only licence with this attribute; others are the Open Software Licence and the Honest Public Licence.) Table 10.2 gives a summary comparison of the effects of typical licences.

An added complication for the cloud service provider is that many cloud services, while running most of the service on servers, do, in practice, distribute some portions of the software to run on the customer's computer – this will typically be relatively small portions of code, or scripts, which are sent to the customer's computer and will be run by the customer's computer in their browser. These components are being distributed, and the cloud service provider will therefore have to comply with the terms of the applicable licences that cover obligations on distribution.

### Open source and software deployed on-premise

For the customer, open source deployed on-premise looks very attractive. The up-front costs are likely to be less than for a proprietary system with equivalent functionality because there are no licence fees. More importantly, there are no ongoing licence compliance costs, because there is no restriction on the number of computers on which the software can be installed or the number of users who can access it. There is no need

**Table 10.2** Summary of the key provisions of popular open source software licences

| Licence | Copyleft (strong/weak/none) | Comments (restrictions, obligations) | Patent-related clauses | Trade mark-related clauses | Commercial use allowed |
|---|---|---|---|---|---|
| Apache License 2.0 | None | Distribution of unmodified, modified or aggregated work is permitted; code can be used in works licensed under proprietary licences | Express patent licence, patent retaliation provision | Apache trademark is not licensed, distributed modifications cannot be called 'Apache' | Yes |
| New and simplified Berkeley Software Distribution (BSD) licenses | None | Conditions for distribution of unmodified and modified works: affixation of copyright notice and related liability disclaimer (source code and binary code); code can be used in works licensed under proprietary licences | n/a | Use of trademarks – names only with permission | Yes |
| GNU General Public Licenses (GPL) | Strong | Copyleft effect covers the work, modifications and derivatives including (usually) linked modules. Breach results in termination, although third parties downstream will be unaffected | 'Liberty or death' clause preventing distribution of software if licensor cannot pass patent (and other) rights to its licensees | n/a | Yes |

*(Continued)*

Table 10.2 (Continued)

| Licence | Copyleft (strong/ weak/none) | Comments (restrictions, obligations) | Patent-related clauses | Trade mark-related clauses | Commercial use allowed |
|---|---|---|---|---|---|
| GNU Library or 'Lesser' General Public License (LGPL) | Weak | Copyleft effect covers the work, modifications and derivatives excluding linked modules, provided that the licensee is given information to enable relinking with the LGPL-covered module. Reverse engineering must be permitted to allow this. Failure to follow licence terms results in revocation of licence, although downstream third parties will be unaffected | 'Liberty or death' clause preventing distribution of software if licensor cannot pass patent (and other) rights to its licensees | n/a | Yes |
| Massachusetts Institute of Technology (MIT) license | None | Simple licence with virtually no restrictions, the only condition: affixation of copyright notice and contract and tort disclaimer; code can be used in works licensed under a proprietary licence | n/a | n/a | Yes |
| Mozilla Public License 2.0 (MPL) | Weak | Distribution of unmodified, modified or aggregated work is permitted, code can be used for non-commercial purposes subject to conditions: source code is published for a period of one year, or six months, from the time the executable version was made available, affixation of copyright notice; and licensed under a proprietary licence subject to conditions: this licence must include the source code for any MPL aspects, for a limited time; allows use of other licences such as GPL | Express patent licence, obligation to inform downstream users about any known third-party intellectual property (IP) rights in the program, patent retaliation provision | Trade marks are not licensed along with the software | Yes |

(Continued)

Table 10.2 (Continued)

| Licence | Copyleft (strong/weak/none) | Comments (restrictions, obligations) | Patent-related clauses | Trade mark-related clauses | Commercial use allowed |
|---|---|---|---|---|---|
| Common Development and Distribution License (CDDL) | Weak | Distribution of unmodified, modified or aggregated work is permitted, code can be used for non-commercial purposes subject to conditions: source code has to be distributed with each unmodified or modified work, affixation of copyright notice and disclaimer; and licensed under a proprietary licence subject to conditions: this licence must include the source code for any CDDL aspects; incompatible with GPL | Express patent licence, patent retaliation provision | Trade marks are not licensed along with the software | Yes |
| Eclipse Public License 2.0 | Weak | Distribution of unmodified, modified or aggregated work is permitted, code can be used in works licensed under a proprietary licence subject to conditions: source code has to be distributed with unmodified or modified work or it must be stated where it can be obtained, affixation of copyright notice and disclaimer. GPL compatibility clause | Express patent licence, patent retaliation provision | Not specifically | Yes |
| Unlicense | None | Distribution of unmodified, modified or aggregated work is permitted; code can be used in works licensed under proprietary licences | n/a | n/a | Yes |

(Continued)

Table 10.2 (Continued)

| Licence | Copyleft (strong/weak/none) | Comments (restrictions, obligations) | Patent-related clauses | Trade mark-related clauses | Commercial use allowed |
|---|---|---|---|---|---|
| Artistic license 2.0 | Weak | Associated with the Perl programming language. Distribution of unmodified, modified or aggregated work is permitted, code can be used in works licensed under a proprietary licence subject to conditions: modified versions must be released under the Artistic licence or a free software licence which meets certain conditions (which GPL meets) | Express patent licence | Trade mark rights are not licensed along with the software | Yes |
| Open Software License | Weak | A permissive variant of the Academic Free License. It has a similar effect to the Apache 2.0 license | Express patent licence, patent retaliation provision | Trade mark rights are not licensed along with the software | Yes |
| GNU General Public License version 3.0 (GPLv3) | Strong | Copyleft effect covers the work, modifications and derivatives including (usually) linked modules. Breach (subject to a cure period) results in termination, although third parties downstream will be unaffected. Allows use with Affero GNU v3 licensed-works; contains anti-tivoization clause | Liberty or death' clause preventing distribution of software if licensor cannot pass patent (and other) rights to its licensees. Express patent licence, knowing reliance | May be restricted by way of an 'additional permission' | Yes |

*(Continued)*

Table 10.2 (Continued)

| Licence | Copyleft (strong/ weak/none) | Comments (restrictions, obligations) | Patent-related clauses | Trade mark-related clauses | Commercial use allowed |
|---|---|---|---|---|---|
| | | | 'provision, anti-discriminatory patent licence provisions, patent retaliation provision | | |
| GNU Lesser General Public License version 3.0 (LGPLv3) | Weak | Copyleft effect covers the work, modifications and derivatives excluding linked modules, provided that the licensee is given information to enable relinking with the LGPL-covered module. Reverse engineering must be permitted to allow this. Failure to follow licence terms results in revocation of licence, although downstream third parties will be unaffected | Drafted as an additional permission to GPLv3 | May be restricted by way of an 'additional permission' | Yes |
| Creative Commons Licenses | Varies | Used mainly for content, and not software. Varies from strong (SA) to permissive (BY and CC0). NC (noncommercial) and ND (no derivatives) variants are not open source (status of others is unclear, but clause excluding a patent licence may bring them outside the definition of Open Source). CC0 attempts to relinquish all copyrights, equivalent to public domain | n/a | n/a | Yes, except for NC variants |

to audit usage and there will be fewer issues with corporate transactions. For example, a restructuring will not require consent to assign the licences (although if the customer has made modifications to the software, or combined software under incompatible open source licences, some care still needs to be taken when transferring the software between different group members).

Open source software by its nature tends to be modular, and to adhere to standards. This is mainly because there is rarely any advantage in an open source project working outside the standards system, whereas proprietary software companies have a vested interest in trying to lock customers in. An advantage for the customer is that it is relatively easy to remove one open source component and replace it with another adhering to the same standards.

**PRACTICAL DIFFERENCES BETWEEN OPEN SOURCE AND PROPRIETARY CODE FOR THE BUSINESS CUSTOMER**

- Since the customer of an open source solution will have access to the source code, it is likely that they will more easily be able to find an alternative provider for services around the software, thus reducing lock-in.

- Some proprietary software contains logic bombs to impair the software's functionality if triggered, to force users to pay maintenance or licence fees. Open source code is extremely unlikely to contain any such logic bombs or other 'malware' such as viruses. The source code is freely available and published, so anyone seeking to disrupt an open source project in this way would be very quickly found out and ostracised, and removing the offending code would be a trivial job for a competent programmer.

- Open source code is unlikely to contain any arbitrary hard-coded limitations. Proprietary software frequently contains such hard-coded limits (e.g. the maximum size of a mailbox a mail server can handle, or the maximum size of a disk that a formatting program can format using a specific file system). These limits are frequently imposed to encourage the user to pay for an upgrade for a higher specified version, but are pointless in open source. First, the higher specified version would itself be open source, and, second, programmers with access to the source code can easily remove the limitations.

For more information on procuring open source software for use on-premise, see 'Procuring on-premise open source' section.

From a legal point of view, the warranties of performance and compliance with specification that apply to an open source contract should in theory be no different from those that would apply to a contract for proprietary software. However, this does need to be considered in context (see 'Procuring on-premise open source' section). There are also some special considerations relating to intellectual property that we consider later.

Note that if, as a customer, you are purely consuming open source software (and do not intend to distribute it yourself), the legal issues are relatively straightforward. If, on the other hand, you are using open source software in products that you distribute to others (usually your own customers, but it could include self-employed subcontractors, or even, in certain circumstances, group companies), then you are, in effect, behaving like a software company, and the legal situation is more complex. The next section summarises the effect of open source on modern software development, but a detailed analysis of open source software as it applies to software companies is beyond the scope of this book.

## Modern software development

Software development projects increasingly involve integrating, configuring and, occasionally, modifying components from different sources, as opposed to writing code from scratch. There is a vast quantity of open source components available from repositories such as GitHub and SourceForge. Professional programmers are aware of these open source repositories, and will be keen to use pre-existing code from them where possible to save time and effort. This means that almost all software development projects are likely to contain open source components, and will therefore have some of the characteristics of open source projects (regardless, in many cases, of whether the programmer's employer intends it or not). Hence, the importance for software development companies to have an open source policy (see 'Open source compliance policies and procedures' section).

A closer look at software released under proprietary licences will reveal it most likely contains code that was originally open source code, acquired by the developer under a permissive licence.

## OPEN SOURCE LICENSING IN GREATER DEPTH

The specific details of the various kinds of open source licensing are less important for organisations that merely consume software than for companies that develop and distribute it. Free and open source software is primarily about granting rights to users, so there should be no direct compliance issues unless the organisation starts modifying the code or distributing it to third parties. However, distribution between companies in a group **may** trigger compliance obligations, as may making the functionality of the software available to third parties though a web interface, for example. This is examined below.

There are hundreds of different forms of open source licence (and unwise software developers sometimes attempt to write their own licences as well), but a vast majority of open source projects provide code that is available under the top 10 licences. The licences vary in their length and what they are trying to achieve, from the incredibly short 'You can do whatever you like with this software',[3] to the GNU GPL version 3, which, as well as being a software licence, has also been described as a call to arms and a manifesto – because it contains clauses designed to ensure that any software using it, or derived from software using it, remains free software. It also aims to prevent

---

3   This is a paraphrase of the text of the licence colloquially known as the 'WTF Public License', the less family-friendly name and definitive text of which can be found at: https://www.wtfpl.net.

companies from leveraging software patents for their own benefit, without extending the same benefit to recipients of the code down the line.

As noted above, open source software licences can be divided into two broad camps: permissive (sometimes called academic) and copyleft.

Permissive licences may be very short and grant broad freedoms, including the freedom to incorporate the code into just about any other project, including a proprietary project.

Copyleft licences are more restrictive, and use the mechanism of copyright to limit the extent to which the code can be incorporated into other projects, especially proprietary ones. The copyleft licences cause most complexity from a legal point of view.

**Permissive licences**

Two common and very similar permissive licences are MIT (named after the Massachusetts Institute of Technology) and BSD (Berkeley Software Distribution, named after the University of California at Berkeley); hence, they are sometimes described as 'academic'. The text of these licences can be found by clicking their names at https://opensource.org/licenses/alphabetical.

Compliance with permissive licences is straightforward. It usually requires accompanying the software, when you distribute it, with a liability disclaimer and copyright notice (these will usually appear in its documentation). It does not require the grant of access to the source code, or the distribution of the code under the same (or another specified) licence, which is why permissively licensed code can be incorporated into proprietary software.

From a copyright perspective, there is a little to be concerned about. However, as the terms of the permissive licences do not require the supplier to provide the customer with source code, businesses should ensure that any contract they sign includes some alternative means of accessing the source code should this be required in the future. (If it is a well-known package, such as the FreeBSD operating system, the source code should reliably be available from elsewhere.)

**Copyleft licences**

Copyleft licences, paradoxically, are intended to guarantee freedom by imposing restrictions. They usually require that if copyleft code is modified and distributed, then the distribution takes place under the same copyleft licence terms, and the source code is made available to the recipient. The idea is that once software has been released as free software, it cannot then pass into proprietary software. This principle was most famously established by Richard Stallman, founder of the Free Software Foundation, in the GNU GPL, which has now reached version 3. Version 3 is gaining ground, but version 2, released in 1991, is still the most commonly applied copyleft licence (it governs the Linux kernel, for example). They are known as GPL3 and GPL2 respectively, and their text can be found at https://www.gnu.org/licenses/licenses.html.

This chapter is not the place for a detailed discussion of licence terms (see Table 10.2 listing some of the characteristics of the more common open source licences). However, the intention is that if a program is distributed under a version of the GPL, and that program is then modified or parts of it are used in another program, then that other program itself can only be distributed under the GPL. From a legal perspective (and there is some debate about this), if a derivative work of a GPL work is created, it may only be distributed under the same version of the GPL (unless the version of the GPL attached to the program explicitly says that any later version may apply).

English law, unlike US law, has no formal definition of 'derivative work', and there has been debate over the extent to which one program released under the GPL has to be incorporated into another so as to require that the latter program can only be released under the GPL.

This is the derivation of the so-called 'viral' or 'cancerous' nature of the GPL (or, if you are less polemical, its 'reciprocal' nature, also sometimes referred to as 'sharealike'). The GPL (like most open source licences) has no jurisdiction clause, so its interpretation may vary significantly according to the local law of the jurisdiction in which it is tested.

There are a number of licences that contain copyleft provisions to a greater or lesser extent. Some of them, like the various versions of GPL and the Open Software Licence, are called 'strong copyleft'. This is because the copyleft provisions apply irrespective of (a) whether the changes are made to the original file and (b) whether they are incorporated in any way into another project. 'Weak copyleft' licences, such as the Mozilla Public License, only apply the copyleft rule in relation to specific files: if parts of the work are extracted and used in different files, the copyleft obligation no longer applies. Simon Phipps helpfully uses the distinction 'file-scoped copyleft' for licences like the Mozilla Public License, and 'project-scoped' for licences like GPL.

## Licence compatibility

Unfortunately, copyleft licences (and especially strong copyleft licences) are rarely compatible with each other. In other words, code released under a specific copyleft licence (e.g. GPL2) cannot be combined into the same project as copyleft code under another licence (e.g. Open Software Licence) and distributed. This is because each licence will require that the resulting project, once distributed, has to be released under that same licence, to the exclusion of the other licence. However, it is becoming more common for copyleft licences to allow relicensing under another copyleft licence in certain circumstances. The Mozilla Public License is an example of this, which allows relicensing under GPL provided specific conditions are met.

One practical effect of licence incompatibility is that it reduces the ability to combine open source projects that may, technically, be highly complementary. This is the reason why some open source projects are released under a number of different open source licences: see 'Dual licensing models' section.

By contrast, permissive licences do not insist that the code released under them is distributed under the same licence, so there is no problem with taking MIT code, for example, and incorporating it into a GPL project, which would then have to be released under the GPL as a whole.

Licence compatibility is a major issue for software companies, but customers need to be aware of it as well. Companies such as Synopsis and Revenera provide tools that can be used to scan code, identify applicable licences and assist in determining whether compatibilities exist. There are also open source projects such as the Linux Foundation's SPDX, FOSSology, Quartermaster and Eclipse Software 360 that are working on automated processes to make licence compliance easier.

In a situation where code derived from material released under incompatible licences is distributed, then the distributor will be in breach of copyright in respect of at least one of the licences.

## Dual licensing models

If a copyright owner chooses to release software under any non-exclusive licence (all open source licences are non-exclusive), there is nothing preventing the same software from being simultaneously released under any number of other non-exclusive licences. Some companies, such as Oracle in relation to MySQL, exploit this ability. When a user chooses to use Oracle's MySQL database software under the GPL, or wishes to create an amended version of the MySQL code and distribute it, they have two options. They can either release the source code to the amended version, as required by the GPL, or pay Oracle a fee and take a proprietary licence of the code that permits the release of amended object code, without being required also to release the corresponding source.

Sometimes, software is made available under different open source licences simultaneously. This can be to assist with licence compatibility (see previous section), or simply as a convenience to customers, who may be more familiar with the terms of one licence than another and so perceive that there will be fewer legal headaches in agreeing to the licence terms that they already know.

## PROCURING ON-PREMISE OPEN SOURCE

As a customer, negotiating a contract for an open source project is little different from negotiating a proprietary software project. The provisions relating to ancillary services surrounding the core development work (such as integration, training, migration and support) will, from a legal perspective, be the same. Under a traditional software development methodology, taking a top-down approach, a great deal of effort is employed defining the needs, requirements and specifications, and that is then tightly circumscribed before any coding commences. Any changes from specification will be subject to a rigid change control procedure, and additional cost.

In contrast, open source development projects tend to be informed by an Agile development methodology and as a result the whole project may be less rigid and structured, and the requirements document less specific. The first stage of a project is frequently to rough out specifications, then generate a prototype, which is refined through constant involvement with the client until, eventually, the project has reached a stage where both parties are happy with it. Agile methodologies are discussed in more detail in Chapter 11.

There are advantages and disadvantages to this approach: the obvious disadvantage, to a lawyer, is the lack of legal and contractual certainty about outcomes at the point that the development work begins. If there was no initial specification, and the project fails to fulfil the client's requirements, how can the client demonstrate to a judge that the supplier has failed? This equally causes issues for the supplier if it is looking for payment from an unsatisfied client.

The advantage to both parties is that, if they can establish an effective working partnership, the project can progress in a freer and less formal manner, with quick decision-making and constant refinement of the prototype until a release version of the product is completed.

The contract itself may well be significantly shorter where the Agile methodology is employed. There may, however, be greater emphasis on process and procedure than the specification of the software. The customer's lawyers will find it more difficult to draft clauses that manage risks in this more collaborative approach to development, and there is no substitute for doing adequate due diligence on the supplier. This will typically involve taking detailed references from previous customers, and asking them pertinent questions about the development process. If possible, the customer should test the supplier by engaging them on a relatively small, non-business-critical project before moving to more significant work. Crucially, the parties will need to ensure that sufficient customer staff time is allocated to working with the supplier, that the customer's staff have sufficient authority to make decisions and that they are sufficiently aware of the business needs to be fulfilled by the project. See Chapter 11 for more information.

In any case where software is acquired, whether open source or proprietary, there is always the danger that the supplier does not have the right to license the software to the customer (possibly because the supplier has inadvertently incorporated some code that it wasn't entitled to, or because a rogue coder incorporated some code that was unlicensed).

These issues can, in extremis, cause the recipient of the code to be infringing (and possibly lose the customer the right to use the software at all, with potentially catastrophic business consequences), which is why appropriate due diligence should be undertaken on any software acquired, whether proprietary or open source. The Linux Foundation is alert to these issues and has implemented a compliance programme called OpenChain,[4] designed to ease compliance from both the perspective of the developer and from the perspective of those procuring the software further down the supply chain (hence the name OpenChain). OpenChain compliance is discussed in greater depth in 'Open source in the supply chain' section. OpenChain is now an ISO standard.

## LICENSING REQUIREMENTS

### Internal use

This section assumes that you (the customer) have contracted with a supplier to develop bespoke software for you, and the software is open source or contains open source components.

---

4   https://www.openchainproject.org/

If you are using the software for internal purposes only (solely within your own business), then there are, in practice, unlikely to be any licensing issues.

If the supplied software contains elements that are licensed under the GPL, for example, you will, irrespective of anything it says in your contract with the supplier, be entitled to receive the source code. However, this does not mean that the supplier is forced to make the source code they have developed for you available to the public in general (even if the component that you have had developed contains GPL code from elsewhere).

As a customer, you may well perceive proprietary advantages in maintaining the confidentiality of the source code that has been developed for you. You will therefore be relieved to learn that you have no obligation to release the source code to any third party (unless you decide that you are going to distribute the software further). If a contract between you and your supplier seeks to prevent you from distributing GPL code, that will put the supplier in breach of the GPL in relation to that code. This is also the case if the supplier fails to give you a copy of the source code on request. This may also mean that you cannot place an obligation on the supplier not to release the source code.

Note that if the supplier is technically in breach of the GPL itself when it distributes to the customer, this will not mean that the customer is in breach. The customer does not derive title to GPL code through the supplier: when a customer obtains GPL code in which the copyright is owned by a number of parties, it receives parallel licences from each of the owners, not a single licence from its immediate supplier. GPL wording explicitly confirms this point. This is typically called the 'cascade' licensing model.

Of course, if the code received by the customer from its supplier was never lawfully issued under the GPL in the first place (e.g. if it was unlawfully pirated from proprietary code), then by using the code, the customer will be an infringer, irrespective of what the supplier's contract or licence says.

A more common issue concerns licence incompatibility. If you as a business are developing software internally, and you intermingle components under different copyleft licences (see 'Licence compatibility' section), then because no distribution occurs, you do not have an issue. However, if you commission a supplier to develop software for you and they distribute software to you under incompatible licences this can be problematic.

In this case, the distribution to you, the customer, will be an infringement by the supplier (although, for the reasons stated above, the code in your hands will not be infringing). A consequence of this will be that the supplier is in danger of losing their own licence to the open source code, as their infringement may terminate their licence (the mechanism for this happening will depend on the specific licence terms). This is clearly not a good thing if you want the supplier to continue to support the software (for which they will no longer have their own licence).

To avoid this, it's possible to draft the supply contract so that when the supplier is developing software for you, they are acting as an agent on your behalf. This means, in effect, that the development is now being carried out internally, albeit by the developer on your behalf. This has the effect that the transfer of the software to you, the customer, is not a distribution from a copyright law perspective, and thus the compatibilities do not apply – it's as if you developed the software internally from the outset. Another option is for the developer to transfer the software to you as source code, and then for your own engineers to run the 'build' script that creates the software from the source.

If you are having software developed, you need also to consider whether you are willing for the code to be reused by third parties (potentially your competitors). This issue will also arise in proprietary software contracts, but it is more subtle in the context of open source code. If it is necessary to retain a restriction on reuse of the code, then the safest mechanism is for the contract to make clear that the customer engages the supplier as an agent to develop code on the customer's behalf, on the same basis as set out in the previous paragraph, and, as a customer, insist on a copy of the source code. It may be possible to negotiate restrictive covenants that prevent the supplier from developing a similar application for a competitor, but detailed advice should be obtained from legal counsel (as this is a tricky area, and may count as an impermissible additional restriction on the exercise of the rights under some licences, such as those of the GPL family).

If the software is to be accessed by the public through the internet (e.g. as software as a service), there are special concerns if any of the code is governed by certain licences such as the AGPL or the Open Software Licence.

## Procuring cloud services (software as a service)

If you are procuring a SaaS solution, it is highly likely that the software will contain open source code. You may want to undertake due diligence on the supplier (as discussed in the 'Procuring on-premise open source' section), but since the code the cloud service provider is using (with the exception of some components that may run in your browser) is unlikely to be distributed to you (as they are running the code on their own systems), from your perspective, as a customer, compliance is very much the service provider's problem. Some licences (e.g. the AGPL) give you a licence to the code and the right to receive the source even if the code's functionality is accessed across a network. From a customer's perspective, this is a benefit; from the service provider's perspective, they need to take care that they are not, in effect, licensing any of this code under terms that they were not expecting to license it.

## External use

Particularly careful attention is needed if you plan to make the software available outside your own organisation, for example by distributing it to third parties (such as your own customers or distributors), and especially if any software is going to be embedded in devices supplied to the public such as mobile phones or Internet-of-Things devices. If there is any question that the source code should not be released to the public, you, the customer, will need explicit verification from your cloud service provider that the licences of software components used in the cloud service are compatible with this aim.

The cloud service provider needs to be aware not only of the technical and legal requirements for the software that provides the functionality they are selling to the customer, but they also need to know what, specifically, the customer intends to do with the software in terms of onward distribution or access by third parties through the internet, in order to ensure that licence requirements are fulfilled.

As well as ensuring that these requirements are dealt with in the contract, they should also be verified by undertaking proper due diligence.

**Warranties and indemnities**

The considerations relating to warranties and indemnities for an open source project are broadly similar to those of any other software project. Two points to bear in mind:

- Warranties and indemnities are of no value if the entity giving them does not have sufficient financial strength to provide a worthwhile remedy if you ever need to sue them.
- Warranties and indemnities are not an adequate substitute for due diligence on the underlying subject matter.

If the customer is being offered very broad intellectual property warranties and indemnities, then it is wise to check that, if there is any question of the supplier's ability to meet them, they are covered by insurance. Insurers are increasingly making insurance available to cover open source-related risks.

Warranties of performance and compliance with specification will mirror those from an equivalent proprietary software project and are not covered in this chapter.

Warranties and indemnities relating to intellectual property may well be more complex than those that can be found in proprietary software contracts, reflecting the difference in software methodology. In particular, the supplier may be prepared only to give intellectual property warranties in respect of the code it has supplied itself, but not any third-party code it has incorporated, and in that situation, the customer will have to assess whether it is prepared to take the risk itself in third-party code. However, even if it is agreed that the customer will take the risk of third-party code infringement, then the supplier should warrant that it has taken reasonable care in selecting the code, bearing in mind the licences under which the customer has asked to receive it, and that it is not aware of anything that would conflict with those licences.

One solution, which is gaining traction, is for the procurement contract to contain an obligation that the supplier complies with certain processes and procedures relating to procurement. They will typically include documentation on the provenance of code. Such policies are required in any organisation, which is compliant with the OpenChain specification. This is discussed in more detail in the next section.

**OPEN SOURCE IN THE SUPPLY CHAIN**

The OpenChain Project, initiated by the Linux Foundation, is aimed at applying procurement best practice to the development of software, and particularly open source software. It is structured like a quality assurance standard, and is intended to provide a framework for organisations developing software using open source code, with the aims of reducing the risk of incorporating infringing and low-quality code, minimising friction in the supply chain, and making open source licence compliance simpler and more consistent.

Companies that comply with OpenChain benefit from a shared framework making open source software readily available to developers. By contrast with a typical supply chain, where every member of the chain has to conduct its own compliance checks in respect of the software of each other supplier, OpenChain allows companies in a supply chain to work together towards open source compliance, thus saving time and resources. Rather than imposing a set of procedures and policies, the OpenChain Project identifies a core set of requirements every quality compliance program must satisfy. There is no fee involved in obtaining OpenChain certification, and any organisation developing open source can use it as a sensible basis for compliance as well as requiring suppliers to adhere to it.

An OpenChain compliant organisation will have the following:

- an open source policy (see 'Open source compliance policies and procedures' section);
- training for relevant staff;
- a licence review policy;
- a defined set of individuals responsible for compliance, with properly empowered and funded roles;
- a bill of materials (i.e. list of components contained in each product that is shipped);
- an open source compliance process to handle common licence issues;
- appropriate compliance materials (which are provided with the software);
- a contribution policy for external projects.

A well-run open source business will already have most, if not all, of the above in place.

The aim is not to eliminate risk, but to assess it, and by implementing procedures, code and contracts, and, potentially, further managing the risk through insurance, to bring the risk within the parameters the business's management is prepared to accept.

## OPEN SOURCE COMPLIANCE POLICIES AND PROCEDURES

A completely prohibitive policy such as 'no open source' is unlikely to be effective in most commercial software development organisations; programmers under a deadline are unlikely to ignore a ready-made open source solution to their specific problem. This is exactly how open source turns up in proprietary software projects without the official knowledge of the company concerned.

Instead, companies that undertake software development should implement open source compliance policies and procedures that focus on (a) compliance with the terms of open source licences and (b) the related matter of protection of their own intellectual property from unintended disclosure or other consequences. Producing documentation that demonstrates knowledge of open source issues, and ensuring that developers actively engage with the compliance process, are critical. The process should encompass everyone involved in code creation, from programmers through to management. Under a mature open source development methodology, any code should be developed with the appropriate compliance materials, and verification of provenance, to ensure licence compatibility. Demonstration of conformance with OpenChain would be evidence of this, as would the provision of equivalent materials (open source development policy, etc.).

In practice, it will rarely be possible to document the precise provenance of every piece of code (especially in GPL code, such as the Linux kernel, where the individual authors will retain their own ownership). There will always be a residual risk of possible infringement. The transparency of open source means that infringing code will be more readily visible to the copyright owner than is the case with proprietary code – but it is, of course, equally possible that proprietary code contains infringing components as well.

A reliable open source usage policy from the Linux Foundation includes six simple rules:[5]

- Engineers must receive approval before integrating any open source code in a product.
- Software received from third parties must be audited to identify any open source code included, which ensures licence obligations can be fulfilled before a product ships.
- All software must be audited and reviewed, including all proprietary software components.
- Products must fulfil open source licensing obligations prior to customer receipt.
- Approval for using a given open source component in one product must not be assumed to constitute approval for another deployment, even if the open source component is the same.
- All changed components must go through the approval process.

## OPEN SOURCE SOFTWARE: EMPLOYEES AND CONTRACTORS

The copyright in employees' work done during the course of their employment will automatically belong to their employer. Independent contractors' work will not. However, questions of code ownership may well arise, and it is sensible, in the case of employment contracts, and critical, in the case of contracts for independent contractors, to set out explicitly the terms on which copyright works generated are transferred to the employer.

A subtle issue that arises in relation to open source code is that employment contracts may contain terms that specifically restrict the freedoms that open source licences may try to guarantee, for example in terms of restrictive covenants and confidentiality. Technically, if these restrictions conflict with the licence terms of software used by the employer, the employer may find itself in breach of the relevant licence.

---

[5] https://www.linuxfoundation.org/resources/open-source-guides/using-open-source-code/#3.

A further point is that an enlightened employer may well request the employee to be actively involved in the community of the software they are working on. It is possible (even likely) that some of this work will take place outside the scope of employment. Employees' contracts therefore need to grant them the freedom to do this, as well as ensuring that their terms do not conflict with the terms of software licences.

Developing a corporate policy will help to specify how your employees contribute to open source projects. It will reduce confusion among the employees and help them contribute to open source projects in the company's best interest. A good example is Rackspace's Model IP and Open Source Contribution Policy.[6]

Many projects request that contributors sign a contributor agreement. There are two kinds of contributor agreement:

- In a Contributor Licence Agreement (CLA), the original contributor retains copyright ownership of their contributions, but grants the project a broad set of rights such that the project can incorporate and distribute the contributions as it needs to.

- In a Copyright Assignment Agreement (CAA), the contributor actually transfers copyright ownership of the contributions to the project, which can then license it however they want since they own it outright. However, a CAA typically grants very broad non-exclusive rights back to the contributor so that they too can use, distribute and sub-license their contribution freely.

The terms of these contributor agreements can vary dramatically, but it is important that the contributor agreement is considered carefully, both from an employment perspective and to ensure that the employer is not giving away rights unnecessarily (e.g. a very broad patent licence) or granting unacceptable indemnities.

Developers may be suspicious that a contributor agreement is handing over too many rights and granting too much power to the project or company that is the recipient of those rights. An alternative to the contributor agreement is the **developer certificate of origin**. These are more applicable to projects that are governed by copyleft licences. Contributor agreements tend to give the project a broad range of rights, which may include the right for the project to release the software to which the contribution is made under any number of licences, including, potentially, proprietary licences. Since contributors to a permissively licensed project would expect this to happen anyway, this is unlikely to be an issue. In contrast, however, contributors to copyleft projects have a legitimate expectation that the project will only be available under a copyleft licence, and will be resistant to the ability to release the code they have contributed under any other licence. For this reason, copyleft-licensed projects frequently have a 'licence-in, licence-out' policy, meaning that the developers license their contributions to the project under the same licence that the project uses to license its code to the outside world. The classic example of this is the Linux kernel, which is licensed under GPLv2 and therefore receives all its contributions under GPLv2.

To ensure that the project retains a minimal level of assurance that the contributors have the right to contribute the code they are providing, and to help the project keep

---

6  https://github.com/todogroup/policies/tree/master/rackspace

track of those contributions, the Linux Foundation provides a much simpler document, the **developer certificate of origin**. By signing it, each developer confirms that they developed the contribution themselves, have the right to license it to the project under the specified licence, and that the personal details they submit will be made public.[7]

## OPEN SOURCE SOFTWARE AND PATENTS

Open source software is not immune from patent infringement suits, so it is important to be aware of the implications of the issue of software patentability. This is discussed in more detail in Chapter 4. Many open source bodies oppose software patents, although companies such as IBM (which are patent holders as well as having a significant open source business) are understandably keener to support patents within the context of open source.

A patent that impinges on open source software will also impinge on proprietary software that does the same job in a sufficiently similar way. On the one hand, the very availability of the source code means that it may be easier for a patent owner to tell whether a piece of open source code infringes the patent than would be the case for an equivalent piece of proprietary code (where the underlying mechanism is obscured). On the other hand, the open source community is likely to respond to a patent threat by quickly replacing the relevant code with non-infringing code (where such replacement is possible). Thus, patented algorithms, such as those for the creation of MP3 files, have prompted the development of free codecs such as Ogg Vorbis, which does a similar job without patent encumbrance.

Where open source licences specifically refer to patents, they do so in one (or more) of three ways:

- First, where a contributor to the code owns or controls a patent that impinges on the code, there may be an explicit licence that will typically grant anyone receiving a copy of the code a non-exclusive right to use the code that the patent protects.
- Second, open source licences frequently contain retaliation clauses, which mean that if a licensee is taking advantage of an open source licence, and they initiate litigation of specified sorts (e.g. patent litigation) concerning the software they are making use of, then various rights under the licence automatically fall away. Depending on the licence, these may simply be other patent licences, or may, more fundamentally, be the underlying copyright licence. The rationale is one of fairness: it is not fair that a licensee can make use of someone else's code while at the time trying to exercise rights that they may have in the same code.
- Third, and limited to the GPL family of licences, is the **liberty or death** clause. This clause has caused much difficulty in interpretation, but it is best understood as a mechanism to ensure that free software (as the FSF understands that term) either remains free for everyone or cannot be distributed at all. If you are making use of exercising rights under the GPL and, to do so, you also need to rely on rights (e.g. a patent licence) you have been granted by a third party, then, unless you can ensure

---

7  https://developercertificate.org.

that anyone who gets the code from you can also make use of the third-party rights, you are not allowed to distribute the software at all. Again, the rationale is one of fairness. The FSF argues that if you are only able to make use of software because of a special deal you have with a third party, then the software is not free software unless anyone to whom you distribute it gets the same rights that you have.

Many open source licences are silent on the issues of patents and trade marks. It is nonetheless possible that there are implied terms (i.e. terms not explicitly stated in the licence, but which the court may imply to give effect to the intention of the parties). There is an increasingly heated debate as to whether patent licences can be implied in this way, but this analysis is outside the scope of this chapter.

Initiatives such as the Open Invention Network (OIN) operate as a shared defensive patent pool to protect the use of significant open source projects (in the case of the OIN, it is what it defines as the 'Linux system' – a list of components defined by OIN and regularly reviewed and extended[8]). Anyone using the Linux system automatically receives a licence from the OIN under their patents, and those of the OIN's members. The intent is that the OIN will acquire patents and patent rights for the benefit of the whole Linux community.

## SUMMARY

Open source software is everywhere, and affects just about every area of technology. As with proprietary software, its use is subject to compliance with the applicable licence terms, although the licence terms for open source differ from those for proprietary software because they are designed around ensuring freedom of use, modification and distribution, rather than just providing a contractual mechanism for enforcing payment of licence fees. Accordingly, the use and deployment of open source requires legal analysis of the licences for the code employed. Tools and mechanisms are being developed under the auspices of organisations such as the Linux Foundation and the Eclipse Foundation to make compliance easier, but, ultimately, legal knowledge is required to make an informed analysis of the risks of deployment of code. One thing is for sure: whatever the risks, open source code is now mainstream, and an understanding of its use and context is necessary for all businesses operating in technology today.

### Associated licences

Outside software, there are other licences that have 'open' characteristics to them. For documentation, the GNU Free Documentation Licence, and certain variants of the Creative Commons suite of licences are available. Creative Commons licenses are also suitable for other content, such as music, photographs, videos and films, but are not themselves suitable for computer software. Open source hardware is a developing area, with two of the most prominent licences being the CERN Open Hardware licence and the Solderpad licence (being a variant of Apache 2.0).

---

[8]   https://www.openinventionnetwork.com/joining-oin/linux-system/.

**FURTHER INFORMATION**

- Free Software Foundation: www.fsf.org
- Free Software Foundation Europe: www.fsfe.org
- Open Source Initiative: https://opensource.org

The Eclipse Foundation grew out of IBM's Eclipse Project in the early 2000s. Eclipse is an integrated development environment (i.e. a set of software tools to help developers write, test and debug software) and the Foundation now acts as the home for more than 350 open source projects. See https://www.eclipse.org.

If you want to get a feeling for what Linux can do, download and burn a 'live CD' or create a bootable USB stick that will load a temporary instance of Linux onto your computer (even if it is running Windows), together with a suite of open source software to try. Although our personal experience has been that it is safe to do this and it has never damaged the existing system on any computer on which we have tried it, as with any trial software, it is wise to try it on a non-critical computer that, if it does contain any important data, has been backed up first. Likewise, you can download any number of open source programs (for Linux, Windows, MacOS or even other more obscure operating systems) from a number of locations – the same warning about using a non-critical computer and backing up applies. To try a Linux distribution, visit https://ubuntu.com.

Other open source software (for a variety of operating systems, and not just Linux) can be found at:

- GitHub, https://github.com (a widely used repository for open source code)
- VideoLAN Organization, https://www.videolan.org/vlc/ (VLC: a great media player)
- Audacity, https://www.audacityteam.org (a versatile program for editing, transcoding and processing audio)
- GIMP, https://www.gimp.org (the GNU Image Manipulation Program – powerful image editing software, not unlike Adobe Photoshop)

**REFERENCES**

Erlang Solutions (2018) '20 Years of open source Erlang: OpenErlang interview with Simon Phipps'. https://www.erlang-solutions.com/blog/20-years-of-open-source-erlang-openerlang-interview-with-simon-phipps.html.

MacDonald, Michaela (2014) 'Open source licensing in the networked era'. *Masaryk University Journal of Law and Technology* 7(2). https://journals.muni.cz/mujlt/article/view/2634/2198.

Microsoft News Center (2018) 'Microsoft to acquire GitHub for $7.5 billion'. Microsoft Stories blog. https://news.microsoft.com/2018/06/04/microsoft-to-acquire-github-for-7-5-billion/.

Moody, Glyn (2002) *Rebel Code: Linux and the open source revolution*. Basic Books.

Open Source Initiative (2007) 'The open source definition, version 1.9, 22 March'. OSI. https://opensource.org/osd.

Raymond, Eric. S. (2018) 'The cathedral and the bazaar'. CatB Writings. www.catb.org/esr/writings/homesteading/.

Red Hat (2019) 'Press release. IBM closes landmark acquisition of Red Hat for $34 billion: Defines open, hybrid cloud future'. Red Hat. https://www.redhat.com/en/about/press-releases/ibm-closes-landmark-acquisition-red-hat-34-billion-defines-open-hybrid-cloud-future.

# 11 AGILE SOFTWARE DEVELOPMENT

## Stewart James

### INTRODUCTION

This chapter begins by outlining the key features common to the major Agile methodologies, such as Scrum and Kanban. It discusses some of the philosophical and practical objections to those methodologies, including the challenges of shoehorning Agile development projects into the framework of traditional forms of software development contract. Finally, it deals with the key issues, benefits and risks of using Agile methodologies in practice.

If you are already familiar with the concepts of Agile, you may wish to skip the Introduction and start reading from the 'Commercial challenges' section. However, the earlier subsection, 'The intransigence of lawyers', provides some useful background to these challenges.

'Agile' is the generic name given to a specific method of software development, application development, project management or the combination of application development and project management. Unlike other development methods, Agile methodologies are characterised by their division of tasks into short phases of work (referred to as 'iterative steps' or 'iterations'), frequent reassessment and adaptation. Agile may also be used to describe the iterative process of continuous development known as 'DevOps'.

The term 'Agile' is derived from the declaration made by a group of prominent software developers in 2001 known as the 'Agile Manifesto'.[1] The manifesto sets out four values and 12 principles for the development of software.

> **THE AGILE MANIFESTO**
>
> We are uncovering better ways of developing software by doing it and helping others do it. Through this work we have come to value:
>
> - **Individuals and interactions** over processes and tools.
> - **Working software** over comprehensive documentation.

---

1 https://agilemanifesto.org.

- **Customer collaboration** over contract negotiation.
- **Responding to change** over following a plan.

Agile software development principles are:

1. Customer satisfaction by early and continuous delivery of valuable software.
2. Welcome changing requirements, even in late development.
3. Working software is delivered frequently (weeks rather than months).
4. Close, daily cooperation between business people and developers.
5. Projects are built around motivated individuals, who should be trusted.
6. Face-to-face conversation is the best form of communication (co-location).
7. Working software is the primary measure of progress.
8. Sustainable development; able to maintain a constant pace.
9. Continuous attention to technical excellence and good design.
10. Simplicity – the art of maximising the amount of work not done – is essential.
11. Best architectures, requirements and designs emerge from self-organising teams.
12. The team reflects regularly on how to become more effective, and adjusts accordingly.

## THE AGILE MANIFESTO

There are numerous Agile methodologies and derivatives available, though all of them comply with the values and principles set out in the manifesto above. This reflects the belief that the manifesto, and therefore methodologies derived from it, does not represent the final answer and that there is always more than one solution (i.e. 'we are uncovering better ways'); in essence, even the manifesto is flexible and subject to further iteration.

Prominent methodologies include:

- Agile Unified Process (AUP);
- Dynamic Systems Development Method (DSDM);
- Extreme programming (XP);
- Feature-Driven Development (FDD);
- Kanban;
- Scaled Agile Framework (SAFe);
- Scrum.

Of these, the best known methodologies are Scrum and Kanban.

# AGILE SOFTWARE DEVELOPMENT

Key components of Agile methodologies include the delivery of working software at regular intervals, flexibility and the willingness to embrace change. The Agile approach is collaborative in nature and consequently requires a high degree of customer involvement in development activities. Different methodologies may incorporate additional values and principles, such as the 'fail fast, fail often' principle, which encourages the parties to try solutions, rejecting those that do not satisfy the requirements in a research and development type approach.

The advantage of Agile is that it is highly flexible, allowing the solution to evolve to meet changes in the needs of the customer or changes in the parties' understanding of its needs.

## Sequential and iterative contracts compared

Early software development methodologies were typically delivered along traditional engineering lines where each stage of the process is completed sequentially, with the parties not progressing to the next stage until the current stage is complete (see Figure 11.1).

**Figure 11.1 Comparison of software development methodologies**

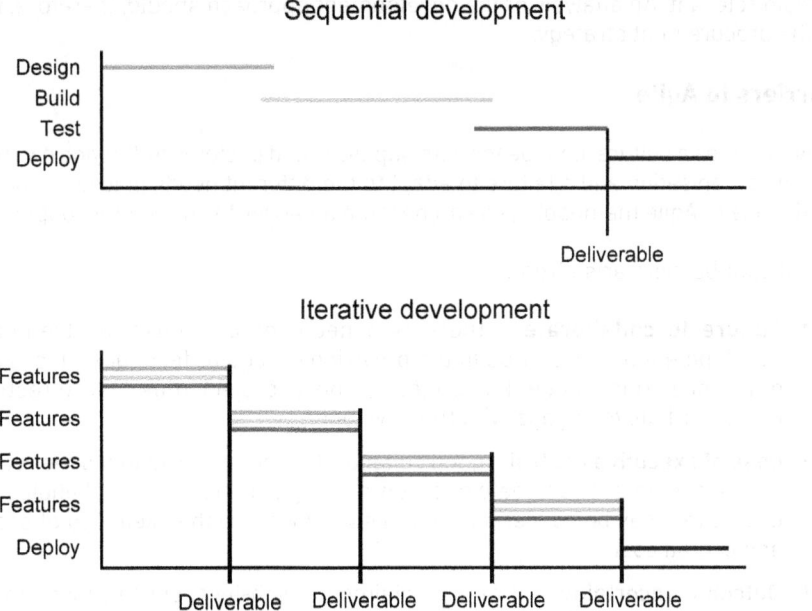

These sequential processes are normally referred to as 'waterfall'. This describes the stepped process of moving in sequence through each stage of the development cycle from the development of a detailed specification, through design, build, testing and deployment. These approaches typically mean that the customer will not receive a working solution until the end of the process and may not have the opportunity to influence the development mid-programme.

199

The use of a sequential methodology may be seen as a very disciplined approach, with each stage of the process being tested and accepted before the developer is permitted to progress or to incur further cost. However, it may take the developer many months or years to develop a solution, during which time the customer's needs may have changed. Additionally, the parties may not be able to identify whether the developer has misunderstood the requirements until a late stage in the programme, when mistakes are harder to resolve and retrospective changes are more costly to implement.

The increasing pace of digitisation also places pressure on the parties to develop software quickly. It is the first to market that is generally best placed to capitalise on an opportunity. Rapidly changing markets demand rapid development of working software, so sequential methodologies are not best suited to meet the demands of business.

The iterative or Agile approach aims to deliver working and tested code at the end of a development iteration, with each deliverable providing an incremental improvement to the overall functionality of the application. This approach enables the early deployment of a working prototype in order to obtain market reaction and permit further refinement and understanding of the requirements. Continued testing and adjustment of the solution in this manner also ensures that only value-adding features are developed in subsequent iterations.

However, Agile is not appropriate for all development projects and sequential methods remain relevant. An analysis of the development approach should, therefore, form part of the procurement strategy.

## Barriers to Agile

Agile requires a cultural change for both suppliers and customers. Change can be difficult for any organisation and a failure to adapt to the different needs placed on the business by the use of Agile methodologies can become a barrier to successful adoption.

Significant barriers arise from:

- **Failure to collaborate** – there is a need for customer involvement in the development process through the provision of regular feedback. This is a cultural difference from sequential projects, and a project may lose direction if the customer fails to engage with the developer.
- **Loss of executive control** – good collaboration normally includes the requirement for the customer to delegate decision-making to more junior stakeholders. Senior executives may be concerned that this will increase the likelihood of scope creep and overall cost.
- **Outcome uncertainty** – it may be claimed a high-level specification results in an uncertain outcome. However, these uncertainties relate only to the **details**, not the general nature of the project. A project for a customer relationship management solution will still deliver that, but, using Agile, only those features and functionality that deliver real value will be developed; anticipated features and functionality that don't deliver value will get discarded during the development phase.
- **Solution risk** – the greater degree of customer involvement and collaboration in the development process may raise concern about the lack of clarity over responsibility

for mistakes. This concern is mitigated by the relatively short duration of each iteration or 'sprint' (typically 2–4 weeks) and the ability to identify issues early.

- **Lack of financial control** – some Agile methodologies promote the calculation of charges on a time and materials basis. This should not be a concern where Agile is conducted properly, but critics may use this as an excuse not to use Agile, claiming that these methodologies are only suitable for low value or for in-house developments.

A key barrier for anyone involved in the drafting of an Agile contract is the general lack of good legal precedents. Unfortunately, client pressure to complete a transaction quickly can drive lawyers to use inappropriate precedents or clauses that do not properly reflect the relevant Agile methodology. Similarly, the drafting of contracts by lawyers who have not properly understood the cultural differences of Agile may result in the misuse of terminology.

## The intransigence of lawyers

Drafting a contract that works with Agile methodologies is difficult. Lawyers are trained to deal with risk and take an inherently conservative approach when drafting. The natural inclination is to use precedents wherever possible; a clause that is known to produce a particular outcome, particularly one that has been tested by the courts, will be preferred over free-text drafting. This approach has the effect of stifling innovation and may result in unforeseen outcomes when templates for sequential contracts are used in conjunction with the different cultural approaches that Agile methodologies require.

Drafting contracts for Agile is not a new practice but there remain relatively few templates to act as precedents. In the early days of computers, software development was sometimes referred to as 'software engineering' and early software development agreements were similarly modelled on engineering and construction agreements. It is still far easier to identify templates for software development contracts based on sequential models than it is for Agile.

Contemporary software development agreements for Agile methodologies need to reflect and enable dynamic, flexible and collaborative approaches. Some of these principles are anathema to the risk-based approach of the past. However, in an environment where the business imperative is to be the first to market, sometimes 'good enough' is sufficient and the contract needs to allow for that.

The increased flexibility of Agile methodologies does not lack the same discipline required of sequential developments. In practice, Agile conducted properly is a more disciplined approach because the constant exposure of results to customer inspection at the end of each iteration means the supplier cannot hide its mistakes or shortcomings.

## COMMERCIAL CHALLENGES

### Agreement on scope

A popular saying attributed to Benjamin Franklin is that 'failing to plan is planning to fail'. Any project needs to identify the need that the solution is intended to resolve. The problem for software development is how, at the start of a project, to deal with the relative uncertainty of the requirements. This lack of clarity has a direct impact on estimates of the time and cost required to achieve the desired outcomes, which may be referred to as the 'cone of uncertainty'. There is a greater margin of error earlier in the project. With sequential contracts, suppliers will seek to mitigate this risk across a series of projects by adjusting their prices accordingly, but this approach is not practicable for Agile projects.

**Figure 11.2 Cone of uncertainty**

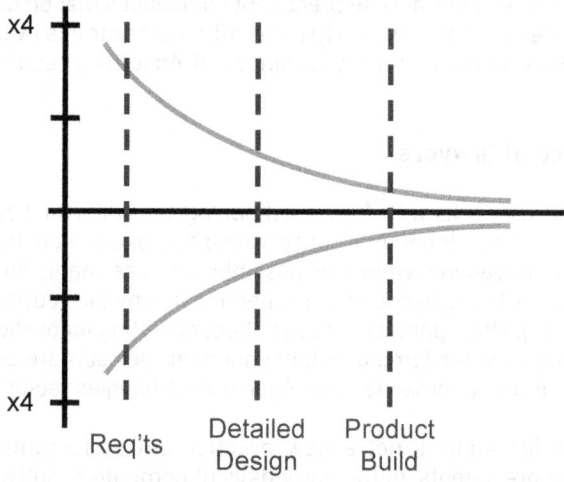

It is still necessary for the parties to estimate the scope of the project in order to understand the appropriate level of resources that are likely to be used in its delivery. Such estimates will be based on the high-level requirements and should be refined during the initial discovery or foundation phases. The degree of uncertainty will also have an effect on the selection of appropriate commercial models (see below).

For larger projects, the requirements may need to be grouped together (sometimes known as 'epics') to allow stories to be written at a higher level for the purpose of setting the scope of the project. These requirement groups will need to be broken down into smaller components during the initial discovery phase. However, trying to base contractual scope on detailed user stories (see explanation below) too early can result in the adoption of a sequential approach.

The requirements for an Agile contract may be written as a series of higher-level statements or use cases, including any constraints or parameters that must be considered by the developer.

Requirements can be:

- **Functional** – these express a function or feature and define what is required, but do not state how the solution is to be achieved.

- **Non-functional** – these define solution attributes such as performance or acceptance criteria, including reliability, maintainability, availability and so on.

Requirements can be written in different formats, depending on the Agile methodology employed. A common format is the 'user story' or 'use case', which is a requirement expressed from the perspective of an end-user goal. For example:

**As a** <role>
**I need** <requirement or feature>
**So that** <goal/value>

Once established, the statement of requirements provides a baseline against which the parties can record future changes. This is a good discipline for the parties to follow, particularly with reference to the reason(s) for any changes.

These requirements will also be ordered into a prioritised list, establishing the initial order in which they will be addressed by the development team. The prioritised requirements list will remain flexible, with the order revised to meet the needs of the development team.

## Maintaining flexibility

Change is inevitable: the need for mid-term change is one of the constant issues that all projects face. Agile anticipates that both parties' understanding of the requirements and the solution will evolve during the course of a project. Additionally, the original requirements may become less relevant due to changes in the business environment.

A key value of the Agile manifesto is prioritisation of the importance of responding to a change over the need to stick slavishly to a predetermined plan. The contractual dilemma is how to encourage flexibility and allow changes to be made without losing control over the duration of the project and its outcomes.

A distinction needs to be made between (1) fundamental strategic changes that have a material impact on the project or the terms of the contract; and (2) operational changes, such as a change in depth and detail of the solution implementation, that do not. Regardless of the nature of the change, it should remain important to understand when and why a change occurred and who instigated it. Establishing an initial baseline and recording variations from it are a necessary step, though suppliers will resist the creation of procedural steps that are cumbersome and time-consuming.

This may give rise to multiple change processes, distinguishing between the processes applied and permissions required for operational and strategic changes. Processes relating to smaller operational changes should not be unnecessarily prescriptive provided they are sufficient to capture information relevant to the purpose of the change. This might be necessary, for example, to enable the parties to reverse the change if the outcome is unsatisfactory and might be limited to the retention of a copy of the pre-change code base.

By contrast, a larger strategic change may still require a degree of rigour, with both parties involved in analysing the reason for the change and its impact on the project outcomes. Strategic changes are, by nature, fundamental to the main purpose of the contract and may result in significantly increased costs. Therefore, the process required for a strategic change may be similar to those normally found in a sequential contract.

## Collaboration

Agile takes an inherently collaborative approach to the development of software applications and project management, with the anticipation that the customer will be actively involved in its processes (e.g. through the provision of regular feedback). Collaboration is built upon mutual trust and good faith, but it is particularly difficult to contract for this. The contract can legally require the parties to collaborate, but this does not necessarily deliver the right behaviours in practice.

Currently, there is no general doctrine of 'good faith' in English law. The courts may imply rules into a contract to ensure that contractual discretions are not used arbitrarily or capriciously, but will avoid implying obligations that are vague or subjective and therefore difficult to enforce.

However, the contract should allocate duties and obligations to the parties so that they have a clear understanding of who holds the responsibility for a particular activity. Examples of the roles within an Agile project include:

- **Product owner** – represents the customer's interest in the project. The product owner has responsibility for defining the customer's requirements, providing feedback and reprioritising work based on the changing demands of the project.
- **Development team** – represents the supplier's resource input in the project. The development team may not be a fixed group of individuals and changes may be made to reflect the nature of the current development activity. Development teams typically contain between five and nine members. Large projects may involve the use of multiple development teams.
- **Agile coach** – represents a moderating function in the project, both between the parties and for the development team. The Agile coach (sometimes referred to as the 'Scrum Master' from the Scrum methodology) may be an independent consultant but is often provided by the supplier from its own employees.

Notwithstanding the allocation of responsibilities, the contract should not prevent the development team from being autonomous and self-organising. This is an important aspect of the principle of flexibility in Agile methodologies and enables the development team to structure itself and conduct development activity efficiently.

## Intellectual property rights

A consequence of the collaborative approach is that both parties may contribute to the development of intellectual property through the project.

A computer program is classed as a literary work protected by copyright under section 3(1) of the Copyright, Designs and Patents Act 1988. The author of a work is the first owner of the copyright in that work or, in the case of a work created by an employee, the employer. However, where the work is produced by the collaboration of two or more authors, in which the contribution of each author is not distinct from the other author(s), it will be jointly owned.

Joint ownership should be avoided where possible. Each owner has the right to grant licences to the work, but, in the absence of an express agreement to the contrary, may not assign ownership or grant licences for some activities without the consent of the other owner(s).

A reasonably high level of contribution is required to establish joint ownership of a computer program. This might arise, for example, if the customer is involved in programming activity in conjunction with the supplier, but would not occur if the customer is only providing feedback on products delivered. However, it should be remembered that preparatory design materials are treated as separate works, which are subject to their own copyright protection and this may result in jointly owned material.

Consequently, it is important that the contract identifies who will own the intellectual property rights in any materials created. If the customer is not the author, the contract will also need to assign ownership to the customer. If the supplier is to own the intellectual property rights, the contract will need to include a suitable licence enabling the customer to use the materials. Consideration should also be given as to whether the customer should be able to use those materials after the contract ends.

## Definition of 'Done'

A key benefit of Agile is the ability of the parties to end the project when the customer's needs have been satisfied. This benefit is often used to justify calculating the supplier's charges on a time and materials basis.

An Agile project will be conducted in a series of phases. For example, the UK Government's Digital Outcomes and Services contract[2] uses the following phases:

- **Discovery** – a preliminary phase to define the problem, understand the users and identify constraints.
- **Alpha** – a trial phase used to build and test prototype solutions.
- **Beta** – development of the best solution from the Alpha phase, which may include a pilot with users.
- **Live** – the solution is put into production and supported, which may include continuous development in a DevOps approach.

Other methodologies may limit the number of phases, use the phases differently or give the phases different labels. They may also include phases that are conducted internally before engagement with an external supplier.

In each case, however, the phases provide a decision point where the customer can end the project for any reason. For example, the opportunity may not deliver the advantage

---

2   https://www.crowncommercial.gov.uk/agreements/RM1043.6.

the customer anticipated, the effort required to develop the solution may not justify the benefit or, quite simply, because the customer has changed its mind.

Similarly, developing the solution through incremental steps provides an opportunity for the customer to identify when its needs for the solution have been satisfied. This may occur before the supplier has delivered all the features set out in the prioritised requirements list.

## Minimum viable product

In theory, ending the development before all the features have been developed should not be an issue for the supplier, particularly if paid on a time and materials basis. However, the supplier will have committed resources to the project and may not be able to recover its costs if the project is terminated early. These costs may include overheads relating to its development team and the purchase of licences for development tools.

The phased approach of an Agile project helps to mitigate some of these concerns. For example, the discovery phase can be conducted as a discrete element with a limited resource commitment.

This issue is more important in the development phase. However, the dilemma can be resolved by the identification of a 'minimum viable product' or MVP. This is the deliverable(s) that provides the minimum level of functionality the solution must deliver in order to meet the basic needs of the customer. Any other functionality or features represent enhancements to the MVP that will or may be delivered if possible (see MoSCoW rules for the prioritisation of features). These additional products provide a profitable margin for the project. The contract can then permit termination of the project following delivery of the MVP to the customer without further financial liability or the need to calculate a compensatory payment for early termination.

## Interim acceptance

Working software will be delivered to the customer frequently. This is not necessarily linked to each iteration, since some iterations may relate to organisational activities and not to the delivery of functionality or features. Development activity will also involve testing, including automated testing processes. However, iterations and the delivery of working software may be linked to the payment profile. Consequently, the question of interim acceptance may arise, including what happens if an accepted deliverable is subsequently rejected by the customer.

Agile mitigates this problem by anticipating that a deliverable must meet the acceptance criteria agreed by the parties at the start of the relevant iteration. Provided these have been met, then any subsequent rejection arises because the features provided by a deliverable are no longer required. This might arise because of a change of requirements or because the feature has been superseded by new features or functionality.

By contrast, if the supplier has not developed the required outcomes in accordance with the agreed acceptance criteria, the relevant features or functionality will be returned to the product backlog for future development activity.

Although the outcome of each iteration is visible to the customer, and the customer has the ability to end the project early if the supplier repeatedly fails to deliver a solution, the supplier may not be sufficiently incentivised if the customer is required to bear the full cost of an unsuccessful iteration. The contract should therefore determine whether the supplier is paid for development activity that does not meet its agreed acceptance criteria.

**Risk and liability**

One of the benefits of Agile methodologies is the much quicker feedback loop established by the release of working product increments to users on a regular basis. Inherent in this principle is the idea that the consequences of failure are relatively small and easier to identify.

The failure of one element of functionality may be a nuisance but it does not impact negatively on the entire project; it is something that can be corrected relatively quickly (in the next iteration) and the cost of correction will be comparatively cheap. This is because it is easier to resolve and there will be little or no concatenation of mistakes. Additionally, the insight gained from the failure can be used to improve the overall outcome.

However, individual releases are components of a larger solution and the failure of one iteration may be disproportionate to the cost of development. Consideration, therefore, needs to be given to the impact of the failure rather than the cost of developing the particular release.

Traditional risk allocation operates on the basis of identifying who should bear the cost of failure, often linked to which party is best able to obtain insurance. These models seek to provide financial compensation, which does not satisfy the customer's need for a solution. Furthermore, even if insurance will provide for the cost of the additional resources required to deliver the solution, it should be remembered that it is always the customer that bears the risk.

**COMMERCIAL MODELS**

A key principle of Agile methodologies is the frequent delivery of working software, closely linked to the iterative development cycle. Consequently, the nirvana for Agile evangelists is to charge for services on a time and materials basis (T&M). Conversely, critics of Agile frequently argue that this objective favours the supplier, both by disincentivising efficient software development practices and by encouraging scope creep, resulting in a loss of financial control.

However, conducted properly, Agile is a very disciplined process, arguably more so than traditional, sequential processes, which can disguise project inefficiencies in longer delivery cycles. The iterative nature of Agile means that the supply of outputs and the creation of deliverables is very visible to the customer, enabling it to constantly monitor the progress of the project.

The high visibility of delivery, when combined with short development cycles and the right of the customer to end the project when its requirements are satisfied, redresses some of this imbalance and enables the customer to retain a high degree of control over total costs.

Remember that the sequential approach to software development, without customer input and feedback during the development phase and the likelihood that requirements will change during this period, can mean that the customer is paying for nugatory development effort. In these circumstances, the Agile approach ensures that the customer is paying for the true realisation of value in the project.

A T&M approach is also not without risk for the supplier. Establishing a development team is expensive and the supplier will need to complete a number of iterations of the project to recover its overheads. This may not be achieved if the customer can terminate the project without financial penalty at the end of any iteration.

This conflict of interests is one of the reasons many Agile contracts seek to employ the concept of an MVP. For the customer, the contract can be drafted to ensure that the developer will deliver a solution that satisfies its basic needs whilst the supplier can be protected from an early termination before it has recovered its project overheads.

The use of an MVP is not compliant with the true intent of Agile, but is a device to balance the parties' risks. It is also a means of introducing alternative commercial models into the contract. For example, the supplier's fixed overheads can be linked to delivery of the MPV, with further iterations providing enhancements at a lower price (i.e. cost plus margin less overhead).

T&M is used for many Agile methodologies. However, there are some Agile methodologies that use fixed pricing, such as DSDM. For these methodologies, the cost of the development effort will be fixed, with development effort prioritised according to the MoSCoW rules (see box).

Ultimately, any commercial model that can be used with sequential models can also be used with Agile methodologies, including capped pricing, unit-based pricing and incentivised models such as target costing and adjustable target costing.

### MOSCOW RULES

MoSCoW is an acronym for a prioritisation technique that enables the development team to understand and manage priorities.

The acronym stands for:

- **M**ust have
- **S**hould have
- **C**ould have
- **W**ould have

Requirements classed as 'Must have' are the features and functions that must be delivered if the solution is to meet the MPV.

Requirements classed as 'Should have' are important features and functions that could be omitted if time and/or cost require otherwise. However, omission of these features and functions will mean the solution may not fully satisfy the customer's requirements.

Requirements classed as 'Could have' are the features and functions that the parties will deliver if time and/or costs permit and requirements classed as 'Would have' are contingent requirements that will be delivered if the opportunity arises.

Prioritisation needs to occur at the start of the project during the discovery phase (DSDM calls this the Foundations Phase). Customers must be dissuaded from categorising all requirements within the first category; if all requirements are classified as 'Must have' the use of fixed price or fixed time is the wrong approach and there is a high risk that the project will be seen to fail.

## CONTRACT DRAFTING

The adoption of Agile methodologies requires a cultural change for the parties. Agile methodologies are inherently collaborative in nature, require different allocations of risk and employ roles with different obligations and responsibilities. There is also a need for greater stakeholder involvement in development activity and the delegation of decision-making.

This gives rise to a number of fundamental drafting mistakes, including:

- Drafting that seeks to describe the Agile methodology without understanding the proper allocation of the encapsulated risks and obligations. It is not normal to describe the 'traditional' sequential methodology in a contract and it should not be necessary, therefore, to do so for an Agile contract. However, it will be necessary to identify the particular Agile methodology and comply with its terminology.

- Conflating Agile and 'waterfall' methodologies in a process that is sometimes described as 'AgiFall'. Obviously, a contract that mixes methodologies is likely to create practical issues during the implementation. It also means that the parties will struggle to realise the benefits of using an Agile methodology.

- Using Agile 'jargon' without changing any of the contracting principles. Such contracts fail to deliver any of the benefit of the chosen Agile methodology and are likely to result in project delivery that diverges from the contractual obligations, making it very difficult to resolve issues should they arise.

Contracts can be divided simplistically into three basic elements:

- Key operative provisions that are always bespoke to the particular project, describing the services that will be provided and setting out key responsibilities. These need to be developed specifically to satisfy the requirements for the project and must be closely aligned to the chosen Agile methodology.

- Boilerplate provisions that govern the relationship between the parties, including standard contractual clauses dealing with matters such as ownership of intellectual property, confidentiality, liability limitations, change management and termination. Although common to all contracts these clauses need to be adjusted to deal with the culturally different approaches applied under Agile methodologies.
- Schedules that provide administrative information, processes and procedures such as pricing information, governance boards and the prioritised requirements list. These also need to be aligned to the relevant Agile methodology but are less likely to contain strict legal obligations.

## TEMPLATE EXAMPLES

Examples of template contracts for Agile methodologies include:

- **Practical Law** – this is a subscription-based legal publisher operated by Thomson Reuters that provides a template contract for legal practitioners. The template is an 'AgiFall' style contract that does not include some of the benefits of Agile, such as the ability to terminate at the end of an iteration or when delivery has satisfied the customer's requirements.
- **LexisPSL** – this is a subscription-based legal publisher operated by LexisNexis that provides a template contract for legal practitioners. The template is closer to a true contract for use with Agile methodologies and includes guidance notes. It attempts to be agnostic of methodology but is loosely based on Scrum.
- **Agile Business Consortium Contract** – this is a template developed for use with DSDM and is maintained by the Agile Business Consortium. DSDM uses a fixed project term and/or fixed pricing, though the template could be adopted for other methodologies. Usefully, the template includes embedded guidance notes that explain how the clauses are designed to operate. The template is free to download from the Agile Business Consortium's website at www.agilebusiness.org/page/Resource_Templates_contract.
- **Flexlite 0.1 Flexible Contract** – this is a simple form contract developed in 2013 and is available to use under the Creative Commons Attribution 3.0 Unported License. The template is structured as a master service agreement with 'call off' contracts agreed under short-term 'statements of target outcomes' (i.e. statements of work) developed by the parties. The template is free to download at http://www.flexiblecontracts.com.
- **DOS v2** – this contract was developed for Government Digital Services, a department of Crown Commercial Services (CCS), as part of the Digital Outcomes and Specialists framework (RM1043). In style, it sits between drafting approaches but with a heavy bias towards sequential models, essentially operating as a series of sequential contracts that can be terminated at the end of each phase. A copy of the contract can be obtained from the CCS website at https://www.crowncommercial.gov.uk/agreements/RM1043.6.
- **PS-2000 Agile Contract** – this contract was developed by the Norwegian University of Science and Technology in collaboration with business and is now maintained by the Norwegian Computer Society. It was last updated in December 2013. A copy

of the template can be ordered from the Norwegian Computer Society, subject to payment of a licence fee, at https://dnd.custompublish.com/the-norwegian-computer-societys-contract-standards.4599105-146042.html.

- **Danish K03 Contract** – this contract was developed for the Danish public sector. In style, it sits between drafting approaches but with a heavy bias towards sequential models. It is available at https://digst.dk/media/12781/endelig-kontrakt-k02-eng-pdf-22-02-08-001011.pdf.

## SUMMARY

When used properly, adopting an Agile methodology for a software development project can produce great benefits in terms of flexibility, transparency, user focus and stakeholder participation. However, it also brings challenges, which are often to do with organisational culture: for example, stakeholders accustomed to a more traditional development approach, involving a conventional business requirements document or a fixed specification, may be unnerved by the fluidity of the early stages of an Agile development.

The key to making Agile work is to ensure that the participants clearly understand the methodology to be followed, that they know what to expect in terms of timings and outputs, and that they commit to collaborate in their respective roles as part of the iterative process.

# 12 SETTING UP JOINT VENTURES

Andrew Katz

A joint venture is an increasingly popular way of doing business, especially in the high-tech arena. This chapter discusses the issues that you should consider when embarking upon a joint venture.

## INTRODUCTION

'Joint venture' is not a fixed legal term; it covers a multitude of different business structures, from straightforward channel-to-market arrangements (like agency and distribution) to collaborative partnerships between two or more parties, which may include the formation of a new business, complete with its own staff, premises, branding, products, supply chain and so on.

What all joint ventures have in common is that each party believes it is offering something complementary to the other party (or parties). In combination, the joint venture is greater than the contributions of the individual parties.

Most joint ventures also have an element of sharing risk as well as sharing the reward (something that brings its own legal problems).

Perhaps the biggest mistake the joint venture parties can make is to concentrate on the mechanism of setting up the joint venture, without giving sufficient thought both to how the joint venture is to be run on a day-to-day basis and to how the parties are to exit from the arrangement. In terms of day-to-day management, the question is really one of managing expectations. Most joint venture documents give extensive thought to the amount of financial commitment that each partner will put into the project. Fewer, however, take time to think in terms of the non-financial input, particularly personnel resources. Even fewer joint venture documents adequately address the question of exit. Is one joint venture partner to be given an option to purchase the other? Is the entire joint venture to be sold as a going concern (and, if so, will it still require any input from the former partners)? The parties need to address those questions to maximise the success of a joint venture.

## JOINT VENTURES AND IT PROJECTS

Perhaps the most compelling reason why joint ventures have been popular in the technology market is that they are perceived to be a quick way of getting a business up and running without a large cash commitment. Almost always, it is theoretically possible for a joint venture partner to buy in the skills it needs, if the cash is available. However, it may be more effective for a cash-strapped start-up to obtain that resource in exchange for a share in the rewards, rather than having to reach into its pocket and fund it. Much of the resource required may have a low marginal cost to the supplier, when provided to the joint venture, but would be much more expensive to purchase on the open market.

**CASE STUDY**

New.com wishes to offer a transaction-based service on the internet. Rather than purchasing both the computer hardware and the software it requires on the open market, it seeks a joint venture relationship with the supplier of the software and with an internet hosting company as a low-risk and low-cost means of bootstrapping the resources needed to run the project.

The software company's cost is little more than providing a copy of its software and the internet service provider can (at least initially) provide a virtual machine and bandwidth for the project that may not have been used in any event.

They are supplying resources at low marginal cost to themselves, in circumstances where they would probably not have made a cash sale to New.com in any event. For them, there is little initial risk, investment or effort, coupled with large potential gains if the project takes off.

Care has to be taken in managing the expectations of New.com and the other partners. For example, can the joint venture expect the same level of support and attentiveness from the software company as its fee-paying clients? Will New.com become resentful of the other partners when the venture becomes successful and it realises that its profits would have been much greater if it had bought the software and hosting for cash on the open market? It's also worth bearing in mind that the initial costs of providing application hosting (e.g. provision of a virtual machine, storage and other necessary ancillaries such as a Secure Sockets Layer (SSL) certificate) have plummeted over recent years as the technical capabilities of the hosts have increased, although the costs do ramp up significantly as the application scales.

Occasionally, a joint venture is the only way forward in a relationship where a party has unique assets (e.g. intellectual property such as patents or software) that it is unwilling to transfer or license directly to the other party. That partner may feel more comfortable where the licence is granted to a third party over which it has some control, rather than on arm's-length terms.

Frequently, the sales staff of the joint venture partners can be used to cross-sell each other's products, thus giving bigger market penetration and the benefit that the names of the joint venture partners themselves will add credibility to the joint venture project.

# ESTABLISHING A JOINT VENTURE

## Non-disclosure agreements

Potential joint venture partners will necessarily spend some time finding out about each other's businesses and plans before committing to final documentation. This will frequently involve the parties disclosing sensitive information and, before any of this information is disclosed, all parties should have entered into a non-disclosure agreement (NDA). Disclosures may involve patentable inventions, so failure to enter into an effective NDA could affect the validity of any later applications for patents. As well as covering secrecy, an NDA can cover areas such as non-poaching of staff during and after the negotiations and ownership of intellectual property created during negotiations. The parties' lawyers can advise on the terms of a suitable NDA.

## Heads of agreement

The heads of agreement (or heads of terms) document sets out the commercial terms on which the joint venture will operate, in less legalistic terms than the full documentation, but nevertheless covering all the commercial bases of the deal. The key here is to negotiate the heads quickly, so that the parties do not end up negotiating the same points twice. The heads are not typically legally binding (in lawyers' jargon they should be 'subject to contract' and the lawyers should ensure that they contain wording that expresses this properly).

Even so, in practice it can be difficult for a party to change its mind on a point once it has been enshrined in the heads. A few points follow on from this:

- Establish what is legally binding and what is not as soon as possible. It is possible for parties to create a contract by exchange of letters alone. To avoid this happening, ensure that all correspondence involving joint venture negotiations is marked 'subject to contract', until the final documentation is ready to be signed.
- Do not start operating the joint venture until you have final, signed documentation. If you do so, you could be deemed to have entered into a contract with your joint venture partner on terms that only a court case will be able to unravel.
- Establish who is going to pay the professional advisers' costs, whether or not the joint venture goes ahead.

Many joint venture negotiations end up nowhere, but that is likely to be better than a failed joint venture for all parties, in terms of cost, loss of management time and market perception. The heads of agreement document allows the parties to reach a red or green light as quickly as possible before too much money and management time have been wasted.

## Managing expectations: the business plan

For a successful joint venture, the extent and nature of the involvement of each party needs to be explicitly agreed and recorded as soon as possible. A software supplier in a joint venture with a hardware supplier may assume that its products are going to be sold by a hardware supplier's sales staff and that the products will be co-branded, but unless this is explicitly stated at the outset, the hardware supplier may turn out to have different expectations. To argue 'we will both make more money that way' is never quite as simple as it seems and the perceptions of the partners must coincide. The documentation setting up the joint venture must address these issues explicitly.

The business plan is a critical document in articulating the joint aims and aspirations of the parties. A plan for regular review and updating of the business plan is vital so that disagreements arising out of the business plan can be dealt with before they grow into larger operational issues. Unstated assumptions tend to lead to disputes and a comprehensive business plan can usually weed out erroneous assumptions ('What do you mean you've put in a £2,000 monthly licence fee for the supply of your software? You're supplying it for free, aren't you?').

## Day-to-day management

The partners need to consider how the joint venture will run on a day-to-day basis. It may seem to be micromanagement to think about things like the design of the letterheads or who will sign off stationery expenses, but it is at this level where real disagreements can surface (as anyone who has ever sat in a board meeting or partners' meeting can testify).

Transpose your own experiences onto the joint venture: think about the processes you are familiar with in your own business and use them as a basis for setting up the business processes in the joint venture. If you have an operations handbook for your own business, use that as a starting point and try to develop a similar handbook for the joint venture. If you do this in conjunction with the other partners then you should end up with a workable model for day-to-day management that has flushed out potential disagreement. This will not be a simple or straightforward process, but working together on the handbook and the business plan will give each partner an invaluable feel for the style and culture of the joint venture.

As an aside, do not fall into the trap of believing that, because you have invested significant time and cost in investigating and negotiating a joint venture, you are obliged to enter into it. If you become sure that you and the other partners cannot work together, walk away.

## Ownership of intellectual property

Joint ventures frequently involve the development of intellectual property (IP). For example, the parties may collaborate to develop new software, based on the software of one of the parties or combining the hardware of one party with the software of another. Generally, the IP will belong to the joint venture, but the parties need to address whether the partners are allowed access to it for their own purposes and, if so, on what terms and what happens to the IP in the joint venture exit arrangements.

Commonly, the joint venture will grant a royalty-free licence on the IP to the partners. If the joint venture folds, rather than have a squabble over who gets the IP, a sensible route is to put in place a mechanism whereby the IP can be exploited by each of the partners as if each partner owned it. Any subsequent developments belong solely to the partners who made them (this is known in the software business as 'forking'). The mechanism for achieving this can be a little complicated, but it is often the fairest way to proceed.

Modern software development almost always involves open source software. Since obligations in reciprocal open source licences are triggered by distribution of the code, and it may be the case that code is distributed between the joint venturers (and any special purpose vehicle, if applicable), special care needs to be taken that this distribution does not cause unintended consequences (see Chapter 10 for more information).

## Exit arrangements

Joint ventures rarely last forever and the partners should have a view as to how the joint venture is to end. Is the business secure enough to be sold on the open market? Can one party buy out the other? For example, if a channel-to-market joint venture establishes a bridgehead into a new jurisdiction, the supplying party is increasingly likely to want to purchase the joint venture to bring it into the group structure, in which case there should be an explicit mechanism for this to happen at an appropriate price.

This is part of the management of expectations: are the partners expecting a capital gain on exit within a defined period or a flow of profits from the venture? The exit aspirations of the venture need to be articulated because a venture in which one partner is keen on maximising short-term profits and the other demands constant reinvestment with a view to growing the joint venture for eventual trade-sale is heading for disaster. Joint ventures in which the partners are at loggerheads are likely to decline and fail very quickly. This is because they are unlikely to have management teams that are sufficiently independent (or have the inclination) to steer the venture away from trouble, and the partners are likely to be providing non-cash benefits to the venture that can easily be withdrawn if a dispute arises.

If the exit aspirations involve a sale of the joint venture company (or if there are plans for raising external finance), then the joint venture company has to be groomed for an inevitable due diligence process, and the partners' involvement in the joint venture company may have to be placed on a more arm's-length basis than was probably the case when the joint venture was established.

The joint venture may be so intertwined with the business of one or more of the partners that it cannot effectively stand alone; in those circumstances the venture has to be viewed as an income-only rather than a capital growth proposition and an orderly wind-down needs to be planned for when the joint venture comes to an end.

## STRUCTURE OF A JOINT VENTURE

Having decided on the aims of the joint venture, the partners need to settle on the most appropriate structure (see Table 12.1). At its simplest, the joint venture may consist of cooperative channel-to-market arrangements. A simple channel-to-market joint venture is characterised by a fairly straightforward distribution or agency arrangement, possibly with some additional items bolted on. For example, there is likely to be a trade mark licence that permits the agent/distributor to use the principal/supplier's trade marks. The principal/supplier may also provide additional resource, in terms of, for example, office space, software, consultancy or administration.

**Table 12.1 Factors to consider when forming an entity**

| | Informal channel-to-market structure | Partnership | Limited company | Limited liability partnership (LLP) |
|---|---|---|---|---|
| **Taxation** | Uncertain | Transparent (but must file partnership return) | Taxed as an entity in own right | Transparent (but must file partnership return) |
| **Third-party liability assumed by partners** | Unlimited, especially if the venture is deemed to be partnership | Partners are jointly and severally liable | Partners normally protected by limited liability | Partners normally protected by limited liability |
| **Complexity** | Simple | Reasonably simple | Moderate to complex | Moderate to complex |
| **Certainty** | Good, unless venture deemed to be a partnership | Good | Good | Fairly good (this structure is still relatively new) |
| **International recognition** | Good | Moderate | Good | Good (but new) |
| **Ease of exit** | Difficult to unbundle | Moderate (can sell business and/or underlying assets, but partners may retain some liabilities) | Good (can sell shares and/or underlying business) | Good (can sell partnership interests or underlying business) |
| **Finances made public** | No | No | Yes | Yes |
| **Identity of partners made public** | No (except in certain cases related to competition law) | Yes | Yes | Yes |
| **Separate audit requirement** | No | Not generally | Yes (above thresholds) | Yes (above thresholds) |

## Distribution and agency agreements

What lawyers call a 'distribution agreement' is probably better known as a reseller agreement. The supplier sells the goods to the distributor; the distributor becomes the owner of the goods and pays the supplier for them.

The distributor then sells the goods on to its client. In this case, there are two separate sales involved: the supplier to the distributor and the distributor to the client.

In contrast, an agency relationship involves an agent appointed by the principal to find clients. The agent may then pass details of the client back to the principal who can conclude the deal or the agent can be granted power to sign on the principal's behalf and conclude the deal for the principal. In each case, the agreement will set out precise limits of the power involved.

A distributor makes its money by selling at a higher price than that at which it purchases. An agent makes its money by receiving a commission on the sales that it makes. Where goods are being sold, the relationship is pretty straightforward. For services (including software), the distinction is more unclear. Legal theory lags somewhat behind what happens in practice and, although there is a billion-dollar industry in reselling shrink-wrapped software, lawyers are still pretty much at loggerheads as to what happens as a matter of legal theory. When dealing with services, the lawyers drafting the documents defining the relationship must take extra care because there are some important legal distinctions between the two models (in terms of liability, regulation and termination).

Both agency and distribution models can form the basis of a simple joint venture relationship, frequently where the supplier (or principal) wishes to use the distributor (or agent) to break into a new market.

## Licensing and royalty deals

Licensing deals are very common in IT and are another form of a simple channel-to-market joint venture arrangement. Where a channel-to-market deal involves licensing, it usually either echoes a reseller model (the owner sells software to the reseller who then sells it to the client, taking a cut in the process) or a royalty model (the owner permits the reseller to duplicate and sell copies of the software, remitting to the owner a percentage of its revenues as royalties). The former route tends to be used for shrink-wrapped software and the latter for Original Equipment Manufacturer (OEM) or component software.

## 'Bolt on' terms

Whenever any of these forms of channel-to-market arrangements are employed, there may well be additional duties and obligations placed on each party that deepen the relationship and make it more of a joint venture.

On the part of the owner, additional obligations are likely to be:

- provision of training;
- provision of marketing support;

- permission to use the owner's names/logos;
- provision of front-line or second-line support to the reseller or its clients;
- provision of updates to the software;
- financial support for marketing;
- protection of its intellectual property for the benefit of the reseller.

On the part of the reseller, typical obligations are likely to be:

- sales targets;
- staffing requirements;
- provision of front-line support to clients;
- localisation of products to local markets;
- provision of marketing information back to the owner and/or other resellers;
- protection of the owner's intellectual property.

Financially, the parties may be tempted to structure the deal so that they set up a new accounting ledger for the venture (without setting up a new company or other legal entity) into which they invest certain sums and then split the profits in a certain ratio. This has the danger that the relationship legally forms a partnership, with some unfortunate consequences.

Distribution and agency need not involve the creation of a new legal entity. Other forms of joint venture usually do. For this reason, and also for reasons of increased flexibility, more transparent exit arrangements and ease of introduction of new players, a large number of joint ventures involve the establishment of a new legal entity to undertake the joint venture activity.

### WHEN IS A PARTNERSHIP NOT A PARTNERSHIP?

Lawyers tend to be more precise about the way in which they use various terms than businesses do. For example, 'partnership' has a strictly defined meaning at law, whereas many companies will refer to their 'partners' in a much looser sense. This can lead to problems.

In summary, where the parties are sharing risk as well as reward, there is always a danger that they will be regarded as 'partners' in the eyes of the law (even if the contract between them states that they are not). This has some undesirable consequences, one of which is that each partner becomes liable to the other for any losses of the partnership (and can bind the other in contracts). Another is that they become intertwined with each other for tax purposes (they may be required to file a separate partnership tax return, for example). A partnership agreement is the classic way of dealing with these issues.

## Partnership agreements

In England and Wales, partnerships are governed by the Partnership Act 1890 (despite its age, this is still the current legislation, albeit subject to some updates since then). Many businesses, including many solicitors, accountants and other professional practices, are run under partnership agreements. A partnership under the Act consists of a number of partners (individuals or companies) who have come together for a common business aim (with a view to making a profit).

The liability of the partners is unlimited, meaning that if the partnership incurs losses, each partner is individually liable for, potentially, all of those losses. Partners agree the proportions in which they share any profits of the venture and also the proportions in which any losses are to be borne. Any business relationship having these characteristics is a partnership (whether the partners like it or not). The burden of unlimited liability is often enough to frighten off partners from using this structure. It is possible, however, to have a complex structure where each of the partners will form a limited company that becomes a partner. This way, the partners can benefit from the limited liability afforded by using a limited company.

It is also worth noting that in circumstances where the parties do not adequately set out the details of the relationship between them, then the Act could be applied to the relationship almost by default. Unless the parties want the Act to apply to the relationship, it is good practice both to ensure that any partnership agreement specifically excludes the Act, and, more crucially, to ensure that the relationship does not have the characteristics of a partnership (such as an agreement to share losses).

Partnerships do not have to publish their accounts.

## Limited partnerships

Another structure is a 'limited partnership'. This is basically the same as a partnership, but with two types of partner. First, active partners, who manage the business and still retain unlimited liability. Second, sleeping partners, who are not allowed to get involved in the business of the partnership but are allowed to limit their liability.

Limited partnerships have to be registered at Companies House. They are rare: do not confuse them with limited liability partnerships (LLPs), which are a totally different animal with a confusingly similar name.

## Limited liability partnerships

An LLP is in effect a hybrid of a partnership and a limited company. Like a limited company, it is a legal person and its existence is independent of its partners (called members). The members are protected from the debts and liabilities of the partnership in much the same way as shareholders are in a limited company.

## LEGAL PERSONS

Limited companies, limited liability partnerships and European Economic Interest Groupings are examples of 'legal persons', meaning that they have a legal existence independently of their directors or members. They can enter into contracts in their own name, they can sue and be sued, they can commit criminal offences. In fact, in the eyes of the law, they can do almost anything that a natural person (generally described as an 'individual' by lawyers) can do. Of course, they always need the intervention of an individual as an agent (such as a director) to make that legal relationship, but when acting in a company's name, a director is not also acting as an individual. If a director signs a contract on behalf of the company, it is the company that is liable, not the director. This is in contrast to partnerships, which (in English Law, but not in Scottish Law) have no separate legal personality. A partner signing a contract on behalf of the partnership is always personally liable for the contract, as are the other partners.

If all the directors and shareholders of a company die in a plane crash, the company continues to exist. If any partner in a partnership dies, the partnership ceases to exist, unless the remaining partners agree otherwise.

LLPs were introduced in the UK in 2000, and since then many partnerships operating under the 1890 Act have converted to LLPs to take advantage of the limited liability and other advantages offered by this business structure. LLPs offer interesting possibilities for tax planning (they are 'transparent' for tax purposes, meaning they are not taxable themselves, but are taxed through their members). Members can be other corporate bodies (e.g. limited companies or other LLPs, as well as individuals).

However, in exchange for receiving limited liability status, LLPs, like limited companies, have to publish certain information, such as their accounts, at Companies House. A further potential drawback is the need to set out what each party receives from the LLP by way of profits.

### Limited companies

Limited companies are legal persons that consist of shareholders, who own the company, and directors, who undertake its day-to-day management.

Shareholders have no right to get involved in the day-to-day running of the company, a right that is entrusted to the directors. The shareholders' control of a company is ultimately enshrined in their power to remove and appoint directors. There is (usually) nothing stopping a director from also being a shareholder of the company.

Normally, the shareholders' liability to the company is limited, in that a shareholder cannot be held liable for the debt or other liabilities of the company. In exceptional circumstances, a director may be held liable for any defaults as a director whereas, as a shareholder, the liability is (almost always) limited. But, of course, a shareholder may lose the value of any shares held if the company folds.

Limited liability is very attractive to companies that want to join forces in an untried area. The parties form a company in which they each hold shares to carry out the venture. If the venture folds and the company fails, the parent companies will (in most normal circumstances) be protected from any losses in the joint venture company (although parties dealing with the venture will be aware of this and may try to protect their interests by entering into a parent company guarantee).

Lawyers are very familiar with the limited company as a vehicle for joint ventures and will automatically think of it as an appropriate structure. The checklist set out in the appendix at the end of this chapter assumes that a limited company is the appropriate vehicle, although the issues will also translate to the other entities.

## Other structures

The structures described above all arise under English Law (the law of England and Wales). Other jurisdictions have more or less comparable structures. When the joint venture crosses jurisdictions, always consider which jurisdiction is appropriate for forming the joint venture vehicle. For example, Limited Liability Corporations (LLCs) in the USA (especially the Delaware LLC) offer flexibility of structure and scope for tax planning.

A European Economic Interest Grouping (EEIG) is a creation of the EU. It is broadly similar to a partnership in that an EEIG has partners (at least two of which must be from different member states in the EU), who have joint and several liability and whose liability is unlimited. Unlike a partnership, the EEIG is a legal person. Like a partnership, it is transparent for tax. As an organisation designed to be non-profit making (although profits are not prohibited), it is perhaps more suited to joint ventures aimed at research and development rather than to profit-making channel-to-market joint ventures. To put EEIGs into perspective, there are currently around 200 of them registered in the UK.

There are other UK structures, such as companies limited by guarantee, unlimited companies, friendly, industrial and provident societies, and companies incorporated by Royal Charter. They may all to a greater or lesser extent be involved in joint venture activity, but their uses are very specialised and are not covered here.

## THE OPERATING AGREEMENT

All joint ventures should have some sort of operating agreement that sets out the main facets of the relationship. What should be covered is dealt with in greater depth in the checklist in the appendix to this chapter.

The names and, to a certain extent, the structure of the various documents comprising the operating agreements will vary depending on the type of joint venture. For example, where a joint venture is formed using a limited company as the vehicle, the core documents will be the articles of association of the company coupled with a shareholders' agreement. There may be separate licence agreements (for the provision of intellectual property to the joint venture), management agreements (for the provision of specific management services by the joint venture partners) and property licences or leases (if one or more of the joint venture partners is providing space for the joint venture at their premises). For a partnership, the core document will be the partnership agreement. However, whatever structure is finally adopted, the fundamental issues that need to be adopted in the agreements are largely the same.

## COMPETITION LAW

Whenever businesses start to collaborate, there may be a suspicion that they are no longer competing with each other, and, as a result, any form of joint venture may fall foul of competition law.

Competition law is complex, and this book has space for no more than the briefest summary. Within the UK, competition law is enshrined, in the main, in the Competition Act 1998, the Enterprise Act 2002 and the Enterprise and Regulatory Reform Act 2013 (the latter did not change the law, per se, but rather the institutional structures that enforce it). Within the context of the EU, competition law is based on Articles 101 and 102 of the Treaty of Lisbon. European and UK law are to a large extent harmonised, in that the 1998 Act was based on the European legislation and there is a strong interrelationship between the two.

UK competition law is concerned with activity that tends to restrict or distort competition within the UK, and European competition law is concerned with activity tending to restrict competition between European member states. International joint ventures may also be subject to the competition law (sometimes called 'anti-trust' law) of other jurisdictions (notably the USA).

Competition law is based on the premise that competition between businesses is a good thing and that if businesses get together to act in concert (such as forming a cartel), they not only decrease competition by effectively substituting one composite business where there were previously two, but the more powerful composite business can dictate terms to the market.

On the other hand, it also recognises that when small and medium businesses get together, they can combine to provide a more competitive force in the marketplace by competing with the larger players in that market.

Competition law is therefore aimed at prohibiting activity that has an anti-competitive effect (such as businesses with large market shares combining to dominate the market), while encouraging activity that (broadly) allows smaller businesses to combine forces to compete with the bigger players.

This means that there is activity that is (almost) always absolutely prohibited by competition law (such as price fixing) and activity that is prohibited unless it is deemed sufficiently low-level enough not to affect the market.

Low-level activity can be determined by:

- A judgment call that what the parties are doing does not distort or restrict competition and is therefore legal (something that is almost impossible to prove and that is therefore fraught with danger).

- Being below certain prescribed thresholds of activity in terms of the market share of the businesses concerned (called *de minimis*).
- Being expressly permitted by the competition legislation because there are specific rules in that market sector (block exemptions).
- The competition authorities examining the arrangement and declaring it permissible.

An anti-competitive arrangement is void. A third party adversely affected by such arrangement can sue the partners for damages and there may be penal sanctions (i.e. fines).

Joint ventures, because of their nature, will almost always raise competition law questions, and it is critical to have the arrangements scrutinised at an early stage so that these questions can be addressed. The worst-case scenario is where two direct competitors, each with a large market share, form a joint venture. At the other end of the spectrum, two small businesses working in different fields or at different levels of the supply chain (e.g. a software developer and a value-added reseller) are unlikely to face many general competition law issues. Price fixing is probably the biggest danger area for smaller businesses, and this can arise indirectly as well as directly:

- Partners dictate resale prices to the joint venture.
- Partners provide a price list to the joint venture from which the joint venture may not deviate.
- Partners set the joint venture's prices at a fixed margin over the suppliers' prices.

Specific advice should always be taken in this complex area.

## Joint venturing and open source

In some circumstances, where two or more parties want to collaborate on developing some intellectual property (generally software, but it may relate to hardware as well), an interesting option, where the venturers are happy to make the IP available to the public at large, is to use an open source model to undertake the development. This is simpler than any of the options discussed above, and also has the benefit of avoiding many of the competition law issues that those structures may entail. For more information, see Chapter 10.

## SUMMARY

Companies get involved in joint ventures with other companies for all sorts of reasons: perhaps to make the most of synergies in their technology offerings by pooling their intellectual property rights; to share the costs of investment in a new product or service; to achieve economies of scale; or to compete more effectively with larger businesses. When setting up a joint venture, it is important to be clear about the precise objectives, but it is equally important to address how the venture will operate on a day-to-day basis, how issues between the participants will be resolved and what happens to its intellectual property rights and other assets if and when the joint venture is brought to an end.

## APPENDIX: CHECKLIST FOR A JOINT VENTURE OPERATING AGREEMENT

This checklist sets out the main points that should be addressed irrespective of which business structure is adopted.

- Are the scope and nature of the joint venture clearly defined?
- What assets, resources (services and people) and finance will the joint venture need, both initially and over time? Which are to be provided by the partners and which from third parties?
- Are the partners providing trade mark licences or other IP to the joint venture?
- Are the partners trading with the joint venture (e.g. agency, distribution, licensing)? Are transfer pricing issues relevant?
- Are there any legal hurdles to overcome from the partners' perspective (e.g. is consent required from an investor to take shares in a joint venture)?
- Where is the joint venture to be physically located? Are the partners to provide premises (and associated services)? If so, on what terms?
- What computer hardware and software will the joint venture need?
- Where is it coming from and who will support it? Will additional licences be needed? Will the systems have to interoperate with the partners' systems?
- Who are to be the professional advisers and suppliers (lawyers, auditors, tax advisers, insurers etc.) to the joint venture?
- Does the joint venture need to be registered for VAT?
- Who handles the day-to-day personnel, management, payroll etc. issues?
- Is the joint venture compliant with its data protection obligations (bearing in mind that it may be a data controller in its own right), and can personal data be legitimately transferred between the partners and the joint venture?
- Are there any sector-specific regulatory issues?
- Are there any restrictions on the partners competing with each other or the joint venture? Have competition law aspects been considered?
- Do you need provisions preventing partners from poaching staff from the joint venture or each other?
- What is the nature and structure of the joint venture vehicle? What capital/income contributions are the partners to make?
- Should there be any restrictions on the sale of the partners' interest in the joint venture vehicle (e.g. shareholdings) to third parties or businesses within the partners' group?

- Who are the partners' representatives on the management team (e.g. appointed directors)?
- How are meetings of the partners (e.g. shareholders' meetings) and joint venture management (e.g. directors' meetings) to be convened and run? What decisions can be made at these meetings?
- What powers should be granted to the management team (e.g. are they allowed to raise bank borrowings without reference to the partners)?
- What is the procedure for introducing new partners or allowing existing partners to leave?
- What is the policy for accounting/distributing profits (e.g. a dividend policy)?
- What value (if any) is attributed to intangibles contributed by the joint venture partners?
- Is there a fixed or minimum term for the joint venture?
- What happens if there is a deadlock in decision-making between the partners?
- How does the management team get paid (if at all)? Are they entitled to expenses?
- Can a defaulting partner be forced to sell its interest? If so, at what price? How is that price calculated?
- What constitutes a default of the agreement? Breach of the main operating agreement? Breach of an ancillary agreement (e.g. a supply agreement)? Insolvency?
- What governing law is to cover the agreements (e.g. English)? Whose courts have jurisdiction? Is there a mechanism for dealing with disputes by escalation, arbitration or mediation?

Reproduced by permission of Moorcrofts LLP, www.moorcrofts.com.

# 13 RESOLVING DISPUTES

## Sara Ellacott

This chapter considers the most commonly used methods of dispute resolution, their advantages and disadvantages, together with a consideration of the relevant procedures associated with each method. Mediation is discussed after litigation and arbitration, but you should note that it continues to gain increasing popularity in the UK with the courts, government agencies and the private sector.

## INTRODUCTION

Taking time to consider how to deal with potential disputes at the very outset of a complex technology project can sometimes be regarded as defeatist; the parties are keen to work together and do not want to dwell on the potential difficulties they may face. The reality, however, is that during the life cycle of the majority of technology projects a variety of disputes will happen for a wide variety of reasons:

- business requirements change (commonly referred to as 'scope creep');
- delays mount up;
- complex terms give rise to various interpretations.

Despite the best intentions of the parties, careful planning and excellent working practices, problems can and inevitably do still arise. Time is therefore well spent considering the various methods of dispute resolution available up front, before the need to use them actually arises in practice.

## OVERVIEW OF DISPUTE RESOLUTION METHODS

There is a wide range of potential dispute resolution methods available, the most common of which are:

- commercial negotiation;
- escalation to senior management;
- expert determination;
- litigation;
- arbitration;
- mediation.

There is no 'one size fits all' method of dispute resolution, and your choice will ultimately depend on what you require out of that process; for example:

- Do you require damages/compensation for a particular breach of contract or misrepresentation?
- Is obtaining interim injunctive relief a necessity?
- Is an ongoing relationship important?
- Is it important to maintain confidentiality as to the issues in dispute and the resulting settlement (if any)?

Depending on your needs, the different methods of dispute resolution will be more or less suitable.

## KEY FACTORS IN DISPUTE RESOLUTION

When deciding on any dispute resolution method, there are a number of common factors that should always be taken into account. These include:

- **Impartiality** – is the adjudicator impartial and, maybe more importantly, seen to be impartial?
- **Expertise** – has the adjudicator the correct level of expertise to deal with the issues in dispute?
- **Speed** – how long will it take the adjudicator to reach a decision?
- **Cost** – how expensive will the process be?
- **Certainty** – will the decision be legally binding and can it be appealed?
- **Confidentiality** – will the decision/settlement be confidential?
- **Motivation** – who, if anyone, has a vested interest in the dispute and its resolution?
- **Impact on business relationship** – can the relationship continue after the dispute is resolved?
- **Ease of enforcement** – can the decision be enforced domestically and/or abroad?

Each method of dispute resolution has its advantages and disadvantages, and we will consider each method against these key factors before addressing the relevant procedures associated with it.

## SPECIFIC DISPUTE RESOLUTION METHODS

### Commercial negotiation

Direct commercial negotiation between the parties is one of the most common, popular and successful ways of resolving disputes. Table 13.1 shows how negotiation relates to the key factors.

**Table 13.1 Negotiation**

| | |
|---|---|
| Impartiality | Not relevant (the parties are negotiating for their own benefit). |
| Expertise | Not particularly advantageous or relevant (although the people involved with the technology project will have first-hand knowledge of the issues in dispute and how they can be resolved). |
| Speed | Good: negotiations can be undertaken as quickly as the parties require (although it is up to the parties to ensure that they do not drag on indefinitely, without any actual formal resolution of the dispute). |
| Cost | Good: the costs incurred will primarily be those of the parties involved in the negotiations (additional costs may be incurred if the parties use internal or external legal advisors). |
| Certainty | Not good: the parties will come to a settlement only if they choose to do so. |
| Confidentiality | Good: such negotiations can be conducted on a 'without prejudice' and confidential basis. This encourages openness between the parties and ensures that the negotiations cannot be used in formal evidence if they break down and the parties end up using another form of dispute resolution. This is important, as the parties may be prepared to make concessions in their negotiating positions for the sake of reaching a compromise, which they would not be prepared to concede if they were litigating the dispute. |
| Motivation | Good: such negotiations usually involve those most heavily involved with the project on a day-to-day basis (the project manager, the IT director, the account manager, the commercial team, etc.). These parties are most closely aligned with the project and therefore have a vested interest in resolving issues. |
| Business relationship | Good: such negotiations often allow for a positive ongoing relationship working (in some cases, it can be stronger than the one that existed before the dispute). This is particularly important for those in technology projects, which often last for a number of years. |
| Enforcement | Not good: any settlement can only be enforced by one party bringing a claim against the other for breach of contract (i.e. breach of the settlement terms). This can be time-consuming and expensive. |

## Escalation to senior management

Some technology contracts require that the parties try and resolve disputes through senior management before resorting to external methods.

The advantages and disadvantages of this method are generally very similar to those of negotiation, but there is a particular 'plus' when it comes to motivation. Sometimes those at the 'coalface' of a large-scale technology project can become too emotionally involved to resolve a dispute: they allow their personal prejudices to prevent them seeing the advantages of a commercial resolution. Escalation to senior management can cut through such prejudices, and so allow for the 'bigger picture' to be considered and a commercial resolution found.

## Expert determination

Expert determination has been very popular method of dispute resolution in the construction industry for a number of years, and it is also well suited to the settlement of technology disputes (although its take-up in the IT sector has not been as widespread as many people had previously envisaged. In fact, take up has in reality been low).

It is a procedure by which an independent third-party expert makes a decision on the dispute. The expert does not act as a judge or as an arbitrator. Table 13.2 shows how expert determination relates to the key factors.

**Table 13.2 Expert determination**

| | |
|---|---|
| Impartiality | Good: the parties have to agree on an expert so they will only agree to someone they both believe to be impartial. |
| Expertise | Good: the parties will choose an individual who is an expert in the technology or project type (e.g. customer relationship management (CRM), enterprise resource planning (ERP)) in dispute. |
| Speed | Good: the process can be set up as quickly as the parties can agree (subject to the expert's availability). |
| Cost | Good: in contrast to both litigation and arbitration, the process is relatively inexpensive. |
| Certainty | Good: the result is contractually binding and thus difficult to appeal. This often brings finality to the dispute. The law on expert determination is, however, not conclusive and is still developing. Moreover, there are no arrangements or laws that allow for the enforcement of an expert's decision abroad. |
| Confidentiality | Good: the procedure is confidential, and this is clearly beneficial to a technology supplier, which would not want its customer base to become aware of any particular problems with its technology offering. |
| Motivation | Not a particularly relevant or overriding factor. |
| Business relationship | Good: expert determination may help to preserve a business relationship because it is slightly less adversarial than litigation or arbitration. |
| Enforcement | Good: failure to adhere to a decision will be a breach of contract. An expert's determination can thus be enforced by obtaining summary judgment and using general enforcement methods. |

The procedure adopted for expert determination depends on the terms of the parties' contract (although they may decide to put a dispute to expert determination by later agreement). The 'terms of reference' set out how the expert is required to act and should include clear definitions of:

- the issues under dispute;
- the material the expert is expected to review;
- what the expert is allowed to consider (matters may arise from investigations that the parties to the dispute feel the expert is not equipped to deal with);
- the procedure and timescale to be followed;
- the nature of the submissions each party is allowed to make;
- what type of hearing is required;
- how the final decision is to be delivered (i.e. orally or in writing).

The expert is usually appointed from a recognised body. The parties may appoint a panel of experts rather than an individual; each person having been selected to provide a different type of expertise and perspective.

The parties may agree grounds upon which a decision may be challenged.

If there is no express agreement, then common law inserts the following grounds as reason for appeal:

- Fraud by the expert.
- Failure by the expert to treat the two parties fairly or equally.
- A 'material departure' from the instructions by the expert (any departure from the instructions that is more than trivial will be a 'material departure' irrespective of the consequences).
- A 'manifest error' by the expert (i.e. a blunder or omission capable of affecting the determination). It must have a significant consequential effect on the outcome of the determination; a minor mistake will not render the decision invalid, unless the parties have agreed that it will in their terms of reference.
- An error in an accountant's certificate that details the adjustment in value of a purchase price when that price is being determined by the expert.

## Litigation

Litigation is the traditional method of resolving contractual disputes. The landscape of civil litigation changed with the introduction of the Civil Procedure Rules (CPR) 1998. The CPR continues to place an emphasis on the front-loading of legal costs, by the parties having to properly set out their claims at an early stage in the proceedings (in what is referred to as a 'letter before action'). Table 13.3 shows how litigation relates to the key factors.

## Table 13.3 Litigation

| | |
|---|---|
| Impartiality | Good: judges are impartial. |
| Expertise | Good: the technical expertise of judges has improved a lot in recent years, particularly those in the Technology and Construction Court (TCC). Judges can also appoint experts to advise them on technical issues. |
| Speed | Still not good: the courts are concerned with giving a decision (based on law) that is fair and objective. The speed of the decision-making process can therefore be secondary to obtaining a correct adjudication and the matter may go to appeal. However, the CPR allows for the courts to manage cases strictly and this has helped to reduce the timescales of litigation. |
| | It is now possible to bring an action to trial within a year of the proceedings being commenced, particularly if the court orders a speedy trial (this is certainly no slower than most arbitrations). Large and complex IT cases can and do, however, still take a number of years to reach conclusion (the *BSkyB* v. *HP/EDS* case being a prime example). |
| | It is possible to make an application for urgent injunctive relief. This can often bring a matter to a very swift resolution; the party against whom the injunction is granted often looks for a commercial resolution at that time. |
| Cost | Still not good: particularly if complex areas of IT law or technical matters have to be considered and expert evidence is required. The winning party does, however, generally have the ability to claim back a proportion of its costs from the losing party, which helps to reduce the financial burden. |
| Certainty | Good: litigation in the UK, and in most other jurisdictions, is governed by the rules of the relevant courts. The rules do allow for some flexibility, but they are not as flexible as other forms of dispute resolution. Litigation has the advantage of finality (although the appeal process can lengthen the final outcome) and results in a binding judgment. |
| Confidentiality | Not good: most court papers and hearings are open to the public (the press can be admitted to the court room). |
| Motivation | Not a relevant or overriding factor. |
| Business relationship | Not good: as an adversarial process, litigation encourages tenacious contests, often bitterly fought by the parties. |
| Enforcement | Good: the binding judgment in a domestic technology dispute is enforceable through the courts. The position is less clear when one looks at international technology disputes: if the defendant is based outside the jurisdiction of the court and has no assets within that jurisdiction, the judgment may have little effect. |

The procedure for litigation is:

1. The party who believes its rights have been infringed (the 'claimant') sends a 'letter before action' to the infringing party (the 'defendant'). It is essential that the letter before action sets out the claim in sufficient detail to enable the defendant to fully understand the case against it. Thus, the claimant generally must undertake a significant amount of preparation before sending this letter. When dealing with IT issues, this preparation can be particularly detailed and time-consuming. Failure to send such a detailed letter can have costs implications at the end of the case.
2. The defendant will usually respond in writing to the claimant's letter before action. At this stage, the parties may also attempt to negotiate a settlement on a 'without prejudice' basis (or explore alternative dispute resolution methods, particularly if required to do so by a contract between them, or the courts).
3. If the parties are unable to reach settlement, the claimant may elect to issue legal proceedings in the appropriate court (most likely the TCC). The claimant must serve upon the defendant a 'claim form' (a formal court form containing brief details of the claim) and 'particulars of claim' (a more detailed document setting out the claim and the remedies sought).
4. The defendant must acknowledge service of the claim and may at that stage elect to admit the claim, or defend all or part of it. If intending to defend the claim, then the defendant must file with the court a 'defence' (a response to the claim, including the reasons why the defendant is not liable). A defendant who also has a claim against the claimant may file a 'counterclaim' (a document similar to the claimant's particulars of claim). If the defendant fails to acknowledge service of the claim or file a defence, the claimant may apply to the court for judgment in default of a defence.
5. The court allocates the claim to the appropriate 'track' (small claims, fast-track or multi-track), depending upon the value and complexity of the claim. Technology disputes are dealt with by way of multi-track. Each party completes an allocation questionnaire providing details about the dispute, to assist the court with allocation.
6. The claimant may also choose to serve a 'reply' to the defendant's defence and a 'defence to counterclaim' if appropriate. (If the claimant fails to defend a counterclaim, the defendant may apply for judgment in default.) Unless there are exceptional circumstances, the claimant's reply and defence to the counterclaim brings an end to the process by which the parties set out their legal positions in writing. The remainder of the litigation process focuses upon the collection and exchange of each party's evidence.
7. The court sets the timetable (or directions) for the further steps in the proceedings, including disclosure and inspection of the parties' documentary evidence, exchange of witness statements and expert reports, dates for any interim hearings (e.g. the trial of a preliminary issue or a pre-trial review). The court is guided by information provided by the parties in their allocation questionnaires, which may include each party's preferred directions. The court may also order that the parties attend a hearing, known as a case management conference, to discuss directions. It is a particular feature of the CPR that the courts now take a very 'hands on' approach towards case management. It is fairly common for the directions to include a short stay of proceedings for the parties to attempt to reach settlement by alternative dispute resolution methods, such as mediation.

Following completion of the steps set out in the timetable for directions, the matter will go to trial. Trial may take the form of a single hearing, or the court has the option of trying a key preliminary issue on its own, on the basis that if this is decided in a certain party's favour it may end proceedings (or encourage an out-of-court settlement) and save the cost of a full hearing. After hearing the parties' cases at trial, the court gives its judgment and may grant leave to appeal.

There may also be a separate hearing to determine how legal costs are to be divided between the parties (generally the losing party pays the winner's costs, although the courts have a wide discretion to order costs on the most appropriate basis). If a party fails to comply with any order of the court, it may be necessary for the other party to go back to court to seek a further order for enforcement.

## Arbitration

Arbitration is seen as the traditional alternative to litigation. It is a private and binding adjudicative process and was conceived as a way of providing a solution for commercial disputes in a practical and cost-effective way. Table 13.4 shows how arbitration relates to the key factors.

**Table 13.4 Arbitration**

| | |
|---|---|
| Impartiality | Good: the parties choose the arbitrator, so it can be assumed that they are happy with the impartiality of the individual. In an international arbitration, it is common to have a tribunal of three arbitrators, with the chair being neutral and each party appointing an arbitrator, who may well be of their nationality. |
| Expertise | Good: the appointed arbitrator will possess particular commercial or technical expertise. If necessary, more than one arbitrator (one technical, one legal, for example) can be appointed. |
| Speed | Good: arbitration offers some opportunities for innovation and for devising an appropriate cost-effective procedure for a particular dispute. The speed of domestic technology arbitrations may well rest on the development of such procedures. (There are also opportunities for doing this in international technology arbitration, but the costs of such arbitrations are generally substantial.) |
| Cost | Not good: a large-scale technology arbitration is likely to be at least as expensive as litigation, if not more so. Arbitration is only cheaper if it disposes of a dispute more quickly and efficiently than court proceedings. Whether this is so depends on the cooperation of the parties to achieve that end and the strength of the arbitral panel. Since the arbitrator's engagement is a matter of contract, dates that are fixed will be kept by the tribunal.<br><br>However, if the parties allow their disputes to spill over into the procedural conduct of the arbitration, this may well nullify such cost benefits. |

*(Continued)*

**Table 13.4 (Continued)**

| | |
|---|---|
| Certainty | Good: there is very little difference between litigation and arbitration in this respect. However, one of the main differences between the two procedures is that an arbitrator may not have to decide according to law. This does not mean that an arbitrator should disregard the rules of law altogether, but the parties can authorise the arbitrator to decide not strictly in accordance with the law (e.g. in order to prioritise commercial fairness over strict legal entitlement). |
| Confidentiality | Good: only the parties to the dispute may attend the arbitration hearing, and all documents prepared by both parties for the purpose of the arbitration are confidential and protected from disclosure in any subsequent proceedings. Although not true in all jurisdictions, non-statutory arbitration in the UK is private. This is a clear advantage because many arbitrations involve an investigation of material that is considered to be commercially sensitive, whether financially or because of the technology under consideration. |
| Motivation | Not a relevant or overriding factor. |
| Business relationship | Not good: like litigation, arbitration is an adversarial process involving procedures that can be tenaciously utilised by lawyers. The outcome is often a breakdown in relationships. |
| Enforcement | Good: The Convention on the Recognition and Enforcement of Foreign Arbitral Awards 1958 (known as the 'New York Convention') provides for the awards from arbitration to be upheld internationally. The Convention has attracted near universal adherence (144 countries have signed up to it). Enforcement under the New York Convention is not always easy, but it undoubtedly gives an arbitral award greater international effectiveness than a court judgment. |

The framework for arbitration is governed by statute. Contracts often contain clauses that refer any dispute to arbitration. If such a clause exists, the parties must adhere to it rather than issuing proceedings in the courts.

The parties to the contract select the arbitrator together on the basis of expertise in the field from which the dispute stems or on which the contract is based.

The arbitrator's conduct is governed by the ordinary rules of natural justice, evidence and the civil burden of proof (the case must be proven 'on the balance of probabilities'). The parties are, however, at liberty to dispense with the ordinary rules of evidence and allow the arbitrator to carry out a more inquisitorial role.

If there is no governing arbitration clause, the parties may opt to engage in arbitration by agreement. In this instance, the parties meet and agree the terms of the arbitration agreement after the dispute has arisen. As is the case when an arbitration clause in a contract is being drafted, the parties are at liberty to determine the timescale, applicable law, procedure and venue of the arbitration as well as the arbitrator they wish to use. In effect, the parties tailor the personnel, procedure and hearings to their particular needs.

During the arbitration proceedings, the arbitrator gives directions and may hold hearings in much the same way as a judge would in litigation proceedings. The arbitrator does this in accordance with the rules adopted by the parties, be they of their own invention or adopted from a particular institution's prescribed rules.

The arbitrator may have to decide on the rules of the arbitration if the parties are unable to agree. The parties are able to refer issues to the courts if the arbitrator is guilty of any misconduct. The courts may also determine points of law and support the arbitrator by making various orders.

The arbitrator will hold a final hearing at which they will make an award to one of the parties. There is no requirement for the arbitrator to give reasons for the award they make. However, if one of the parties asks for reasons and they refuse to give them, then the court (on application from the party concerned) may order them to do so. The award made is legally enforceable against the other party, but a party is allowed to appeal to the court against an award on a point of law.

## Mediation

Mediation involves the appointment of an independent, qualified mediator (or mediators) to assist the parties in reaching an agreed settlement. A mediator does not usually have an adjudicative role in the proceedings, nor is it the mediator's role (unless expressly asked to do so by the parties to the mediation) to pass judgment, or to give an opinion on the merits of the parties' individual cases. Rather, the mediator's role is to facilitate the resolution of the dispute in question.

The use of mediation in the technology industry has continued to increase, particularly as parties to a dispute now face increasing pressure from the courts to resolve their differences through alternative dispute resolution methods rather than court proceedings. The CPR state that the court must further the overriding objective by actively managing cases, including 'encouraging the parties to use an alternative dispute resolution procedure if the court considers that appropriate and facilitating the use of such procedure', and there has been a corresponding increase in court-ordered mediations.

Moreover, the government has encouraged the use of mediation in the public sector. Under the Lord Chancellor's Pledge, alternative dispute resolution methods should be considered and used in all suitable cases wherever the parties accept it. This covers government departments and agencies.

If a party in a technology dispute refuses an invitation to mediate, without a legitimate reason for such a refusal, it may risk being criticised by the courts should the dispute result in legal proceedings. That party could also face cost penalties regardless of the outcome of such legal proceedings, should a court consider a refusal to mediate to constitute unreasonable conduct.

Table 13.5 shows how mediation relates to the key factors.

**Table 13.5 Mediation**

| | |
|---|---|
| Impartiality | Good: the parties choose a mediator, so they will be able to select a person who they regard as possessing impartiality. |
| Expertise | Not relevant: the mediator's expertise does not necessarily need to be legal or technical; it is more important that the mediator is well-trained and able to facilitate an open and constructive discussion. If necessary, the parties could appoint an additional, more technical, mediator. |
| Speed | Good: mediation ends when the parties reach a settlement, or when a party or mediator decides to terminate the process. Commonly, mediation does not last more than a day (much less time than arbitration or court proceedings). The time spent preparing for a mediation is also much less than the time spent preparing for litigation or arbitration. |
| Cost | Good: the costs are a fraction of those that would be incurred were legal proceedings to be initiated. Moreover, the significant costs orders and damages awards that may be awarded in court proceedings can be avoided. |
| Certainty | Moderate: if successful, mediation results in the resolution by an agreement of the parties. It may not be a 'correct' legal decision, but resolution will in general be 'fair' because it will be consented to by both parties. |
| Confidentiality | Good: mediation is a strictly confidential process. All representations made during this process (whether written or oral) are also 'without prejudice' and therefore any documentation produced for the purposes of the mediation and admissions made during it cannot, in most cases, be relied upon as evidence by the parties in court proceedings should the mediation prove unsuccessful. |
| Motivation | Good: parties who agree to mediate are usually committed to reaching a commercially acceptable resolution, particularly if an ongoing business relationship is a possibility. |
| Business relationship | Good: the mediation process is significantly closer to business negotiations than to adversarial courtroom procedures, so business relationships can better be preserved. |
| Enforcement | Not good: the process of mediation is non-binding and the parties cannot be forced to settle their dispute unless a consensus to do so is reached. If a settlement is agreed, it only becomes binding upon the parties once the terms have been recorded in a settlement agreement and the agreement is executed by all parties concerned. If a party refuses to carry out the terms of settlement, it is necessary to commence an action on the settlement agreement, to obtain judgment and then to seek execution of the judgment.<br><br>Experience, however, suggests that parties who have mediated a settlement of their dispute tend to voluntarily carry out the terms of settlement and that a formal enforcement procedure is rarely necessary. |

The parties are expected to agree upon a choice of mediator. The choice of mediator will invariably be determined by the nature of the dispute, and the mediator may be a lawyer, an accountant or a technical expert. In the IT industry, a legally qualified mediator with knowledge of the industry, or possibly a technically qualified expert, is often preferable. A venue for the mediation also needs to be agreed upon. This is usually a venue independent of the parties.

The process usually follows this format, although it is open to the parties to agree to any suitable process between themselves:

1. The parties prepare written case summaries that are exchanged with each other and provided to the mediator in advance of the mediation. This allows the mediator to understand the issues in dispute and the parties' respective positions. The case summaries should highlight any facts and issues that have been agreed by the parties as well as those that remain in dispute. These summaries are usually supported by an agreed bundle of relevant documentation to which the parties can refer in their summaries. This is usually made up of contracts, correspondence, notes of meetings, relevant technical papers and so on. The mediation takes place shortly after the exchange of case summaries and copy documentation.

2. The mediation commences with a joint session attended by all the parties (and their legal representatives) and the mediator, at which the parties are invited to give a short presentation of their positions in relation to the dispute.

3. The parties retire to separate rooms and a series of what are termed 'caucus' sessions commence. The sessions involve the mediator visiting each of the parties to discuss and explore their respective legal positions. The mediator will use these caucus sessions to establish if there is any middle ground between the parties that may form the basis of a negotiated settlement.

4. The mediator may call the parties back for further open sessions to discuss any progress that has been made or issues that have been raised.

5. If the parties are successful in establishing a commercial resolution to the dispute, the mediator will expect them to sign up to written terms of settlement prior to the close of the mediation. Most mediation organisations insist upon the parties making available personnel with the appropriate authority to settle the dispute. Mediators are particularly keen on any agreement reached being drawn up and signed by the parties on the day of the mediation because this avoids the parties subsequently disputing the terms of any agreement reached.

## SUMMARY

There is no 'right answer' when choosing a dispute resolution process. Each method has advantages and disadvantages that will play a part in the decision-making process.

The courts, and the increasing range of arbitration bodies, continue to take action to improve their offerings as dispute resolution providers. Mediation also continues to gain popularity in the UK as a commercial and cost-effective way of resolving disputes. A refusal to consider the available dispute resolution methods could have heavy cost implications, and they are accordingly worth addressing properly during the contract negotiation phase of a technology project, as well as in the early stages of any actual dispute.

# INDEX

acceptance testing 6, 8, 12, 23
action plan 148
Adobe 15, 53, 195
agency agreements 218
Agile computing contracts 11, 199–200, 201, 203
Agile software development 197–211
   Agile Manifesto 197–8, 203
   barriers 200–1
   collaboration 204
   cone of uncertainty 202
   contract drafting 209–10
   copyright 204, 205
   ending a project 205–6
   flexibility 203–4
   intellectual property rights 204–5
   intransigence of lawyers 201
   iterative contracts 199–200
   methodologies 185, 186, 198, 199, 201, 207, 208, 209, 210
   MoSCoW rules 206, 208–9
   MVP 206, 208, 209
   principles 198
   project roles 204
   project scope 201–2
   risk and liability 207
   sequential contracts 199–200, 201, 202, 210, 211
   statement of requirements 202–3
   template contract examples 210–11
Amazon 13, 14, 17, 19, 20, 69, 165, 171, 175
APT 28 60
arbitration 234–6

Ashley Madison 53, 59
ASP (Application Service Provision) 14
automated processing 104, 109–10, 129
AWS (Amazon Web Services) 13, 14, 17, 19, 20

bandwidth 14, 15, 213
BCR (binding corporate rules) 101, 103, 136
boilerplate 1, 2, 210
'bolt on' terms 218–19
Brexit 36, 37, 39, 49, 50, 74, 139
business continuity provisions 29–30
business emails 147–8, 150
business plans 214–15
BYOD (bring your own device) 57, 66, 77, 81, 94

CAA (Copyright Assessment Agreement) 192
Chambers' Guide to the Legal Profession 2
charging arrangements 6, 7
Chartered Institute of Patent Attorneys 50
Chartered Institute of Trade Mark Attorneys 50
CIF (Cloud Industry Forum) 23, 91
CISQ (Consortium for IT Software Quality) 77, 90
CLA (Contributor Licence Agreement) 192
click-wrap agreements 21, 22, 39
cloud computing 13–20
   benefits 16–18
   community cloud 16

   contracts 11, 21–35
   definition 13
   disadvantages 18–20
   environmental impact 18
   evolution 13, 14
   hybrid cloud 16
   private cloud 16
   public cloud 16
   security 79–80
   standards 91–2
cloud computing contracts 11, 21–35
   business continuity provisions 29–30
   compensation 28
   liability provisions 24–5
   negotiation 23, 24
   pre-contractual steps 22–4
   risk management 22
   security 27–8
   service availability 26–7
cloud strategies 15
Competition Act (1998) 223
competition law 223–4
Computer Misuse Act (1990) 73, 147
confidential information 12, 47, 48, 54, 63, 150, 155
consultancy services contract 4
Consumer Price Index 7, 9
contingency 4
contractually binding 3, 230
controller 96, 99, 100, 101, 105, 106, 112, 113
Convention on the Recognition and Enforcement of Foreign Arbitral Awards (1958) 235

239

Copyleft licence 167, 169, 172, 175, 183, 184, 187, 192
copyright
  Agile software development 204, 205
  intellectual property law 36, 38, 40, 41, 42, 44, 45, 46–7
  IT contracts 5, 8
  IT in the workplace 143, 148, 154
  open source software 167, 169, 183, 185, 187, 191, 192, 193
Copyright, Designs and Patents Act (1988) 168, 204
corrective maintenance 9
Counter-Terrorism and Security Act (2015) 73
CPR (Civil Procedure Rules, 1998) 231, 232, 233, 236
cross-browser testing 15
cyber espionage 59
cyber Essentials 77, 84, 85–8, 90
cyber security 51–94
  case study 55–7
  checklist 92–4
  confidential information 63
  cyber espionage 59
  cyber security plan 75–85
  cyber threats 52
  cyber warfare 60
  data protection legislation 74–5
  data storage 68–9
  definition 51–2
  guides and frameworks 85–9
  hacking 57, 58, 59, 60–1, 64, 65, 67, 68, 69, 73, 79
  impact of breaches 53, 54, 63–5
  implementing measures 54
  insider threats 68
  laws and legislation 69–75
  main threats 60–2
  measures to protect ICS 62
  passwords 65–6
  policy 66–7
  RDSP 71–2
  responsibilities 55–7
  security breaches 52–3
  standards 89–92
  technical flaws 67
  threats to ICS 62

types of cyber attack 57–9
WannaCry and Petya attacks 53
*Cyber Security Small Business Guide* 52
Cybersecurity Act (2019) 72–3
cyberspace 52, 69

data ownership 32
data protection 19, 34
  *see also* GDPR
Data Protection Act (2018) 19, 74, 75, 96, 105, 112, 135
Data protection in practice 116–42
  after Brexit 139
  anonymous data 118
  children's personal data 127–9
  consent 123
  controllers and processors 130–1, 133
  data breaches 139–42
  by default 117
  by design 117
  DPA 131–3
  DPIA 117, 122, 125
  DPO 134–5
  drafting policies 124–5
  international data processing 138
  international transfers 135–8
  lawful basis for processing 120–3
  legitimate interest 122–3
  objections 127
  processing personal data 117
  pseudonymous data 118–19
  recognising personal data 117–18
  record of processing 119–20
  requests from subjects 125–7
  SAR 125–6
data security 16, 17, 20, 104, 117, 124, 139, 140, 141
database right 36, 40, 41, 45, 46
DDoS (Distributed Denial of Service) 58
deliverables 3, 4, 10, 200, 206, 207
Digital Outcomes and Services contract 205
Digital Single Market Strategy 70
disclaimers 147

dispute resolution 2, 43, 227–38
  arbitration 234–6
  escalation 229–30
  expert determination 230–1
  key factors 228
  litigation 231–4
  mediation 236–8
  negotiation 228–9
  overview of methods 227–8
  specific methods 228–38
distribution agreement 218
DoS (Denial of Service) 58
DPA (data processing agreement) 131–3
DPIA (Data Protection Impact Assessments) 117, 122, 125
DPO (data protection officer) 116, 125, 134–5, 140, 141
draft contract 4, 12
Dragos 62
DSE (Display Screen Equipment) Regulations (1992) 158–60, 162, 163
DSP (Digital Service Provider) 70
dual licensing models 170, 185
*Durant v. Financial Services Authority* (2003) 115

EEIG (European Economic Interest Grouping) 222
employment law in the workplace 161–3
  Equality Act 162–3
  recruitment 161–2
ENISA (European Union Agency for Network and Information Security) 70, 72
Enterprise Act 2002 223
Enterprise and Regulatory Reform Act (2013) 223
entire agreement 2
Equality Act (2010) 156, 161, 162–3
estimated maximum price 4
EU Cybersecurity Strategy 69
European Agenda on Security 69
European Court of Justice 106
European Data Protection Board 100, 135, 136
executable code 91

Facebook 13, 127, 153, 165, 171
feasibility study 4

fixed price 4
force majeure 2, 25, 30
FSF (Free Software Foundation) 166, 167, 175, 193, 194

GDPR (General Data Protection Regulation, 2018) 19, 20, 65, 96
GDPR and data protection 96–115
   accountability 104
   accuracy 103
   automated processing 109–10
   consent 100–1
   data covered 96–7
   data minimisation 103
   data protection principles 98–104
   enforcement powers 112–13
   exemptions 110
   fairness 101
   fines 113–14
   individual rights 104–10
   integrity and confidentiality 104
   privacy notice 101
   purpose limitation 102–3
   remedies 111–12
   special categories 97–8
   storage limitation 103
Gh0st RAT 59
GENIVI alliance 174
Google 19, 106, 115, 153, 165, 171, 175
Google Cloud 13, 14
GPL (General Public Licence) 175, 184, 185, 187, 188, 192

hacking/hacktivism 57, 58, 59, 60–1, 64, 65, 67, 68, 69, 73, 79, 147
hardware
   licence 4
   maintenance 4
   maintenance contracts 9
   purchase 4
   purchase contracts 8–9
heads of agreement document 214
health and safety 156–61
Health and Safety at Work Act (1974) 156, 157
HPL (Honest Public Licence) 175

IaaS (Infrastructure as a Service) 13, 14, 24
IASME (Information Assurance for Small and Medium Enterprises) 77, 90
IBM 15, 172, 193, 195
ICO (Information Commissioner's Office) 19, 58, 64, 112, 113, 119, 123–5, 131, 134–6, 137, 141
ICS (industrial control systems) 60, 62
identity theft 58, 61
IEC (International Electrotechnical Commission) 77, 89, 90
Impact Team 59
insurance 5, 51, 61, 83–4, 94, 189, 190, 207
integrators 23, 24
intellectual property law 36–50
   authorised sales 37
   copyright 36, 38, 40, 41, 42, 44, 45, 46–7
   databases 40–1, 46
   decompilation 39
   designs 49–50
   domain names 42–3
   hardware 37
   licence transfer 39
   main types of intellectual property 36
   moral rights 46
   patents 46–7
   software 38–9
   trade marks 43–5, 48
   websites 41–2
intellectual property rights 5, 32, 37–8, 40–2, 154, 167, 170, 204–5
Investigatory Powers Act (2000) 73, 144
invitation to tender 4
IoT (internet of things) 52, 62, 188
ISO (International Organization for Standardization) 77, 89, 90, 186
IT contracts 1–12
   Agile computing 11
   cloud computing 11
   consultancy services 4
   copyright 5, 8
   form 1
   hardware maintenance 9
   hardware purchase 8–9
   letter of intent 3

   main points 11–12
   SaaS 30–4
   SLA 10–11
   software development 7–8
   software licences 5, 6
   software maintenance 6–7
   supplier's terms 3
IT in the workplace 143–55
   action plan 148
   business emails 147–8, 150
   copyright 143, 148, 154
   disclaimers 147
   DSE (Display Screen Equipment) Regulations 158–60
   hacking 147
   health and safety regulations 157–61
   health and safety responsibilities 156–61
   interception of communications 145
   monitoring internet use 144–5
   policies 143–7
   private email 146
   social media 152–3
   social media policy example 153–4
   staff policy 146–7
   staff policy example 148–52
   unauthorised websites 146
iterative methodology 197, 199, 200

joint ventures 136, 212–26
   agency agreements 218
   'bolt-on' terms 218–19
   business plan 214–15
   case study 213
   competition law 223–4
   day-to-day management 215
   distribution agreement 218
   establishing 214–16, 217
   exit arrangements 216, 219
   heads of agreement document 214
   intellectual property 215
   licensing and royalties 218
   limited companies 221
   limited liability partnerships 220
   limited partnerships 220

operating agreement 222, 225–6
partnership agreement 219–20
structure 216

key personnel 5
keylogger 66
keywords 45

Law Society 2, 50, 137
*Legal 500* 2
letter of intent 3
level of risk 2, 69
LIA (Legitimate Interest Assessment) 122, 123
licence agreements 5, 6, 222
'licence-in, licence-out' policy 192
linking and framing 44–5
Linux 171, 172, 175, 183, 185, 186, 189, 191, 192–3, 194–5
litigation 231–4
LLP (Limited Liability Partnerships) 217, 220–1

maintenance contracts 6–7, 9, 38, 40
malware 57, 58, 59, 61, 62, 68, 87
Management of Health and Safety at Work Regulations (1999) 157
mediation 236–8
metatags 44, 45
MFA (multi-factor authentication) 62, 79, 82
Microsoft 15, 36, 67, 159, 165, 172, 175
Microsoft Azure 13, 14, 20
MitM (man in the middle) 67
multi-tenant 14
MVP (Minimum Viable Product) 206, 208, 209
Myanmar 60

National Cyber Security Centre 52, 84
NHS (National Health Service) 5, 51, 53
NIS (Network and Information Systems) Regulations (2018) 71, 72
NIS/Cyber Security Directive (2016) 70

NIST (National Institute of Standards and Technology) 13
cyber security framework 88–9, 93

object code 90, 91, 165, 167, 175, 185
OEM (Original Equipment Manufacturer) 218
OES (Operator of Essential Services) 70, 71
OIN (Open Invention Network) 194
Open Office 172
open source software 165–96, 216
benefits and risks 170
business models 172–3
cloud 174–5, 188
compliance 190–1
copyright 167, 169, 183, 185, 187, 191, 192, 193
definition 165–7
deployed on-premise 175, 181
developer certificate of origin 193
dual licensing models 185
employees 191–2
four freedoms 166
FSF 166
GENIVI alliance 174
in the supply chain 189–90
legal protection 167
licence compatibility 184
licences 167–9, 182–5, 186–8, 192, 194
Linux 171, 172, 175, 183, 185, 186, 189, 191, 192–3, 194–5
open source code 170–2, 174, 181, 182, 187–9, 191, 193, 194, 195
open source community 171–2
OSI 166
patents 193–4
procured on-premise 185–6
table of licences 176–80
warranties and indemnities 189
OpenChain Project 186, 189, 190, 191
operating agreement 222, 225–6
OSI (Open Source Initiative) 166, 167

OSL (Open Software Licence) 175, 184, 185

PaaS (Platform as a Service) 13, 14, 24, 69, 80
Partnership Act (1890) 220
partnership agreement 219–20
passing off 44, 45, 48
passwords 65–6, 79, 87
patents 36, 37, 46–7, 167, 193–4
payment arrangements 4, 7
PCI DSS (Payment Card Industry Data Security Standard) 77, 91
penetration tests 78, 93
permissive licence 167, 169, 173, 182, 183, 184
perpetual licence 5
Ponemon Institute 52
preventive maintenance 9
Privacy and Electronic Communications Regulations 2003 74–5, 96

ransomware 51, 53, 57, 61, 83
RDSP (Relevant Digital Service Providers) 71–2
Regulation of Investigatory Powers Act (2000) 73, 144
right of access 104, 105–6, 108
right to data portability 102, 104, 108
right to erasure 104, 106–8
right to object 46, 104, 105, 109
right to rectification 104, 106
risk assessment 2, 19, 27, 30, 156, 157, 163

SaaS (Software as a Service) 13, 14, 15, 21, 24, 30
SAR (Subject Access Requests) 125–6
'scope creep' 200, 207, 227
sequential methodology 11, 199, 200, 207, 208, 209
shadow IT 66, 67
SLA (service level agreement) 10–11
social media 13, 80, 82, 93, 127, 152–4, 165, 171
Society for Computers and Law 2
software
application software 4
development contracts 7–8

intellectual property rights 38–40
licence agreements 5, 6
licences 5, 6, 38, 39, 169
maintenance 6
operating system 4
security 84
source code 8, 12, 39, 90, 91, 165–7, 169, 181, 183, 185, 187, 188
SSD (solid-state drive) 14
staff policy 146–52

*Study on Global Megatrends in Cybersecurity* 52
subscription agreement 14

termination 5, 7
'The cathedral and the bazaar' 171
time and materials 3, 4, 8, 201, 205, 206, 207
Torvalds, Linus 171
trade marks 36, 41, 42, 43–5, 48, 49, 194, 216

UK design right 50

vulnerability assessments 78, 93

WannaCry and Petya attacks 53
'waterfall' development 11, 171, 199, 209
WhatsApp 13
WikiLeaks 59
Workplace Regulations (1992) 157
World Intellectual Property Organization 43